What they said about
Thomas Myler's previo...

Boxing's Greatest Upsets: Fights That Shook The World
A respected writer, Myler has compiled a worthy volume on
the most sensational and talked-about upsets of the glove era,
drawing on interviews, archive footage and worldwide contacts.
Yorkshire Evening Post

Fight fans will glory in this offbeat history of boxing's biggest
shocks, from Gentleman Jim's knockout of John L Sullivan in 1892
to the modern era. A must for your bookshelf.
Hull Daily Mail

Book of the Month
Lonsdale Sports

Myler's ability to dig deep, gather plenty of background
information, coupled with his easy-flowing style of writing, paints
a fascinating scene building up to the contests. We urge you to add
this book to your collection.
Boxing News

Myler doesn't just deal with what happened inside the ropes but
also provides a balanced overview of the controversies,
personalities and historical contexts that make these fights
worth reading about.
Ring

Ringside with the Celtic Warriors
The offering from this highly respected boxing writer is well up to
the standard we expect from him.
Boxing News

Thomas Myler has come up with another gem. His credentials and
easy, readable style make this a must book for fight fans.
The Sun

As a ring historian, Thomas Myler has few peers.
Belfast Telegraph

THE
MAD
AND THE BAD

BOXING TALES OF MAYHEM, MENACE AND MURDER

THOMAS MYLER

First published by Pitch Publishing, 2018

Pitch Publishing
A2 Yeoman Gate
Yeoman Way
Worthing
Sussex
BN13 3QZ
www.pitchpublishing.co.uk
info@pitchpublishing.co.uk

A CIP catalogue record is available for this book
from the British Library.

ISBN 978-1-785313950

Typesetting and origination by Pitch Publishing
Printed and bound in the UK by TJ International, Cornwall

Contents

Dedication

To Betty, Jacqueline, Sinead, Ciaran, Colin and Vivian, always in my corner

Thomas Myler is a well-known and established boxing historian, journalist, author and broadcaster. This is his ninth book, eighth on boxing, his most recent being the best-selling *New York Fight Nights*, published by Pitch. Myler has spent a lifetime around boxing, meeting boxers, promoters, managers, trainers, matchmakers and publicists, and has interviewed many of the sport's greats. His work has appeared in many magazines and newspapers. He lives in Dublin.

Acknowledgements

THIS book would not have been possible without the help of so many people too numerous to mention. But a special mention must go to *Boxing News* and *Independent News and Media* for their always helpful assistance, as well as their fine writers including Bob Mee, John Jarrett, Claude Abrams and Vincent Hogan, all good friends and true experts in the noble art. What they don't know about boxing is not worth knowing. My family, too, were always by my side, Jacqueline, Sinead, Ciaran, Colin and Vivian, not to mention my wonderful late wife Betty.

The photographs are by kind permission of Getty Images, with some from the Thomas Myler Collection. Last but certainly not least, full credit must go to Pitch Publishing for having the foresight, dedication and care to get the book into print. Credit here must go to publishing executives Paul and Jane Camillin and their excellent team.

Thank you all.

When archaeologists discover the missing arms of Venus de Milo, they will find she was wearing boxing gloves.

John Barrymore, actor

Introduction

THE world of sport has thrown up many individuals who would certainly come under the heading of wild cards. There was George Best, a wizard on the football field and a demon off it. Once asked what happened to the fortune he earned, he quipped, 'I spent the lot on booze, birds and fast cars. The rest I just squandered.' Another football star, Eric Cantona, may have held on to his money but there were no excuses for his shameful antics on the field. He once launched a kung-fu kick at a fan followed by a hail of punches.

Alex 'Hurricane' Higgins certainly lived up to his name, whether he was at the snooker table or away from it. His misdemeanours included head-butting officials, assaulting a 14-year-old boy, being stabbed by a girlfriend he angered and spending time as a homeless man. There was, too, John McEnroe, the superbrat of tennis. He swore at officials, called an umpire a 'jerk' and was reprimanded for his countless on-court outbursts. More recently, he was even critical of modern great Serena Williams, a 23-time Grand Slam winner, saying she would not be in the world's top 700 if she played on the men's circuit, although he later apologised for the comment.

Then there is the drug culture, which is rampant in sport. In swimming, Michelle Smith-de Bruin won three Olympic gold medals before her career ended in shame following allegations of tampering with a urine sample. The claims were never proven but the stigma has remained. Bad boys in athletics as far as

3

drugs are concerned include Ben Johnson and in cycling Lance Armstrong's name stands out. The list goes on and on.

What of boxing? Yes, the noble art has come up with its bad boys. Some were wacky warriors and others were masters of menace, with many careers ending in tragedy. The mad and the bad.

Nigel Collins, the esteemed author, columnist and former *Ring* magazine editor, put it well when he wrote, 'For many true boxing legends, the glory of victory was quickly superseded by physical and mental ruin, illness and sometimes tragic death. Some were involved in crime, some were murdered, some committed suicide. There have always been exceptions, of course, but the stereotype has ample basis in fact.'

Going back to the bare knuckle era, there was Dan Donnelly, an Irish fighter of much promise until he took to the bottle and died at the age of 32. Still in the bare knuckle days, there was Jack Slack, said to be the inventor of the notorious rabbit punch, long since outlawed. This was a blow to the back of the head or to the base of the skull, which could damage the cervical vertebrae and kill instantly. The punch's name is derived from the technique used by hunters to kill rabbits with a quick, sharp strike to the back of the head. The heavyweight champion of England and a butcher by trade from Norfolk, Slack was also a celebrated fight fixer, and crooked fights were common by the time he lost his title.

Henry 'Hen' Pearce, from Bristol, known as 'The Game Chicken', was another. Pearce was drunk more times than he was sober while he was champion of England. He would contract tuberculosis and other ailments and died at the age of 32 'a physical wreck', in the words of a contemporary chronicler.

Yankee Sullivan, the Irish bare-knuckle battler born in County Cork and raised in east London, also found himself on the wrong side of the law when he was arrested in San Francisco during a round-up of underworld suspects. He was found dead in his prison cell but whether he was secretly killed by a visiting member of the Vigilantes, an organisation that took the law into its own hands, or committed suicide remains a mystery.

Even the great John L Sullivan was a victim of his own success. John L was the man who made the transition from bare knuckles to gloves and in 1892 became the first universally recognised heavyweight champion of the world. Storming into a bar, he would bang his ham-like right fist on the counter and declare, 'My name is John L Sullivan and I can lick any son-of-a-bitch in the house!' There were never any takers. Addicted to the bottle at an early age, he would spend much of his retirement lecturing on 'the evils of drink'.

Many survived the pitfalls of success in those far-off days, as have many modern greats, because boxing will always have its wild cards and wacky warriors. It is the nature of the sport that has survived over the centuries.

Historians can trace the origins of boxing back to ancient Greece, where excavations at Knossos on the island of Crete have revealed that a form of the sport was known among its inhabitants as early as 1500 BC. Other research revealed that boxing's roots date back to as early as 5000 BC, to a time when the Pharaohs of Egypt attended fights in which contestants bound their fists in rawhide straps, known as the cestus, leaving their fingers bare. These were also used by the gladiators in ancient Rome and the most perfect example is the seated figure wearing the cestus that can be seen in the National Museum in the Eternal City.

Over the years and up to the present day, boxing has fallen victim to reformers, lawmakers, abolitionists and so often the ineptitude of its own management. But it has come through, though certainly not unscathed, because of the boxers themselves, who put their lives on the line every time they climb into the ring. Many had their ups and downs, their good days and their bad days, as you will read in the following pages.

Some were all-time greats, others were not so great. But they all had one thing in common. They were fighters. Some were wayward warriors, others masters of menace, often both. But they had that indefinable characteristic – they could fight, and fight like hell. Some ended in tragedy while others survived the pitfalls of success. In the final analysis, they were all knights of the squared circle and have embellished the long, rich history of what the great A J Liebling of the *New Yorker* called the Sweet Science. You will meet many of them in the following pages. Enjoy the journey.

Chapter 1

Eight weddings and two suicide notes

THE hotel manager and the detective stood looking down at the man on the bed, who had killed himself during the night. 'He's Norman Selby, that's the name he checked in,' said the manager. 'Yes,' said the detective. 'He was also known as Kid McCoy. He was a famous boxer in his day and a world champion at that, one of the best.'

It was the night of 18 April 1940 and the scene was the Tuller Hotel in Detroit. McCoy/Selby had checked into the hotel alone and asked for a call at 10am the next day. When he failed to answer the call, the manager went upstairs with a passkey and found him dead on his bed, fully dressed, and called the police. An overdose of sleeping pills had put him out. Beside his body were two notes, both signed Norman E Selby.

One was to the local paymaster at the Ford motor company, where he had been working, to pass on his salary as was due to him to his wife, his eighth and final spouse. The other, which was longer, said, 'For the past eight years I have wanted to help humanity, especially the youngsters who do not know nature's laws, that is, the proper carriage of the body and the right way to eat etc.

'Everything in my possession I leave to my dear wife Sue Ellen Selby. To all my dear friends I wish the best of luck. Sorry

7

I could not stand the madness of this world any longer. In my pockets you will find $17.75.'

McCoy's suicide has remained a mystery all these years. The 'madness' was of his own creation. Several of his friends confirmed his health had been good in spite of his wild and erratic lifestyle. At 66, there was a bit of grey in his curly hair but his fair-skinned face was devoid of wrinkles and he was nearly as neat, trim and supple as when he was world middleweight champion and a claimant to the welterweight title.

Even the detective suspected a trick as the body lay there, half expecting McCoy to suddenly open his eyes and jump up. It would not have been a surprise because Norman Selby, alias Kid McCoy, was one of the world's greatest tricksters, inside and outside the ring. He also happened to be one of the ring's best ever boxers. In over 100 fights, he was beaten in only six of them, with 64 ending in either clean knockouts or stoppages. In 1991, he was inducted into the International Boxing Hall of Fame in New York.

Remarkably, McCoy was just a middleweight at around 160lbs yet he was able to take on and beat some of the world's leading heavyweights.

Active from the 1890s into the early years of the 20th century, McCoy's record is studded with illustrious names such as James J Corbett, Tommy Ryan, Joe Choynski, Jack Root, Tom Sharkey, George LaBlanche, Mysterious Billy Smith and many others. The Kid is credited with inventing the corkscrew punch, a blow delivered with a final punishing twist that could tear an opponent's skin in an era of skin-tight gloves in many states. McCoy was able to slash and maul opponents, sometimes to excess, to gain victory.

McCoy, too, was also a notorious womaniser, with most of his earnings, estimated at over a quarter of a million dollars, spent on satisfying his boundless thirst for pleasure. Of his eight wives, he married one of them three times – and shot another to death. There was vanity in him as well as guile, wit and cruelty.

Above all, there was the self-satisfaction of setting himself a task – and carrying it out whatever the circumstances.

McCoy got tremendous pleasure in many psychological ploys and illegal tactics that went unnoticed by referees and away from the gaze of ringside officials. If McCoy felt he could get away with it, then he would try – and more often than not succeeded. A clever boxer in his own right, he often feigned sickness before a bout or told the media he had failed to train, hoping to lure his opponent into a false sense of confidence. Naturally on fight night, McCoy was usually fully fit and ready, and it was too late for the opponent to do anything about it.

One night in Paris, he boxed a local hero called Jean Charlemont, who was a champion in the art of *la savate*, which is fighting with the feet, with kicking allowed. McCoy, however, figured that such tactics called for urgent measures. Keeping well out of the way of the Frenchman's flying kicks for two rounds, the Kid jerked his head towards the overflowing gallery. Puzzled, Charlemont asked McCoy in a clinch, 'Why are you indicating something or someone up there?' 'Well,' said McCoy, 'there's a beautiful girl up there who keeps waving.'

When Charlemont turned his head to where McCoy indicated, the Kid lashed out with a big left hook and the Frenchman went down for the full count. Back in the dressing room as the fully dressed McCoy was about to leave, Charlemont walked in and asked him why he had resorted to such trickery. 'No hard feelings, Jean, but I thought I would teach you a little lesson,' said McCoy. 'Never let a woman turn your head, you might really get hurt.'

On another occasion, against an opponent whose name has been lost in the mists of time, McCoy filled his mouth with loose teeth and at an opportune moment spat them out. When his horrified opponent dropped his guard and started to apologise for the damage he had done, McCoy flashed across a hard right and dropped his man to the canvas for the full count.

Against a bare-footed black fighter in South Africa, simply known as King of the Kaffirs, McCoy sprinkled his own corner with tacks. In the first round, the Kid lured his opponent into the corner as the King screamed in agony after stepping on the tacks. When the fighter looked down at his bare feet, McCoy swung a right hand and knocked his man senseless.

On another occasion, against Bob Day in Toronto, McCoy purposely tripped up his opponent. As Day struggled to get to his feet, he foolishly grabbed McCoy's outstretched left hand. 'Upsa daisy,' said McCoy, as he pulled Day towards him and let him have it with a smashing right cross. Day was out for six minutes.

Other times, McCoy boxed fairly and squarely with no hint of underhandedness, displaying a fine upright style with a wide variety of punches. This led a New York newspaperman to write after one of these bouts, 'Last night we saw the real McCoy.' The term would grow into popular usage in describing someone or something as the genuine article.

McCoy was born on a farmland in rural Rush County, Indiana on 13 October 1872 to Francis and Emily Selby. The baby was christened Norman. In common with parents everywhere, they had all sorts of ambitious plans for Norman's future. Emily envisioned the boy becoming a doctor while Francis could see him as a lawyer. On occasions, after downing a few drinks too many, he pictured Norman in the White House. But their dreams ended when it became apparent that their offspring was allergic to classrooms and books, both of which he considered boring.

After four years, and now aged 15, Norman could stick it no longer and stuffing his few belongings into a bag one night, climbed out of the back window and hurried off to the local railroad station. The plan was not to get a ticket, as he had no money, but to jump on to the side of a freight train, or even under it, and hang on. This practice was known as riding the rails, or riding the rods.

As to how Norman Selby became Kid McCoy, it seems that on one occasion after his father had reported him missing, two policemen nabbed the teenager as he hopped off a train pulling into Cincinnati, Ohio. 'Are you Norman Selby?' asked one officer. 'No,' said Selby. 'I'm Charlie McCoy.' The night before, he had seen a sign for McCoy Station. The police officer released him and ever afterwards Norman Selby was Charlie McCoy, later Kid McCoy.

'I lived off the land and, while it was a gruelling life, it kind of prepared me for what was to come,' he recalled in later years. 'I got into all kinds of fights with railroad cops, brakemen and other hobos. I was a skinny runt who looked like fair game to anyone who wanted some punching practice. I learned plenty from those railroad scraps and reckoned I might do well as a boxer.'

Skipping the amateurs, which he regarded as a place for sissies anyhow, McCoy made his professional debut with a four-round decision over Pete Jenkins in St Paul, Minnesota at the age of 17. It would be several years before he invented the 'corkscrew punch'. It happened in his own backyard on another of his infrequent visits home. Sitting on the front step, McCoy idly watched the family kitten toying with a cloth ball. Quick to note that the kitten's paw shot towards the ball at an angle instead of a straight line, he wondered what would happen if he hung the same twisting stroke on the end of a jab, like the spin given a bullet by a gun's rifling.

Going quickly to the Selby family barn, he filled a large bag with grain and suspended it from a rafter to practice his new blow. 'It worked fine,' McCoy remembered. 'It hurt my knuckles but I ripped the bag to shreds. There was grain spilling all over the floor. I had discovered a deadly new punch.'

Twitching with excitement, he made for the nearest bar, where he deliberately picked a fight with the biggest fellow he could find. The fight did not last long. As the big fellow came forward, McCoy cocked his left fist and let him have it with his 'corkscrew punch'. The fellow fell backwards clutching an ugly wound to his face. 'You have a knife in your hand,' the man said, demanding the Kid open his fist. McCoy did so for all to see. Just a pair of bony hands.

McCoy made steady progress in the professional ranks and was learning all the time. When he heard that Bob Fitzsimmons, the world middleweight champion from Cornwall, was training for a fight in Louisiana, he made his way there and got a job as a cook and general utility man for the champion. More importantly, he watched Fitzsimmons working out in the ring and claimed he picked up valuable tips. He even got to spar with the Englishman.

In his first three years McCoy had 26 fights, winning 19, losing one and drawing six. By the end of 1895, he had added another nine wins, one loss and a draw. By now, McCoy was one of the leading contenders for the world welterweight title held by Tommy Ryan, a talented New Yorker of Irish extraction.

Although largely forgotten today, in his time and for many years afterwards Ryan was considered one of the greats. A brilliant boxer and hard puncher with both hands, Ryan honed his ring skills in lumber camps and it seemed only natural he would become a fighter, and a good one at that. In July 1894, at the age of 24, he won the world welterweight title by outpointing Mysterious Billy Smith over 20 rounds in Coney Island, New York.

He defended the title successfully by stopping Nonpariel Jack Dempsey, not to be confused with the heavyweight champion of later years, in three rounds. Ryan would subsequently win the world middleweight title.

At ringside for the Dempsey fight was McCoy – and for good reason. He wanted a title fight with Ryan and felt he could beat him. They were old friends. Ryan had befriended the Kid a year or so earlier by engaging him as a sparring partner, giving him a bed and three meals a day. McCoy's unscrupulous temperament and manipulations, even against friends, would now manifest itself in a scheme designed to bring about the downfall of his generous benefactor.

Even though they had boxed hundreds of rounds together, Ryan never tried to hurt McCoy, although there were times when the Kid retreated to his quarters with a bloody nose and large red welts decorating his lily-white skin. He took his lumps without complaining but he never forgot. Inwardly, he developed a bitter hatred towards the world champion. It was not so much the punishment he received as jealousy. McCoy envied Ryan's lofty position in boxing, with his fat bank account, his luxuries and his aloof attitude.

McCoy had stayed in Ryan's camp a little over a year and made good use of every minute. He studied the New Yorker's style and made mental notes about his strong and weak points, including how he pulled back or slipped inside jabs and how he hooked to the body and often stood back to admire his handiwork. By the time McCoy left the Ryan camp, he reckoned to know more about Tommy than he knew about himself.

McCoy's association with the world champion gained him much publicity and enabled him to gain bouts with established boxers. Before long, he had strung together some impressive wins and boxing writers were taking notice of this cocky kid with fast hands. McCoy now wanted to fight for the world championship but he realised he would have to qualify by defeating some leading contenders. Instead, he took the short cut. When Ryan left the ring after stopping Nonpariel Jack Dempsey, McCoy publicly challenged him to a title fight. Ryan said he would talk to his advisors and let McCoy know. The Kid's masterplan was beginning to unfold.

When the challenge was printed in the New York newspapers, Ryan dismissed it as a publicity stunt. 'Let him go through the contenders and let's see what he is worth,' Ryan told reporters. But McCoy was in a hurry. He did not reply to Ryan's comments but instead went to the champion's training camp just outside New York City and sought him out. Even though Ryan might not have a fight coming up, he always insisted on keeping in shape.

After exchanging pleasantries, the pale McCoy put his plan into action. 'Tommy,' he said, almost with tears in his green eyes. 'Please don't get the wrong idea about what you read in the papers. It's all poppycock. I know deep down that you can lick me any day in the week but you see, I'm down on my luck. Sure, I get fights but there's no big money in them. I'm looking for one big payday to pay my debts and nothing would help me more than a fight with you for the world title.'

Ryan said nothing at first, allowing McCoy to state his case. The Kid praised the champion's fine natural ability and said he hoped he would hold the title for a long time. 'I'd really appreciate it if you would accept my challenge as an old friend,' pleaded McCoy, 'and you could carry me along for a few rounds for the fans' sake and I'd get a good purse to ease my financial worries.

'Remember when you'd hold me up in the ring after landing a good shot in those old sparring sessions? Ah, those were the days. In fact, nobody knows this except my doctor but I'm dying of consumption. You only have to look at my pale face. My medical bills are still unpaid.

'With that in mind, you might persuade the promoter to increase our purses. A little more for me and a little more for you. I wouldn't even mind if the promoter made it more for the winner and leave the loser's purse the same. You deserve as much as possible for doing me this great favour, Tommy.'

Ryan listened to it all before rubbing his chin reflectively. 'OK, you're on,' he said finally. 'But I won't put my title on the line. Later on, we could talk about a title fight. As to the purse monies, I'll talk to the promoter and I'm sure he'll agree. But don't worry about the result or getting hurt. I'll carry you for a few rounds as you suggest and all will be fine. I'd do anything to help out an old pal, that's for sure. I can assure you that you can count on me.'

As McCoy was leaving the camp, he couldn't help a smile crossing his face. He fully respected Ryan's ability and a fully trained and mentally alert champion might be more than he could cope with. But a half-trained Ryan might be a different matter altogether. There would be no title on the line but the Kid reckoned that an impressive showing would force the authorities to demand they meet for the championship. Ryan might even retire, which would leave the division wide open, with McCoy the top contender.

In any event, the Kid was sure Ryan would take things easy on his 'down-and-almost-out' challenger. Why, Ryan might not even train hard, even though he always stayed in light training just to keep ticking over. The fight was set for 2 March 1896 at Maspeth, a small residential and commercial community in the Queens borough of New York and founded by English and Dutch settlers in the 17th century.

Boxing writers and sports editors in New York and across the nation gave McCoy little chance of upsetting the talented champion, who entered the ring as a solid favourite to dismiss his opponent in the early rounds. Even if the battle went the scheduled 20 rounds, there was unlikely to be a different result. Ryan's overall skill and hitting power would be too much for the untested McCoy. After all, the Kid did not look very sharp in training whereas Ryan was his usual buoyant self, even if he often cut short his sessions for what he considered an easy fight.

McCoy looked sluggish when the newspapermen visited his camp, but it was a trick. When they left, the Kid got down to hard training, pounding the heavy bag, punishing his sparring partners, doing his roadwork and getting into what he would call 'the physical and mental condition of my life'. He told one of his team that Ryan would get the shock of his life. 'The guy expects a walkover,' he said. 'Wait until he gets into that ring.'

McCoy reached the arena early and quickly donned his boxing togs. Ryan arrived soon after and instead of undressing, he rested on the rubbing table. Before Ryan could doze off, there was a knock on the door and in walked McCoy. Ryan couldn't believe it. His opponent was no longer the sorrowful figure he had met earlier to first discuss the fight. McCoy was bright eyed, cheerful, cocky and more importantly looked in prime condition. Where was that pale look? Ryan discovered later that McCoy had put a light powder on his face.

Extending his right hand, McCoy said, 'Good luck out there, champ, because you'll certainly need it.' Before the flabbergasted Ryan could reply, McCoy turned on his heels and walked out. The champion had been conned, and it was too late now to do anything about it. His title was safe but he could not afford to lose in a non-title match and lose all credibility as a world champion.

McCoy entered the ring to a faint, half-hearted ovation, compared to the cheers that greeted Ryan. At the bell, the Kid moved around and landed a few light left jabs, followed by Ryan. In a clinch, McCoy whispered to his rival sarcastically, 'Don't forget your promise, Tommy. No surprises. You wouldn't want to double-cross me now, would you?' In Ryan's poor physical and mental condition, he was in no state to pull off any surprises or any double-crosses. Whenever Ryan shot a left jab or a hook with either hand, McCoy simply brushed them off as if swatting flies.

For round after round, McCoy punished the champion with all kinds of combination punches, left jabs followed by damaging hooks from both gloves and uppercuts on the inside when they were in the many clinches that marred the bout. McCoy also used his deadly corkscrew punch at every opportunity. No matter what Ryan tried, the Kid went one better. Witnesses to the one-sided battle claimed that McCoy could have knocked out Ryan at any stage but preferred to torture the champion for his own satisfaction. In the 12th round an overhand right staggered Ryan, who now had cuts over both eyes and a bloody nose, but McCoy grabbed him and held him up.

Finally, in the 15th round, a powerful left hook followed by a smashing right landed flush on Ryan's jaw and sent him to the blood-stained canvas. He rolled over a few times then just lay still as the referee counted to ten and out. At the age of 23, Kid McCoy was technically the best welterweight in the world, even if he did not have the title.

Instead of staying in the welterweight division, where he would have been a strong favourite to win the title officially, McCoy changed his mind and decided to go for the big boys, with the heavyweight championship of the world his ultimate target. In any event, he had outgrown the welterweight division, with its limit at 145lbs. McCoy now weighed around 156lbs and could easily make the middleweight limit of 160lbs if he wanted to. Why not? A world title was a world title.

The Kid's old sparmate, Bob Fitzsimmons, had relinquished the middleweight title to pursue the heavyweight crown, so McCoy was matched with Dan Creedon from Bridgeport, Connecticut for the vacant world middleweight championship in Long Island City on 17 December 1897. The Kid won on a stoppage in the 15th round.

McCoy never bothered to defend the title because he still wanted bigger fish – the heavyweight championship. The light-heavyweight division, with its limit at 175lbs, would not be established until 1903, so the heavyweight class was the next logical step and where big money could be made. Besides, McCoy felt he could beat most of the heavyweights anyhow. 'As my old pal Bob Fitzsimmons used to say, the bigger they are, the harder they fall,' he would tell newspapermen.

McCoy started his heavyweight campaign on 20 May 1898 with an impressive 20-round decision over tough Gus Ruhlin in Syracuse, New York. Ruthlin, who boxed out of Akron, Ohio, was a good fighter with a strong wallop in his right hand, but he was inclined to be erratic.

When he was good, he was very good but when he was bad, it was an altogether different story. Ruhlin gave McCoy some worrying moments but the Kid was always on top with his fast, shifty style. By now, there were stories circulating that the rugged Irishman Tom Sharkey was being considered as an opponent for McCoy.

From County Louth on Ireland's East Coast, Sharkey was one of the toughest heavyweights in the business, even though he was only 5ft 8ins in his bare feet. The fifth of ten children born to James Sharkey, a railwayman, and the former Margaret Kelly, he had very limited schooling. He always had a sense of adventure and yearned to see the world. Going to work on the small merchant ships that plied their trade to Liverpool and ports in Scotland, he would subsequently work as a cabin boy on larger vessels before getting jobs on bigger ships that took him all around the world.

'I enjoyed my time at sea,' he recalled in later years. 'I would often take the wheel with permission of the captain and would stay at it for 18, 19, 20 hours at a stretch without sleep. I travelled the seven seas, from London to Cape Town, from Hong Kong to Sydney, from San Francisco to the coast of China, through the Indian Ocean and ports where no white man had ever set foot.

'I had my share of moments with typhoons in the Indian Ocean and hurricanes in the Pacific and no fewer than four shipwrecks. Many a day and night I spent in an open boat with not a drop of water passing my lips. You could say that my experiences read like something out of *Sinbad the Sailor*, only mine were true.'

A few weeks after sailing out of New Orleans port, Sharkey found himself in New York harbour, when he decided to leave his own ship for good, make his way to the Brooklyn navy yard and enlist in the US Navy. It was while watching the training sessions aboard ship every evening from 7pm to 9pm, with officers acting as referees, that he got the boxing bug. Soon, he was invited to join the sessions and enjoyed them so much that he made up his mind to become a boxer. He quickly established himself as a formidable opponent for any of his shipmates to tackle.

His training period completed, Sharkey was assigned to the cruiser, the USS *Philadelphia*, when it was rushed to Honolulu early in 1893 to protect American interests during a revolution that had broken out against the ruling native dynasty. It was on the Hawaiian island that Sharkey began his actual ring career and after blasting his way through the heavyweight championship of the American fleet, rivalry developed with British sailors stationed there. As it happened, they were no match for the powerful Irishman with a heavy wallop in both hands.

At one stage, the British Navy imported its own champion, Jim Gardner from England, 'to give this little Irishman a lesson and restore pride to their fleet', but Sharkey put him down and out in four rounds. Even though neither boxer was paid and the match was technically an amateur contest, some sources claim that the Gardner bout was Sharkey's first as a professional. Indeed there are conflicting contemporary reports as to when the Irishman actually began his professional career, with several historians coming up with different dates.

Record compilers also differ and not even his recent biographers Moira Sharkey, a distant relation, and Greg Lewis are certain. *Ring* magazine was, and still is, unclear as are the various websites that are always a good source of information. The *International Boxing Register*, published in association with the International Boxing Hall of Fame in New York and regarded universally as the world's official record book, lists the Gardner fight in Honolulu as Sharkey's first official fight, which took place appropriately enough on St Patrick's Day, 17 March 1893.

Wherever the facts lie between his amateur and professional careers, Sharkey put in 18 months in Honolulu and in that time had 14 fights, all ending in knockout victories. Some sources show that he lost one, George Washington putting him away in seven rounds in February 1894, though it has never been officially verified. During that summer, the USS *Philadelphia* left Hawaii and pulled in at the Mare Island naval base in San Francisco. With his naval service coming to an end, Sharkey became a civilian and continued his ring activities in the Bay areas of Colma, best known to historians as the burial place of the Wild West gunfighter Wyatt Earp, and nearby Valejo.

Sharkey took on all-comers in a busy career but he is probably best remembered for his two titanic battles with the great James J Jeffries, particularly the second one for Jeffries's world heavyweight championship at the Coney Island Athletic Club, New York on 3 November 1899. It turned out to be one of the fiercest fights in ring history and was held under the glare of 400 blazing arc lamps radiating 100°F heat, set up so the fight could be held in the brightest light possible for the benefit of the Biograph Company that was filming it. Both boxers later complained that because the lights were so low, their scalps were blistered by the halfway stage, even though a large umbrella had been placed over each corner as a shade during intervals.

For 25 torrid rounds, both fighters battled away without giving as much as an inch. At the final bell, with both contestants on the verge of exhaustion and very glad to hear the welcome sound of the gong, referee George Siler, who combined his ring duties with his day job as chief sportswriter on the *Chicago Tribune*, raised Jeffries's right hand as winner and still champion. Sharkey complained he was robbed, stamping his feet and shouting, 'I won, I won', but to no avail. Big Jeff was still king of the heavyweights and would successfully defend his title six more times before retiring undefeated in 1904, only to make an ill-advised comeback six years later and lose to Jack Johnson.

Almost a year before the second Sharkey-Jeffries fight, the tough Irishman accepted an offer to take on Kid McCoy over 25 rounds at the Lenox Athletic Club, New York. The date was 10 January 1899 and he agreed without any hesitation. The winner was promised a shot at the world heavyweight title held by Bob Fitzsimmons, Jeffries's predecessor. For the wily McCoy, it was a chance too good to miss. Yes, he would be giving away considerable weight but at 5ft 11ins he was three inches taller and would use that to his advantage by jabbing and hooking, picking up the points, while the occasional corkscrew punch would not go astray either. Sharkey brushed aside McCoy's chances. 'He's only a middleweight, for god's sake,' he retorted. 'It'll be all over in a round or two.'

It was snowing heavily on the day of the fight but that did not stop the fans from packing the arena for what promised to be a great night of action. When they stepped on to the scales the previous day, there were gasps from those in attendance at the vast difference in their respective weights, though it should not have come as a surprise. Sharkey weighed 178lbs, a fully fledged heavyweight, while McCoy tipped the balance at 156lbs, four pounds inside the middleweight limit. But McCoy vowed not to allow the 22lbs pull in the weights to deter him. He had a job to do and he would do it.

Billed as 'A Battle Between Science and Strength', McCoy was reported to have bet $100 on himself while Sharkey allegedly placed $200 on his own chances. The purse money of $20,000 would be split, 75 per cent to the winner plus a percentage of the gate. When they climbed into the brightly lit ring to do battle, 'Sharkey looked disgustingly healthy alongside McCoy,' recalled Mike Sherry in *Boxing and Wrestling* magazine in 1955. 'His arms and legs were at least twice the width around, and his ruddy suntanned skin was in deep contrast to the Kid's sickly yellowish complexion. McCoy looked like a fugitive from a graveyard.'

When Sharkey removed his green dressing robe, his green trunks had an American flag for a sash. McCoy wore a white robe and white shorts, with the stars and stripes draped around his middle. As both men were having their gloves put on, referee Tim Hurst observed that there was too much tape on McCoy's hands and ordered the American to take at least two feet of it off. The Kid's handlers sheepishly obliged.

When Hurst called the two men together for their final instructions, McCoy placed his right hand on Sharkey's massive chest, which was decorated with tattoos of a four-masted sailing ship and a large star, a legacy of his days in the US Navy. 'You and that ship are going to sink soon, Mr Sharkey,' said McCoy. 'Don't be a fool, McCoy,' said the Irishman, his face turning an angry red. 'That ship stays upright and so will I. You'll see.'

The opening round set the pattern for the fight. The heavy-shouldered Sharkey attempted to reach the taller McCoy but the Kid nimbly danced away. 'While Sharkey was shorter, McCoy looked like a mere stripling in comparison,' reported the *New York World*. 'Sharkey looked gigantic, enough to make two of him. It seemed a match between Hercules and Apollo.' As two rounds passed, McCoy had a clear advantage, having won both sessions on his better boxing and nifty footwork.

The pattern changed dramatically in the third round when McCoy connected with his corkscrew punch to the jaw. Sharkey, caught by surprise, went to the canvas but did not take a count. Seconds later, another corkscrew punch exploded on his jaw and he went down for the second time. The roaring crowd were on their feet now and Sharkey took a short count. It was not looking good for the Irishman and at the bell he looked decidedly worried.

McCoy seemed to slow down in the fourth round, perhaps conserving his energy for what could well be a long encounter. But Sharkey was still very much in the fight and fans and newspapermen began to notice a slight shift in the battle. The Kid was still reaching the shorter Sharkey with his long jabs and hooks but the blows were beginning to lack authority. Also, Sharkey's solid smashes to the body were producing a weakening effect on his opponent's wind and legs.

By the seventh round, McCoy appeared to be falling behind on points as the persistent Irishman kept on the attack. The Kid connected with a long left hook, only to get a powerful right to the face in return. Quickly, Sharkey connected with a left hook to the stomach and McCoy went down. Lying on the canvas groaning and with his face contorted as though he were in terrible pain, he was yelling, 'Foul, foul', but referee Hurst wasn't having any of it as he was familiar with McCoy's tricks.

The wily Kid would take advantage of any opportunity to win. Hadn't Hurst known about McCoy's tricks and schemes, particularly the time he conned the great Tommy Ryan into believing he was sick and went on to trounce the world champion into a humiliating defeat?

Sharkey was turning out to be McCoy's toughest opponent and despite his skilful boxing, clever footwork and regular foul tactics, the Kid was losing as the rounds went by. Sharkey was by far the stronger puncher and several times rocked the lighter man with heavy blows from both hands. In the tenth, he connected with the powerful right cross that sent McCoy down to be counted out. But nobody heard the count amid all the din. As McCoy struggled to his feet, Sharkey rushed in and threw a smashing left hook over the referee's shoulder and the Kid went down for the second time.

Hurst immediately sent Sharkey to his corner. Was he being disqualified for hitting after the fight was officially over? 'I wish I knew what's going on,' the bewildered Sharkey said to one of his seconds. Hurst then held up his hands, called for silence and said, 'The referee decides that McCoy is too weak to continue and awards his decision to Sharkey on a tenth-round knockout.'

The next day, Hurst explained to newspapermen at a press conference that both boxers attended, 'I counted the Kid out and waved my hands to signify that the fight was over. But for whatever reason, I wasn't understood. Sharkey couldn't get it into his head that he had won and to make sure he ran over and flattened McCoy for the second time. I couldn't actually believe that Tom had fouled deliberately and inasmuch as the fight was over when the act was committed, I felt my ruling was just and fair.'

McCoy said, 'I was defeated but I still think I can whip Sharkey and I demand a return match. I made the mistake of being too cautious and waiting too long to apply my best shots. I should have been able to avoid his wild punches but it was clearly my fault that they landed. There were two punches in the eighth and ninth rounds which were fouls and which the referee did nothing about. I knew I was going in against a heavier man but I felt I could handle him, and I did until the sudden finish. I would dearly love to fight Sharkey again and I think you all agree that I would have a very good chance of beating him.'

Sharkey said, 'I won the fight fair and square. I simply knocked the man out and that's all there really is to it. I thought I had him by the tenth round and that is what happened. The Kid can hit hard and he is fast, and while I have some speed myself the public know that I can hit hard. McCoy is a good, game fellow and I give him all the credit in the world for that, but he can't beat me and deep down he knows it.'

They never fought again as Sharkey's team had their sights firmly set on a world heavyweight title fight against Bob Fitzsimmons, and feelers had already gone out. But Fitz lost his title to James J Jeffries in June 1899 and Sharkey would go on to meet the new champion in Jeffries's first defence five months later. As recounted earlier, the rugged Irishman went the full 25 bitter rounds and lost the decision.

Meanwhile, McCoy made up his mind to continue taking on all-comers, irrespective of weight. In his first fight after the Sharkey encounter, he fought the formidable Jewish heavyweight Joe Choynski in the latter's hometown of San Francisco on 24 March 1899 and won over 20 rounds. It was a notable performance as Choynski had been in the ring with past and future world heavyweight champions such as John L Sullivan, James J Corbett, Bob Fitzsimmons and James J Jeffries, and would establish himself as one of the outstanding heavyweights around the turn of the 20th century.

It would be first of three classic encounters between the pair. They boxed a six-round draw in Chicago seven months later and on 12 January 1900, in New York, McCoy left no doubt about his superiority by knocking out Choynski in the fourth round. 'I always found McCoy a tricky customer,' Choynski would recall in later years. 'I found it extremely hard to nail him. He was all over the place.'

McCoy said in an interview in 1937 with Nat Fleischer, editor of *Ring* magazine, 'My good record at the time, especially the knockout over Choynski, should have gotten me a title fight with Jeffries, but Jeff wasn't having any. He was running scared of me. What other conclusion can you come to, Nat? I continually challenged Jeffries to no avail. I had started off that year, 1900, in good form by knocking out the Irish heavyweight Peter Maher in five rounds. Then followed four more wins, including the Choynski victory, and I was in a good position for a title shot but nothing happened.'

When an offer came to fight the former world heavyweight champion James J Corbett on 30 August 1900 at Madison Square Garden, New York, McCoy accepted. Once again, he would be the lighter man but he told newspapermen he had discovered a weakness in Corbett's defence and would exploit it to the fullest. However, two weeks before the fight, there were rumours that the bout was fixed. George Siler said in the *Chicago Tribune* that he had been told by a prominent manager that McCoy would take a dive and pocket 'a substantial sum' from a betting syndicate.

A rumour that both boxers had agreed to equally share a purse of $33,810 instead of the normal 75 per cent to the winner and the remaining 25 per cent to the loser lent credence to the allegations. Both boxers denied the claims, declaring that the split would be 50-50, but the rumours gained such widespread attention among the public that the arena was far from full and the $35 box seats were empty. Corbett had all the physical advantages, being two inches taller than the 5ft 11ins McCoy, and at 190lbs had a 20lb pull in the weights. James J entered the ring as a 2/1 on favourite.

Scheduled for 25 rounds, few expected the fight to last even ten. After referee Charles White called both men to the centre of the ring to explain the rules, 'the prizefighters waived the formality of shaking hands and eyed each other with anything but friendly glances,' reported the *New York Times*. It was clear that there was no love lost between them.

At the bell, McCoy took the offensive and crowded in on Corbett but no blows were struck. Both missed with long jabs and McCoy neatly sidestepped a right cross and countered with a fast left hook that glanced off Corbett's chin. The round ended with both contestants feeling each other out. James J opened the second round more aggressively, driving back the lighter man with jabs and swings and for the first time McCoy was looking worried. Corbett increased the pace further in the third and while some of his swings missed the target, the blows that did land hurt McCoy and the Kid was staggered by a long right to the jaw. McCoy hung on and the bell sounded before the two could be separated.

Corbett continued his assault in the fourth round and McCoy was now looking decidedly jaded. In the fifth, encouraged by the shouts of his followers, Corbett landed effective blows to the head and body. McCoy tried to save himself by holding on but Corbett was now anxious to finish the fight as soon as possible. The Kid made a brief recovery by getting through with some hard blows to the chest, but James J pushed him off and landed some sharp uppercuts and swings that the tired McCoy failed to avoid.

There was no escape now for the lighter man. McCoy rushed into a clinch but Corbett pushed him away and landed powerful rights and lefts to the body that sent McCoy to the canvas. The Kid managed to get to his knees with his head down and remained in that position as the referee counted him out. The time of the knockout was 2:03 of the fifth round.

The *New York Times* report, under a heading 'McCoy Knocked Out by Fierce Blows to the Body', seemed satisfied that the fight was genuine. 'The fight while it lasted was as ferocious an encounter as ever has taken place in the city,' the paper said. 'What was looked for was a craftily contested bout between the most skilful glove fighters of the time, long drawn out by cautious and scientific masters of sparring. What was really seen was a modicum of scientific boxing, then a rough grappling and swift exchange of blows, all in favour of the heavier man, and a clean knockout after a furious attack by Corbett.'

George Siler, who had brought up the 'fake fight' story in the *Chicago Tribune* in the lead-up to the bout, reported, 'It was hard to believe that the fighters were not acting. At the end, one had the same feeling as a person coming away from a clever but decadent play – he wants to take several long breaths of good, fresh air and a drink of cool, clear water to take the taste out of his mouth.'

McCoy insisted to his dying day that he threw the fight and got a 'nice little financial reward' for his efforts, but Corbett was adamant that the fight was on the level. 'The accusation hurt me more than anything else that has ever been said about me,' he wrote in his autobiography *The Roar of the Crowd*. 'I saw no evidence of McCoy's reported efforts to "lie down" and he fought very hard in the fight. I had bluffed my opponents sometimes but it was beyond me ever to descend to fixing a fight.'

The fix-or-no-fix story eventually died down, especially after the US vice-president, Theodore Roosevelt, declared that he had enough evidence to suggest that the fight was on the level. McCoy continued his career, taking on all-comers, and managed to get a fight in April 1903 for the world light-heavyweight title, a newly formed weight division created by a Chicago newspaperman named Lou Houseman to bridge the gap between the middleweight and heavyweight divisions. Matched with Jack Root in a ten-rounder in Detroit, McCoy lost the decision.

Undaunted, the Kid turned his attention to anybody who was willing to take him on – anywhere in the world. He turned up in Nice in January 1912 and outscored the Irishman Petty Officer Matthew 'Nutty' Curran over 20 rounds. Not satisfied with the verdict, Curran demanded a return. It was not until

August 1914 that they met again, this time at the old Blackfriars Ring in London in a scheduled 20-rounder.

McCoy was 40 years of age at the time and feeling it after 23 long years in the ring. By the 15th round he looked tired and worn, although still ahead on points. Suddenly, the timekeeper sitting by the ring in evening dress took a tall glass of whisky and soda from an attendant and placed it carefully on the apron of the ring. A moment later, McCoy ran into a right cross from Curran, fell to the floor near the timekeeper's seat, snatched up the highball and drank it off. It rejuvenated the Kid and he went on to win the remaining rounds and the decision.

McCoy carried on with his ring career for another two years before making his final ring appearance on 4 August 1916, when he won a decision against Artie Sheridan in Mission, Texas. 'I always wanted to go out a winner and I'm happy I've now achieved that,' he told newspapermen in his dressing room.

As it was, McCoy made more front-page headlines during his hectic and often wild private life than for anything he achieved in the ring. Some years earlier, the Kid was hanging around with Mrs Elizabeth Ellis, a wealthy widow worth $7m whose late husband had made a fortune building locomotives in New York. McCoy and Ellis eventually married and the Kid, now wearing a dignified moustache, spent most of his days riding round in Elizabeth's fleet of luxury cars or aboard the family yacht. The fact that McCoy had been married six times already was neither here nor there.

To nobody's great surprise, the couple divorced on the grounds that 'Charles simply refused to end his playboy lifestyle and settle down,' in the words of the latest Mrs McCoy. The Kid was called up for army service in 1917 and did a year with the 29th Infantry Division, and sold bonds. On being demobbed, he worked as a salesman and a private detective, as well as opening a bar and a gym in New York.

In the ensuing years, there were periods of bankruptcy and modest affluence, of riding horses in Hollywood B movies and making friends with the likes of Charlie Chaplin and the director D W Griffith. He made personal appearances at boxing venues and social gatherings but became addicted to alcohol and was now broke. McCoy's unusually quiet life might have gone on indefinitely had he not met one Mrs Teresa Weinstein Moers at a party in Los Angeles.

A wealthy antiques dealer and wife of Wilbert E Moers, Teresa was literally swept off her feet – and out of her marriage – by the charming former world champion. The couple moved into an apartment and were described by neighbours as 'a devoted couple'. But the cosy arrangement did not last. There were frequent quarrels over his womanising and heavy drinking. It all came to an end on the night of 12 August 1924 when, after a wild drinking party at their place, McCoy shot Teresa through the head.

McCoy was arrested the following morning when, dishevelled and apparently drunk, he rushed into Mrs Moers's antique shop a few blocks away, terrifying customers and staff as he waved a gun before dashing out into the street, where he shot and injured two men and a woman. The police nabbed him as he was running blindly through nearby Westlake Park.

Charged with murder, McCoy was defended by a promising young attorney called Jerry Geisler, who would later become famous as the lawyer for troubled movie stars. Despite Geisler's contention that Teresa had argued with McCoy and that the gun he had in his hand went off accidentally, the jury, which was out for a record 78 hours, found him guilty of manslaughter. Judge Charles Crail sentenced McCoy to 24 years in San Quentin, the state penitentiary near San Francisco.

A model prisoner, the Kid served just seven years before being released on parole. He lectured on the evils of drink, worked for the Ford motor company in Detroit for several years and married again, for the eighth time. Tragically, his life would come apart for the last time with two suicide notes scrawled in a hotel room in the spring of 1940.

Chapter 2

Nightmare on 41st Street

BOXING'S long and colourful history has produced some unusual and controversial characters, to say the least, but it is debatable if there ever was, or ever will be, an oddball to match Battling Siki, the first African to win a world title.

Known as the 'Singular Senegalese', on the one hand Siki was a brawling wild man who knew no fear inside or outside the ring.

He once paraded a fully grown lioness on a leash down the boulevards of Paris, much to the terror of pedestrians and the consternation of gendarmes who threatened to jail him. Often, he could be seen in full evening dress with a mischievous chattering monkey perched on his shoulder. Other times, he would fire a gun into the air to attract attention and induce his two Great Danes to do some tricks.

On the other hand, Siki was a well-educated person who spoke eight languages and was decorated for his bravery on the battlefields of World War 1.

A national hero in Senegal, then a French colony on West Africa's coast, Siki's life ended tragically just before Christmas 1925 in New York when a police officer on his dawn beat found him face down on the sidewalk. He had two bullet wounds in his back. The killing remains one of the city's many unsolved murders.

Light-heavyweight champion of the world in the Roaring 20s, Siki, a Muslim, was born Baye Phal in the sprawling Senegal port city of Saint-Louis on 22 September 1897. 'Baye is a Senegalese name corresponding to Louis, so I am Louis Phal,' he would tell an interviewer. 'I called myself Battling Siki when I became a boxer as Siki is a Senegalese word which parents apply to their children, like darling in English or cherie in French. I adopted it because I thought it was one that people would remember.'

Boxing writers in the US and Britain believed Siki was born 'in the bush' but it was far from the truth. He told Ed Cunningham of *Ring* magazine he resented stories that he had 'hopped from a coconut tree in the jungle and straight into a boxing ring'. He pointed out that 'Saint-Louis, where I was born, is a big city with streetcars and everything that a modern city has'.

Coming from a poor family, Siki grew up diving for coins in the harbour. He claimed his father was a wealthy trader dealing in plumes, feathers, cigarettes and monkey fur, and his grandfather was a slave captured by the Moors tribe before escaping to Saint-Louis, where he married. Siki would recall he was bitten by the wanderlust bug, ran away from home as a boy and made his way to Paris. While there, the ten-year-old was spotted doing handsprings on the streets by an affluent German dancer, Elaine Grosse, who had been touring France and took him into her act as her servant, dressing him in red velvet.

By day, she taught him to read and write, provided him with nice clothes and they toured several European capitals to wide acclaim. At the end of the tour, they went back together to her villa on the French Riviera. Elaine said she wanted to adopt Siki and planned to take him back to Germany, but French immigration officials refused her request unless she got written permission from the boy's parents. The consent never arrived and she finally and reluctantly said goodbye to Siki in Marseilles after giving him 1,000 francs. 'That'll tide you over until you get a job,' she said.

'I never heard from her again,' Siki recalled. 'I repeatedly tried to get in touch with her and wrote to various theatrical agencies in France and other countries to no avail. She was a wonderful lady and was very kind to a black boy. Only for her, I would have been slogging away in Senegal's hot climate.'

Having had a taste for travel, Siki hitchhiked his way to Paris and received some assistance and schooling from the charitable organisation La Francais de Bienfassance, but was generally left to his own devices. He managed to get several menial jobs, mainly as a dishwasher in various hotels and cafes. In one hotel, part of his job was to throw out bad patrons who refused to pay their bills. A boxing official once witnessed an incident such as this and told him that with his fine physique and muscular body, he should give the sport a go.

Making enquiries, Siki discovered that there was an amateur boxing academy in Marseilles run by a wealthy sportsman named Paul Latil. Making his way to the port city in southern France, he joined the academy as a sparring partner for established boxers. Siki's innate athletic ability and knack of absorbing heavy punishment without weakening made him a popular choice for the big hitters. He had a heavy punch, too. 'One afternoon in the ring, I closed my eyes, swung a big right and knocked my man down and out,' he later recalled.

After learning the basic rudiments of the sport from Latil, who showed him how to hit the other fellow without being hit himself, and how to weave and duck, Siki felt his skill would develop and add to his natural hitting power to make him a good fighter.

On 13 October 1912, Siki turned professional with Latil's approval and best wishes. Although he lost his first two fights and didn't record his first win until his seventh, he was on his way. By his own admission Siki had a succession of managers, changing them regularly as he tried to find the right one.

Siki had limited skill but possessed a good punch in both hands, though he often missed more than he landed. Promoters were not exactly falling over themselves to put him on their shows. It was always a question of 'Siki who?' His early record was anything but auspicious with just six wins, six losses and a draw in his first 12 months, but he was picking up valuable experience that he would put to good use later.

'The main thing was that I was learning,' he told a Parisian journalist. 'Things were starting to look good and I was getting to fight good men for better purses. I was getting stronger and learning from each man I fought. Often, I would get into the ring, act nervous, shuffle around and when the bell sounded I would swing my arms wildly. People would laugh and the opponent would think he had a frightened man before him.'

At the outbreak of World War 1 in 1914, Siki joined the French army and was assigned to the 8th Colonial Infantry Regiment composed only of Africans. He never liked the life of a soldier and was reprimanded twice for overstaying his leave, drinking wine and having fun with the local girls until a squad of soldiers came to take him into custody. 'For most men, the squalid living conditions in the trenches made for a thoroughly miserable existence,' wrote Nigel Collins in Boxing Babylon. 'For Louis Phal, however, it was just another adventure, one of the countless hair-raising episodes that punctuated a life of reckless abandon.'

Inside two years, Siki had become a national hero for bravery in the Battle of the Somme in France, the bloodiest conflict of World War 1, which lasted for over three months. On the first day alone, 1 July 1916, over 57,000 British Army troops were killed or wounded by German infantry.

'I felt honoured to join the army and do my duty as a French citizen,' remembered Siki. 'My four brothers joined up, too, and three of them were killed. I was in all the early campaigns and I was fortunate to receive my only wounds around the Somme in the summer of 1916. Bomb fragments went through both my legs in the middle of the calf. After a short spell in hospital, I was transferred to Toulon and wound up as a corporal in the 73rd

Regiment of heavy artillery. I became the champion thrower of hand grenades. I could throw them 75 metres and it was exciting. I went into what sportswriters were calling my "jungle crouch" and let the Germans have the grenades.

'When hostilities ended in November 1918, my artillery regiment was sent to Versailles near Paris and I was demobbed shortly afterwards. I was Corporal Louis Phal and I was decorated twice, receiving the Croix de Guerre and the Médaille Militaire and seven citations "for conspicuous bravery in action." That was nice and I was glad I had done my part for my country.'

After the armistice Siki resumed his boxing career, determined to make something of himself, far away from the world of blazing gunfire, bursting shells and dense smoke. Getting down to serious work in the gym and with a new manager in tow, Siki had a particularly good 1920, with 15 wins and one loss.

'By now I was much bigger and stronger, a fully blown middleweight at close to 160lbs, the division's limit, and I often boxed at light-heavyweight,' he recalled. 'The newspapers and magazines were featuring me in their pages and I felt good. I felt I was achieving something and getting places in boxing. In interviews, I told writers for a story that I was a wild beast from the jungle and had a skull so thick that punches just bounced off me. The ones I didn't knock out just ran away from me, scared.'

Now managed by Jim Harris, who knew his way around the pitfalls of the fight game and had many connections, Siki fought in Paris, Strasburg, Brussels, Algiers, Barcelona, Amsterdam, Antwerp and Marseilles, gaining a reputation as a good fighter with a strong wallop in both gloves. Continuing to keep busy, in 1921 he had 14 fights, all wins. Having developed into a light-heavyweight, rarely weighing a few pounds over the 175lb limit, he frequently took on heavyweights.

Siki's big problem was his growing addiction to drink. He would often round up his pals, head for the nearest bar, get drunk and start throwing his weight around, sometimes turning up tables. More often than not, the gendarmes were called to restore some kind of order and haul off Siki to the local station, where he would either be jailed overnight, forced to pay a fine or let off with a caution. 'The police have something against me,' he would complain. 'They just don't like me.'

Nevertheless, when he was sober and got down to the serious business of keeping in shape, Siki looked capable of beating any boxer. In 1922 he fought Harry Reeve, from London's East End, a former British light-heavyweight champion now campaigning as a heavyweight, three times, winning the first bout over ten rounds, a no-decision in the second fight and finally knocking out Reeve in six rounds in their third meeting. 'I have a feeling you'll make something of yourself in the fight game,' Reeve told Siki in the dressing room. Prophetic words.

Louis Golding, the Manchester-born author and novelist, was one who was impressed by Siki's style and attitude. 'Big and strong, there was terrific power in those long, pendulous arms, which could be unleashed with devastating effect when he was aroused,' wrote Golding in later years. 'Crowds flocked to see him in action. His appearance, as he shambled under the arc lights, monstrous and as black as midnight, terrified audiences and opponents alike. Without exactly being sensational, his record was impressive and a number of good men were put away in style, some in the knockout mood.'

Shortly after Siki's win over Harry Reeve in Marseilles in July 1922, feelers were put out by his manager for a world light-heavyweight title fight with Georges Carpentier, the Frenchman who had been champion for over a year. But Carpentier's canny manager, Francois Descamps, was reportedly looking for too much money and too high a percentage of the gate. Negotiations fell through.

Carpentier, an extremely talented boxer with a knockout blow in both hands, would have been formidable opposition for Siki but Harris felt his boxer had a real chance of winning and was prepared to back his man heavily. But every time Siki's managers contacted Descamps with a challenge for a title fight, the answer was always no. Descamps would tell reporters stories like 'Siki hasn't proven himself against legitimate contenders' or 'a Siki-Carpentier fight would not draw a nickel' or 'Nobody knows who the hell this African is.' Everybody, however, knew the real reason – big money or no fight.

Questions were nevertheless being asked in boxing circles, such as, 'Was the financial issue a convenient cover-up by the Carpentier camp for avoiding Siki?' 'Unlikely,' agreed the experts. In any event, Georges feared no man. Hadn't he taken on the great Jack Dempsey for the heavyweight championship of the world the previous summer, conceding 16lbs? If he did not fear Dempsey, why should he be afraid of the untested Siki?

With no official world championship organisation to control and determine who should fight who in title fights, it was left to promoters in the main to set them up – and more often or not, the biggest drawing cards got the championship bouts rather than legitimate contenders. With Americans showing little interest in a fight between a Frenchman and an African, it was a Parisian newspaper article that brought on a Carpentier-Siki match. 'Georges Carpentier has not boxed in the capital for three years and should he not now give fans a chance to see him?' said *Paris Soir*. Other papers such as *Auto* and *Echo des Sports* followed.

Finally, giving in to public opinion and with no other legitimate opponents around anyway, Carpentier and Descamps signed contracts for a world light-heavyweight title defence against Battling Siki. The venue was the Vélodrome Buffalo on the outskirts of Paris and the match was scheduled for the afternoon of 24 September 1922. It would be Siki's big chance to make ring history and become the first African to win a world title. But the boxing public asked, 'Could he do it against a superb champion like the talented Frenchman?' The experts shook their heads. Little or no chance.

'In reality, there was no justification for the match,' Carpentier would tell this writer in later years. 'But the public wanted to see me in action and as there was nobody else around, we took it. Marcel Niles, the heavyweight champion of France, wanted to fight me but his manager wanted nothing to do with the fight. In any event, I felt a match with Siki would be an easy one. He was a well-built fellow, a middleweight in actual fact, who had attracted a certain amount of attention to himself with some unimportant victories, but he lacked a lot of class. I figured I could handle him.'

Georges was boxing's matinee idol. A handsome, dashing figure, he was responsible for bringing hordes of female admirers to boxing matches in the years leading up to World War 1. He competed at all weights, from flyweight to heavyweight, and was heavyweight champion of Europe for nine years. While never weighing more than a light-heavyweight, it was in the 175lb division that he became champion of the world.

Considered by many as the greatest French boxer of all time, Carpentier was born just outside the mining village of Lens in northern France on 12 January 1894. The youngest of five children, his father was of peasant stock and graduated from working in the fields to driving a horse and cart for a factory for little pay.

Soon after Georges was born, the family moved to a miner's cottage in Lens, where his father got work in brewery as a maltster. The youngster was actually weaned on the local light pale ale, which he drank from a baby's feeding bottle and retained a lifelong taste for.

When he was ten years of age, Carpentier and his mother travelled to Paris as guests of a neighbour in the capital. 'I found the whole experience fascinating,' he recalled. 'The journey on a train, the Arc de Triomphe, the lovely restaurants and the drive through the streets in a carriage. The lovely girls, Paris, the good living. This was the life I wanted, the life for me, and I vowed someday I would return and become rich and famous.'

Back in Lens, and getting into street fights with usually bigger boys, one day he was spotted by Francois Descamps, who ran a travelling one-man show that entertained the country folk with acrobatics, hypnotism and political oration. He took a liking to Georges, which was reciprocated. Descamps also ran a gymnasium in Lens and invited the boy to train at his gym as an alternative to fighting in the street.

Georges proved his skill at boxing and gymnastics and was soon part of the team at sports displays in the area. Descamps also taught his club members a French version of the noble art called *la savate*, which permitted the use of feet like kick boxing, said to be a forerunner of martial arts so popular today. Descamps now expanded his repertoire in the show to include exhibitions of *la savate* and conventional boxing, which turned out to be very popular with customers. Georges was now becoming something of an all-rounder, boxing in what he called 'the English style' and *la savate* in the French method.

Carpentier, meanwhile, attended school regularly and came out at 12 years of age with very good marks. He worked at a variety of jobs, including a riveter's assistant and an insurance collector, but always at the back of his mind was Paris, the city of opportunity. Someday he would make it big in the City of Light and make his parents proud of him.

Descamps felt Carpentier had the making of a world champion and following a long talk with the lad's parents, he got their consent. All they wanted was for Francois to look after their boy as if he was his own son and ensure that he came to no harm. The ambitious manager and the equally keen student set off together on a journey that would lead them to fame and fortune.

Conventional boxing was unknown in France at the time and fighting for sport was conducted in the *la savate* style. But Descamps had heard of 'the English form of boxing' and as soon as he and his protégé had seen a performance of *la box Anglais*, they quickly added it to their repertoire of entertainment.

When a German circus came to Lens, Descamps heard about an acrobat named Ali, who was roughly the same age as the 11-year-old Carpentier. Francois arranged a match between the two and Georges knocked out his opponent inside 15 seconds with a fast right hand to the chin. Descamps was impressed and felt that the lad had tremendous potential as a boxer. But that would be in the future.

One day a major amateur boxing tournament was held in Béthune, some eight miles from Lens, and Descamps put Carpentier's name forward. Georges ended up reaching the semi-finals. This encouraged him to give up his day job as an insurance collector and, with his family's full approval, become a professional boxer under Descamps's managementship.

Carpentier and Descamps would go on to become one of the standout boxer-manager relationships in ring history. Descamps was entitled to 30 per cent of his boxer's earnings but would accept 20 per cent until Georges became successful. Carpentier would tell this writer in later years that they never had a written agreement or contract of any sort throughout their 18-year partnership, from the time of his first bout to his final one. 'We were always the best of friends, from beginning to end,' he confided.

On 1 November 1908, at the Café de Paris in Maisons-Lafitte, on the outskirts of the capital, Carpentier made a successful debut in the paid ranks in a scheduled 20-rounder when his more experienced opponent, Ed Salmon, accidentally fouled him in the 13th round. The 14-year-old Carpentier had held his own up to that point in the fight, which was made at 103lbs, nine pounds below the flyweight limit and which by today's standards would fall under the minimum weight division.

The fighters met in a return at the same venue a month later, again scheduled for 20 rounds, but this time Descamps retired his charge in the 18th round after Georges had been down ten times in the previous three rounds and was exhausted. Carpentier felt he could have gone on but Descamps said, 'No point in taking unnecessary punishment. Your day will come, don't worry.'

Around this time, Carpentier met 19-year-old Maurice Chevalier, who was making his name as an entertainer. Chevalier had come into the gym for a workout and the two lads who would become world famous in a few years developed a lasting friendship. Each would follow their respective careers and always kept in touch.

By now, Carpentier had gone to live in Puteaux on the fringes of Paris while Descamps remained in Lille, but they travelled together for fights and Georges was a busy boxer. Through 1909 and 1910 he had 41 fights, winning 32, 18 inside the distance, and losing just four. He was turning into a big attraction with a large following, especially among the ladies.

'Carpentier was a very, very handsome man, even to the end of his days,' said the historian Gilbert Odd, who edited the trade paper *Boxing News* for many years. 'Women loved him. He was the idol of France, not only for his amazing performances in the ring but also because he grew into an athlete of beautifully proportioned physique, with handsome features that attracted women to boxing as never before. His lightning right-hand punches that won him so many victories also earned their admiration and hero worship.'

Georges scored a notable win in November 1909 when he defeated Charles Ledoux, a future world bantamweight champion, over 15 rounds in Paris, and received rave notices in the press. A month later, again in Paris, he won the French lightweight title by outpointing Paul Til over ten rounds while still only 15 years of age. The lad had not yet cultivated the deadly, accurate punching power that would characterise his later ring life, but he was putting on weight and gaining strength and confidence.

Within 18 months, Carpentier won the French welterweight championship by stopping gritty Robert Eustache in 16 rounds, following it up with impressive victories in European welterweight and middleweight title fights. Two visiting American boxers, Frank Klaus and Billy Papke, proved too good for the Frenchman in 1912. Klaus, who had a claim on the world middleweight title and was an experienced battler, won in the 19th round in Dieppe when Descamps threw in the towel to save his man from unnecessary punishment.

Papke, who had two classic fights with Stanley Ketchel, the feared 'Michigan Assassin', was too strong for Georges and won on a stoppage in the 17th round, with some sources listing it as a disqualification defeat. It would be Carpentier's last fight as a middleweight. From now on, he would campaign in the more comfortable light-heavyweight division.

Carpentier duly won the vacant European light-heavyweight title on his onward march to the top as he set his sights on the heavyweight championship held by his former sparring partner Bombardier Billy Wells. A Londoner by birth, Wells was good looking and debonair but was something of an enigma in the ring. He had the build to become a world champion but suffered the most amazing lapses, losing to opponents one day when he might easily have beaten them on another. In all but two of his professional fights, he either knocked out his opponent or was counted out himself. He was never beaten on points.

The Carpentier-Wells title fight was set for Ghent, Belgium on 1 June 1913. Billed as 'David v Goliath,' the taller, rangier Englishman was a strong favourite to turn back the Frenchman's challenge. It was Wells who started strongly, dropping the Lens fighter with chopping lefts and rights in the opening round. It was all Wells in the second round, too, with the younger Frenchman barely surviving the session. In the third, and on Descamps's advice, Carpentier concentrated on the Londoner's body with hooks and uppercuts, which slowed down the Bombardier. In round four, a hard left hook to the body followed by a jarring right to the chin dropped Wells for the full count. Europe had a brand new heavyweight champion.

When Wells claimed he was unlucky to lose, a return was set for the National Sporting Club in London for 8 December. This time, and knowing the Englishman's strength and mainly his weakness, Carpentier got to work quickly. Slipping under the Bombardier's long left hand, he landed some powerful lefts and rights to the body and Wells sank to the canvas for the full count. The time was 73 seconds. Wells was booed as he left the ring and Jim Driscoll of Wales, who had recently retired as a world featherweight title claimant, called him a coward.

Carpentier was in England when World War 1 was declared in August 1914 and enlisted in the French air force. After passing several examinations as a pilot, he was involved in regular air battles behind a machine gun on a swivel and, like Siki, became a war hero, being awarded the Croix de Guerre and the Médaille Militaire. He was demobilised in August 1919 after completing a course as a PT instructor and trainer.

Resuming his boxing career, Carpentier took on the British heavyweight champion, Joe Beckett, who had succeeded Bombardier Billy Wells, at Holborn Stadium in London on 4 December 1919. Promoter C B Cochran charged £25 for ringside seats but all the fans got were 73 seconds. Beckett succumbed to a stunning right cross to the chin that sent him down for the full count.

Ten months later, on his American debut, Carpentier knocked out Battling Levinsky in four rounds in Jersey City to win the world light-heavyweight title. Flushed with success, he challenged Jack Dempsey for the heavyweight title on 2 July 1921, again in Jersey City, but the powerful 'Manassa Mauler', outweighing his opponent by 20lbs, put his man down for a count of nine in the fourth round. On rising, Dempsey dropped him a second time for the full count. The historic match, promoted by the flamboyant Tex Rickard, drew over 80,000 fans, who paid a record gate of $1,789,238, the first fight to pull in over a million dollars.

Carpentier returned to London in 1922 and had two early wins, a fourth-round knockout over Australia's George Cook at the Royal Albert Hall and a defence of his world light-heavyweight title against local favourite Ted 'Kid' Lewis at Olympia. This one ended in less than a round. A former world welterweight champion, Lewis claimed he was complaining to the referee about a foul punch when Carpentier knocked him down for the full count.

Now it was time for his second defence, against Battling Siki. Normally, any boxer would jump at the chance-of-a-lifetime opportunity to fight for a world title, but Siki did not think he was ready for such an important bout and wanted at least one warm-up. However, with his manager Jim Harris having already consented to having Siki in the ring on 24 September 1922, there was no turning back. In any event, the Vélodrome Buffalo had been extended in anticipation of a large crowd, with a canopy put over the ring so that the fight could go ahead in bad weather.

With Siki still arguing that he did not want the fight just yet, an agreement was finally reached between both managers that it would technically be an exhibition bout, though, peculiarly enough, the world title was still on the line. It was agreed that Carpentier would treat Siki lightly for four rounds before knocking him out in the fifth. Both boxers were also told by their mentors that the film rights had been sold on the proviso that the fight would last at least four rounds.

'That was the arrangement,' Carpentier would later tell this writer. 'The plan was that for four rounds I would tap Siki lightly and he would make it appear he was trying to knock me out. The crowd would never know. With this in mind, I did little training.'

At the weigh-in, Carpentier scaled 173lbs and Siki 174lbs. It was something of a grudge match, certainly as far as Siki was concerned. While a smiling Carpentier merely told reporters that he was confident of winning and left it at that, Siki was more forthright.

'I'm glad this match is taking place,' he said. 'Carpentier's handlers have been saying I'm not a worthy challenger, which is not true. I'm the number one contender and everybody knows it. The strange thing is that for the last two years I've been racing around France, Belgium, Holland and Germany fighting everybody who would get into the ring with me. Who else is Carpentier going to fight? He even went up to heavyweight to take on Jack Dempsey, and lost. No honest observer can say that Battling Siki, a black brawler from Senegal, has not earned the opportunity. I'm told I only got the fight because I agreed to lose. We'll see.'

With a crowd of over 55,000 in attendance, the contest was on, exhibition or not. This was for real, with the winner as world champion. Carpentier danced round his opponent for two rounds, tapping home light left jabs as Siki swung and missed. In the third, Siki was short with a left hook but connected with a right swing that dropped a shocked Carpentier for a count of four. Flushed with success and ignoring any pre-arranged agreement between the respective managers, Siki went on the attack in the fourth round as the crowd roared and he bloodied the Frenchman's nose with a stinging right cross. By the fifth round, the fight had turned into a brawl, with both fighters headbutting, punching low and ignoring all the rules, but there were no warnings from referee Henri Bernstein.

Siki was looking fresh and strong when the bell rang to start round six whereas Carpentier was badly cut and seemed jaded. Shortly into the round the Frenchman went down, holding his right leg and obviously in pain. Referee Bernstein moved in and indicated to the three judges that he was disqualifying Siki for tripping. This prompted an angry reaction from the crowd and boos broke out. The big crowd were now on the underdog's side. With Carpentier still on the canvas, his bloodied face masked in pain and with little chance of beating the count, it was all over. Bernstein called a hurried meeting with French Boxing Federation officials at ringside and the verdict was changed.

Forget that silly exhibition tag. Siki was now the winner on a knockout in the sixth round, becoming Africa's first world boxing champion.

'By the end of the third round, I wanted to win,' said Siki in the dressing room. 'I decided I was not to take a beating from a man I knew I could defeat. We both landed good punches in the fourth round but in the fifth, most of the best shots were mine. Just before the bell ended the fifth round, Carpentier slipped and as I helped him to his feet, he sneakily lands a left hook to my head. That enraged me. Starting the sixth, I charged him and landed a powerful right uppercut to the chin and more uppercuts and body shots. He collapses stiffly, clutching his right leg, and it doesn't look like he'll be able to get up.

'He was struggling to get to his feet but couldn't make it. He must have been down for at least 30 seconds. Meanwhile, the referee was bending over the ropes talking to the judges and next thing he announced he was disqualifying me for tripping. With utter confusion around the ring and the crowd booing, he eventually comes over to me and raises my right hand as winner and new champion. It was a great feeling.'

A sullen and badly marked Carpentier, finally conceding that it was not an exhibition but the real thing, told the newspapermen who crowded into his dressing room, 'Siki definitely tripped me up. There is no doubt about that and the disqualification result should have stood. Bernstein said he had seen Siki deliberately trip me up and in agreement with the three judges, he disqualified Siki and proclaimed me the winner on a foul. But the tumult was so enormous that the decision of Bernstein and the judges was squashed and Siki was announced as the winner. But the wrong man won and Descamps and I were furious that we were double-crossed. Also, why did the crowd, my own faithful fans, boo? I think they don't like to see the same men winning all the time, not even their own.'

With his new-found fame, Siki announced he wanted to take on world heavyweight champion Jack Dempsey. But the

American's promoter Tex Rickard was unhappy about a white v black heavyweight title fight, remembering the race riots during Jack Johnson's reign, and a Siki-Dempsey bout never happened. In any event, Siki was fast losing his head. Always fond of drinking, wearing flashy clothes and escorting beautiful white women around fashionable Parisian nightclubs, he was constantly in bother with the gendarmes for troublemaking.

'Me Siki, me different,' he would say, beating his chest like King Kong. Siki's only concern was enjoying himself, whatever the consequences. After all, it was the Roaring 20s, the decade of fun and frolics, and Battling Siki was the champ. Soon, he found himself barred in restaurants, cafes and bars. It was only a matter of time before the French Boxing Federation suspended him as he had degenerated into a public nuisance and brought discredit on the sport. Issued with deportation papers 'to leave the country as soon as possible', Siki now planned a British trip for a proposed fight with the native heavyweight champion Joe Beckett, but the Home Office announced that if he ever set foot in the country he would be placed under immediate arrest.

Siki still wanted to go to America but an offer from an Irish promoter, Tom Singleton, to defend his title against Mike McTigue, a veteran from County Clare, in Dublin on 17 March 1923 changed all his plans. Siki's new manager, Charles Brouillet, received the offer but did not tell his boxer, whose only interest was the USA and the big time. Brouillet and Singleton hit on a plan. They would tell Siki they were sailing from Cherbourg to New York when in fact they were heading for Dublin via the port of Cobh, in County Cork. To make sure the plan worked, they filled Siki with wines and spirits, which made him so drunk that by the time he sobered up, he was heading down the gangplank in Cobh.

Furious at first that he was conned, Siki soon cooled down when informed by Brouillet and Singleton that McTigue was well past his best and was essentially an overblown middleweight who would not cause any problems. In reality, the Irishman was a crafty, cagey and experienced warrior with many big names in his record.

'He'll be no trouble,' said Brouillet to Siki on the train to Dublin, conveniently keeping quiet about the fact that the country was in the throes of a bloody civil war that had come after the 1916 Rising and the War of Independence. Executions and homes being burned down were commonplace, and the guerrilla war had, in the words of a commentator of the time, all the appearances of a colonial dogfight. The visiting party might well all be blown to pieces. The manager also said not a word about the scheduled date, which happened to be St Patrick's Day, a national holiday, when the Irish on both sides of the troubles would have no time for anybody but their own.

Michael Francis McTigue was born in the small village of Kilnamona, just outside Ennis in County Clare, on Ireland's west coast. One of 13 children, Mike's pet gag was, 'I just ran out of pocket money in a 13-horse race. I was the youngest. There was never enough to go round.' He always had a wanderlust in his bones. At the age of 18, he ran away from home and finished up across the Irish Sea in Sheffield before making his way back to Ireland. In Cobh, he set off on the SS *Baltic* bound for New York and the start of a new life 'in the land of the free and home of the brave', as he cheerfully put it.

The 21-year-old Mike stayed with his brother Patrick John in the Bronx and got a job lugging sides of beef around. He was encouraged to take up boxing when he defended his boss, who was smacked by a drunk and sent sprawling into a pile of raw steak. 'I sailed into the three thugs and knocked one of them to the ground before the other two ran off,' he would remember in later years.

'When my boss regained his feet, he told me I should go in for boxing and I'd make a lot of money as I had a good wallop in both fists. He gave me the address of an old-time lightweight named George 'Elbows' McFadden, who trained boxers at his gym on East 59th Street near Madison Square Garden. George was a good guy and I hear he got the "elbows" tag in his ring days because if he missed with a left or a right, he would bring his elbow back and catch his opponent, bloodying his nose, always away from the referee's glance, too, of course. He fought many greats and held his own.'

Through McFadden's connections, McTigue got in touch with Dan Hickey, who was the boxing instructor at the New York Athletic Club. Hickey got him started as a professional in 1914 when Mike was 21, a relatively late age in those days, but McTigue was confident he could make up for lost time by boxing regularly and learning as he went along.

Mike developed into a clever middleweight boxer with a good, solid punch in both gloves and often fought in the light-heavyweight and heavyweight divisions. 'In his first ten years, he crowded close to 100 fights into his career,' recalled Jersey Jones in *Ring* magazine. 'His style was not flashy or spectacular. Nor was his physical appearance particularly impressive. He was scrawny, almost frail, in build. But he was of the rangy, wiry type, and a lot stronger than he looked.'

McTigue took a break from the ring in early 1918 to join the famed Fighting 69th, an infantry division of the American army, and saw active service in the bloody Battle of the Argonne in France, which lasted seven weeks and brought an end to World War 1. Mike won the Distinguished Service Cross for 'exceptional bravery' on the battlefield.

Resuming his boxing career on demobilisation in 1919, McTigue fought anybody willing to share a ring with him, many in no-decision bouts, including the former world light-heavyweight champion Battling Levinsky, future title-holder in the same division Tommy Loughran and two encounters with Harry Greb, who had still to win the world middleweight title. In 1922, McTigue decided to visit his folks back home and have a few fights in England while he was at it. He had three contests, two in Sheffield and one in Liverpool, all resulting in knockout wins, each in less than four rounds. It was at ringside after the Liverpool contest that McTigue met the Irish promoter Tom Singleton, who would put the Siki fight together.

'Probably no championship fight in ring history had ever been staged amid more fantastic conditions,' recalled Jersey Jones in *Ring* magazine in March 1948, the 25th anniversary of the Siki-McTigue fight. 'Spectators walked to the La Scala Theatre in the centre of Dublin city between rows of armed men and were searched for firearms before being allowed inside. Armoured cars loomed around corners. Machine guns poked their menacing noses from points of vantage. It was a weird setting for a title fight.'

Not surprisingly McTigue, with home advantage, was installed favourite at 6/4 but many of the foreign journalists were not so sure. They felt that the veteran McTigue, who was five years older than the 25-year-old Siki, would tire around the halfway stage of the 20-rounder, when it was expected the stronger champion would come on with his hooks, uppercuts and swings and wrap up the decision. Mike scoffed at such stories. 'The only prominent boxer that Siki has beaten is Carpentier and that was something of a fluke,' he told the *Irish Independent*. 'I will use my better skill and move around the ring to confuse him. No man is going to stop Mike McTigue.' When this was relayed to Siki, the champion replied, 'I haven't come to Ireland to lose my title and McTigue will find that out when we get into the ring.'

As the crowd filed into the La Scala with an estimated 25,000 people in the street and surrounding areas, there was a deafening explosion about 50 yards from the venue. Miraculously, nobody was seriously injured, the only casualty being a young boy struck by flying glass while standing by his mother's fruit stalls.

For whatever reason, there was no weigh-in but it was felt that Siki was around 14lbs heavier. McTigue was essentially an overblown middleweight and his opponent a fully fledged light-heavyweight, with the fight officially made at the light-heavyweight limit of 175lbs.

After Manchester referee Jack Smith called the two fighters together for their final instructions under the white glare of the arc lights, they returned to their corners. Both looked very fit and confident. From the opening bell, McTigue's plan was to keep on the move and pepper Siki with left jabs while at the same time keeping a close watch on the African's strong hooks. Siki's intention was to keep the pressure on the Irishman, back him up as much as possible and get him into range. As it happened, McTigue was as slippery as walking on ice.

According to collective reports of the fight, Siki was apparently ahead after six rounds, with his constant aggression nullifying McTigue's stick-and-move style. He would pound the Irishman to the body and drive Mike back to the ropes. There were many clinches, making referee Smith earn his money, and the heavier blows were coming from Siki. Both the French newspaper *La Populaire* and the Paris edition of the *New York Herald* gave Siki a commanding lead after ten rounds with his constant aggression and body shots. Several other newspapers, though, had McTigue marginally in front on his better boxing.

There was big trouble for Mike in a busy 11th round when he emerged from a clinch with a cut on his left eyebrow. Ringsiders claimed it was caused by a short, sharp right hook but McTigue's corner said it was inflicted by a headbutt. When the referee intervened to inspect the injury, one of his seconds, Ted Broadribb, who would later manage such famous British boxers as Tommy Farr and Freddie Mills, said there was no problem and took the opportunity to tell him to warn Siki about the repeated use of his head. Smith nodded and waved the contestants on.

The injury had been cleared when McTigue came out for the 12th round but he had another problem now. His right thumb was hurting after being damaged, probably in the 11th, but he would conceal it from Siki by using it sparingly, mainly by jabbing away with that fast, stinging left jab and picking up points. The *Irish Times* had McTigue in front after 12 rounds, 'penetrating the African's defence with punches to the head and body'. When Siki returned to his corner at the end of the 12th round, he said he heard former champion Georges Carpentier taunting him from his ringside seat and shouting, 'Go for it, Mike' and 'kill him'. Siki was threatening to climb out of the ring and attack the Frenchman there and then, but was restrained by one of his cornermen.

The Irishman was cleverly slipping Siki's punches in the 13th and 14th rounds, encouraged by shouts of encouragement from his supporters. McTigue's right hand was hurting badly by now after he aggravated the thumb by landing a hard right to the champion's head. While Mike would use the hand sparingly in the closing rounds, Siki never suspected anything was wrong.

McTigue's biographer, Andrew Gallimore, in his book *A Bloody Canvas,* described the finish like this, 'The last round began amidst intense excitement. A hush of expectancy fell on the crowd, with only the occasional isolated cheer to break the silence in the packed venue. The cigarette smoke drifted towards the lights that illuminated the soiled canvas as the two weary warriors fell into a clinch – needing each other to remain upright. Mike won the 20th because he was marginally less tired than the champion.'

Referee Smith's scorecard was never disclosed but at the final bell he had no hesitation in walking over to the Irishman's corner and raising his right hand in victory. One of McTigue's cornermen, overcome with emotion, fell to the floor unconscious. Some of Mike's jubilant fans clambered over seats, made their way into the ring, hoisted their hero and new champion on to their shoulders and carried him out of the ring. This was truly a night to remember for the Irish.

In a packed and noisy dressing room, McTigue said, 'I thought I won comfortably and only for the fact that my right thumb was injured, I might have stopped him. I beat him to the punch two to one. He didn't land a clean blow and I had no doubt at the finish that I had won. Siki had only two punches all night, a long left and a overhand right, and I was able to block them and score on the counter. He's lucky I only had one hand from the 11th round.'

Siki was crestfallen in his dressing room. 'We will have to lodge a protest that I deserved to win the fight,' he said. 'All McTigue did was move, move, move. I did all the punching. I felt I won at least 17 of the 20 rounds and my corner thought so, too. I was robbed of my title and this is the last time I will box in Ireland. I'm now going to America, where I will get a fair deal.'

While some felt that Siki and his team had a case, with the Parisian newspaper *Le Journal* calling the decision 'iniquitious' and ex-champion Georges Carpentier saying the verdict was 'incomprehensible and indefensible', most observers felt that while the fight was close, McTigue's better boxing and ring technique were the deciding factors. Their view was that it was a victory for skill and scientific boxing over big punching and aggression.

Referee Smith could not be located in the packed theatre for his after-fight view but in a statement the next day, he justified his verdict, 'I understand there is considerable controversy over my decision. Some, I believe, think that a draw might have been a better verdict but McTigue had secured a sufficient lead on points, which left me in no doubt as to the rightful winner. Granted that Siki was the aggressor for the greater part of the contest, yet in his retreats and evasions the Irishman was continually scoring and generally outboxing his opponent. Siki was the better fighter but as a boxer he was distinctly outclassed. Except when he caused McTigue's eye to bleed, Siki never had his opponent in difficulty.'

There was much talk of a return fight, this time in Paris, where Siki had beaten Carpentier six months earlier, but it never happened. McTigue soon left for New York and continued his career there. Siki returned to France, where he had two wins and a loss before packing his bags for America, where he planned to redeem himself. 'America hasn't seen Battling Siki in the flesh and I want to go there and show them what I can do,' he told pressmen in France.

Nat Fleischer, founder and publisher of *Ring* magazine, recalled that Siki entered the US quietly. 'Most fight fans did not know a lot about him, except that he could hit hard and take a lot of punishment. He was a fighter of the dock variety and when he rolled his eyes, he looked terrifying. American sportswriters took to him and he in turn enjoyed the attention he was receiving. I heard many stories of him – that he drank like a fish and was a nasty customer when riled. I also understood he paraded a lioness on the streets of Paris.'

All the rumours were confirmed to the satisfaction of Fleischer and two other newspapermen when they came upon Siki directing the traffic with his cane in the middle of 42nd Street and Broadway, but without the lioness this time. Dressed in formal evening clothes, with a flowing French cape lined with purple satin over his broad shoulders, he wore bright red gloves and grey suede shoes. One of the writers remarked, 'This guy was dressed to kill!'

When a policeman, a former Olympic hammer thrower named Pat McDonald, approached to see what all the commotion was about, a chattering monkey leapt from underneath Siki's cloak and landed on the officer's head. There was a shriek from the crowd that had gathered as McDonald gathered his composure, grabbed Siki by the arm and bustled him away with a stern warning, 'No more of these commotions, mister, or you'll find yourself in jail.'

Siki took on a new manager, a veteran New Yorker named Pa Levy and made his American debut against Kid Norfolk on 20 November 1923 at Madison Square Garden. A crowd of 12,180 was in attendance but it was quite clear that Siki was out of condition. The Baltimore fighter, a ringwise veteran and 6/5 favourite, won all of the 15 rounds and only a knockout could have saved Siki. It never came. In the early rounds, Norfolk used an effective left jab and often crossed over hard rights to the chin to break up Siki's limited defence. As the fight wore on, the American became more aggressive and used punishing body shots to slow down the former world champion.

The decision by referee Eddie Purdy and all three judges was a formality. All that could be said about Siki was that he was game.

Siki lost again a month later and determined to get himself into reasonable shape, though he was still drinking heavily and partying until the early hours. Staying on in the US, he returned to the ring in January 1924 with a win in two rounds and ran up a reasonably good record. But a heavy defeat in March 1925 by Paul Berlenbach clearly indicated that his career was definitely over.

Berlenbach, a hard-hitting New Yorker of German extraction and an Olympic heavyweight wrestling champion in the 1920 games in Antwerp, Belgium, was on the attack from the start and gave Siki little chance to get going. A powerful right hand to the body in the ninth round almost doubled Siki in two. In the middle of the tenth, with Berlenbach, known as 'Punching Paul,' still aggressive and scoring well, he shot over a smashing right cross that sent Siki down for the full count. Years of unchecked high living, carousing and a minimum of training had robbed him of his sharpness.

Berlenbach paid tribute to his game opponent after the fight. 'He came to fight and did his best, and that's all a man can do really,' he said. 'He took all I could hand out and gallantly went down fighting.' Ironically, in his next fight two months later, Berlenbach would take the title from Mike McTigue, Siki's successor, on a 15-round points decision.

No longer a headliner, Siki had six more meaningless fights around the New York area, winning two, with two no-decisions and two losses, the final one on 13 November 1925 against Lee Anderson, after which he announced his retirement.

Living in the tough Hell's Kitchen section of New York's West Side, Siki was regularly in trouble with barmen and taxi drivers for failing to pay them and was twice beaten up in a dark alleyway by an unknown assailant. To many, it would come as no surprise that Siki could end up bad.

On the early morning of 15 December 1925, Patrolman John J Meehan of the West 13th Street Police Department was walking his beat along 9th Avenue when he chanced to look up 41st Street and saw a body lying face down at the kerb. He turned it over and being a sports fan recognised it was Siki. Meehan summoned a doctor, who pronounced the boxer dead from internal haemorrhage caused by two bullets, one of which had penetrated his left lung. The other had lodged in his kidneys.

Judging by a pool of blood discovered nearby, two detectives who had come on the scene deduced that Siki had staggered to his feet after being shot and attempted to find his way home before finally collapsing and bleeding to death. On the opposite side of the street, in front of 33 West 41st Street, one of the detectives found a small .32 calibre pistol, with two of the cartridges discharged. The two bullets recovered during Siki's autopsy showed the revolver was the murder weapon.

'You know, Siki was mild and affable when sober but dangerous and argumentative when drunk,' Patrolman Meehan would tell reporters. It later transpired that the boxer had become involved in an earlier skirmish in a nearby speakeasy after failing to pay for drinks in the company of two male friends and a girl. Within a few hours, the story was all over the New York papers. The 'Singular Senegalese' had lost his last fight – at the age of 28. His murderer or murderers were never found.

On 18 December 1925, Siki was buried in Flushing, in the Queens district. The Rev. Adam Clayton, who presided over the ceremony, said, 'No man who ever came out of Africa had a more dramatic life or had a more tragic ending. A lack of proper preparation or a noble purpose were the two dreadful mistakes of his life. Our civilisation is perhaps more to blame for these dreadful mistakes than he was.'

Over the years, there were a number of campaigns to have Siki's remains returned to his native Senegal. It was not until March 1993 that Haffini Hamouda, then president of the South African Boxing Union, persuaded the United Nations Special Committee Against Aparthied to honour their national hero. The World Boxing Council came into the picture and subsidised the transfer of the body from a Muslim tomb to the boxer's birthplace in Saint-Louis. Battling Siki had finally come home.

Chapter 3

Lord of the manor

THE media called Chris Eubank 'the man you love to hate'. He would enter the ring by vaulting the top rope and, on landing, would adopt a statuesque pose – 'the pose of a warrior', he would say. A household name, there were as many fans who hoped to see him knocked out as there were hoping to see him win. Supremely confident, even when the odds were against him – which was not very often – his theme music as he walked to the ring was Tina Turner's 'Simply the Best'.

Through his best years and beyond, Eubank developed a reputation for eccentricity. Speaking in affected upper-class tones, he dressed as a stereotypical Englishman, in jodhpurs, a bowler hat and riding boots. He carried a silver-tipped cane and wore a monocle. He was lord of the manor in Brighton. Eubank was voted Britain's Best Dressed Man four times and in a poll published by *BBC Homes and Antiques* magazine in January 2006, he was named the second most eccentric personality after the Icelandic singer/actress Bjork.

Obsessed with his appearance, Eubank would fly a barber once a week from Manchester to his home in Brighton, a distance of 204 miles (or 328km), to cut his hair for £250 plus travel expenses.

Seemingly, it did not matter that he had his own barber shop fitted in his house with swivel chairs, mirrors and special sinks.

Eubank's collection of vehicles included a customised Harley-Davidson and a huge American Peterbilt 379 truck cab, said to be the largest in Europe. At one stage he owned the only US military vehicle, a Hummer, in Britain. Manufactured in Detroit and used by several Hollywood stars, the pick-up truck, used in two wars, was said by one dealership to be 'a great way to impress the neighbours'. A difficult man to live with, his former wife Karron went on record as saying, 'Chris Eubank lives on another planet – Planet Eubank.' A notoriously big spender, he was said to have gone through a £10m fortune.

Eubank professed to dislike boxing and once called it 'a mug's game' on national television despite the sport having made him rich and famous. He later defended his remarks by explaining (a) that he was referring to the shadier side of the sport such as beatings taken by journeymen for little money, (b) fighters being ripped off by promoters and (c) he was boxing so often that he had grown tired of the sport. While he was used to being called a clown and an egomaniac outside the ring, whenever he pushed his hands into boxing gloves and the first bell rang, he was all business. No messing. No tomfoolery. By his own admission, he said, 'I thought I lacked the natural ability of a truly great fighter, so I focused on being a showman.'

Yet he was much more than that, as his record illustrates – just five defeats, three at the tail-end of his career, and two draws in 52 fights. Eubank was a world champion at two weights, middleweight and super-middleweight, and is ranked by the website BoxRec as the third best British super-middleweight of all time. His world title fights with fellow Britons Nigel Benn and Michael Watson, as well as Irishman Steve Collins, helped British boxing ride a peak of popularity in the 1990s, the nation's last golden era, according to many. Eubank defended his super middleweight title 15 times and scored victories over six world champions. Credited for his bravery in the ring, win, lose or draw, he was able to take considerable punishment from power punchers. Possessing a solid chin, he was never knocked out, his only loss inside the distance coming on a stoppage in his final fight, when he challenged Mancunian Carl Thompson in a rematch for the WBO cruiserweight title.

Christopher Livingstone Eubanks (he later dropped the 's') was born in Dulwich, south London on 8 August 1966, the youngest of five children. From the time he was two months old up to the age of six years, he lived in his native Jamaica. On the family's return to England, he lived in several London boroughs before settling in Peckham in a largely impoverished environment. Eubank had a troublesome youth, frequently getting into trouble with the law over shoplifting. At the Thomas Calton secondary school in Peckham, he was suspended 18 times in one year for various misdemeanours and was finally expelled, despite claiming he was trying to protect classmates from bullies.

When Eubank was 16, his mother, tired of her husband's womanising, took him to New York and settled in the tough South Bronx district, where shoplifting and muggings were accepted as a way of life. His mother insisted on an education and he enrolled at the local Morris High School, where he took North American history, Spanish and geography.

It was in the South Bronx where the young Eubank got his first introduction to boxing when he joined the local gym. The sport was in the family as his father was a fight fan and his two elder twin brothers, Peter and Simon, were boxers. Peter would develop into a good featherweight and inflict the first defeat on Barry McGuigan, the future world featherweight champion and TV analyst. Chris would admit that he got the drive to be a good boxer because of subjective bullying from Peter and Simon. In 26 amateur contests, he won 19, culminating in the Spanish Golden Gloves light-middleweight title in 1984 and reaching the semi-finals of the New York Golden Gloves tournament, also at light-middleweight, the same year.

By now, Eubank felt he could make a good living as a professional. Still based in New York, he switched to the paid ranks on 3 October 1985 with a points win over four rounds against Timmy Brown in Atlantic City. His purse was $250, more money than he had ever seen in his life. Putting some money into a computer course, he graduated from Morris High School and began a course at the College of Technology in the South Bronx. 'I was a good student because I didn't have any friends, not even acquaintances, to distract me,' he recalls.

Eubank had four more fights, all wins, in Atlantic City before homesickness took over and he decided to return to England. Settling in Brighton, where Peter and Simon trained, the brothers introduced him to Ronnie Davies, a trainer who had been English Southern Area lightweight champion in 1967. Davies worked as a site manager for a building company during the day and in the evenings he could always be found in the local Jack Pook gym. Davies worked out with Eubank four evenings a week. Eubank would tell this writer in 2003 when he was in Dublin to promote his autobiography, 'Ronnie was a great guy, a real friend. He knew the pitfalls of the fight business and he made me laugh, too. I'll always love Ronnie.'

Eubank ran up a string of victories in British rings and worked with small-time promoters, but his career really took off when he signed with the Essex promoter Barry Hearn, who guided him to a world middleweight title shot against Nigel Benn, the reigning World Boxing Organisation champion.

Benn was one of Britain's most successful and popular champions. Possessing a style built on constant aggression, with a powerful punch in both gloves, Benn had an indomitable will to win. The sixth of seven brothers born to Barbadian parents, Benn was born in Ilford, Essex on 22 January 1964. He came from a sporting family that included former Premier League midfielder Paul Ince, who would often accompany Benn to his fights. In the early 1980s, Benn joined the army and became Private Nigel Gregory Benn, serving four and a half years as an infantryman in the Royal Regiment of Fusiliers. He was stationed in Germany and then Northern Ireland during

The Troubles. During his army years, Benn won titles from welterweight to heavyweight, as well as acting as trainer to his regiment.

As an amateur with West Ham Boxing Club, the Ilford man built an impressive record of 41 wins and one loss, winning the English ABA and London middleweight titles in 1986. 'When the selectors sat down to pick the team for the Commonwealth Games in Edinburgh the same year, I was passed over for allegedly missing a training session,' Benn remembered. 'The ABA had favoured Rod Douglas and he was selected, even though I had already beaten him. I felt cheated and humiliated by their decision. The chance to win that gold medal should have been mine.'

Benn turned professional on 28 January 1987 with a two-round win over Graeme Ahmed in Croydon. Before the end of the year, he had become a major sensation with a large following, with 11 more victories, all inside the distance. His winning streak continued through 1988 with eight more victories, six inside two rounds and two in the first. By now Benn had won his first professional title, the Commonwealth championship, and was billed as the 'Dark Destroyer'. In his final bout of 1988, he successfully defended his Commonwealth title by finishing Trinidad's David Noel in one round.

Benn had his sights now set on becoming world champion. Eubank sought the same title so it was a race to see who would get there first. As it happened, it was Benn, who scored an eighth-round stoppage of WBO middleweight champion Doug DeWitt of Yonkers, New York, billed as 'The Cobra', in Atlantic City in April 1990. After Benn successfully defended his title with an impressive one-round win over another New Yorker, Iran 'The Blade' Barkley, in Las Vegas four months later, the stage was set for the Benn-Eubank showdown. The date was 18 November 1990 and the venue the National Exhibition Centre, Birmingham. It turned out to be a gruelling battle. Eubank was so confident that he bet £1,000 at 40/1 to win by a knockout in the first round. When news of the bet reached Benn, Nigel scoffed, 'What rubbish! Eubank will be a sad loser.'

A lot of pre-fight hate was generated in the press and while Eubank entered the ring as favourite, according to *Boxing News*, Benn had his supporters, including *The Times*. The paper described him as a 'wild animal' in the ring, adding: 'We have rarely if ever seen anything like that in our country. He is the epitome of an all-out warrior, bringing a rage and fury into the ring that one might only encounter in the United States. Only Mike Tyson and Marvin Hagler have exuded such menace.'

Over 150 celebrities were in attendance – 'the largest turnout for a sporting event Britain had ever seen,' Benn commented. During the introductions, Eubank stood for long periods in his corner as though he were locked in some kind of trance. Ringsiders agreed he was playing mind games. Gloves together with his torso twisted in a bodybuilder's pose, Eubank was motionless apart from an occasional flexing of his neck and presented an extraordinary sight. Benn wondered what he was facing. After Las Vegas referee Richard Steele called the two boxers together for final instructions and they returned to their corners, the first bell rang. Eubank came out in a crablike sideways stance hoping to disconcert the champion with an unorthodox right lead.

It didn't work and Eubank settled into a jab-and-move routine, dropping in rights occasionally and making Benn miss with sweeping hooks. When they clinched, Benn lifted the challenger up and hoisted him on his shoulder, as if to demonstrate that he had the physical power to manhandle his opponent as he pleased. But the opening round went to Eubank and so too did the interval as he strode around the ring for a full 15 seconds before trainer Ronnie Davies got him back to his corner. It was no doubt all part of the psychological war.

In round two, Eubank was admonished by Steele for leaning on Benn. On breaking, Benn landed two chopping rights to the chin that forced the challenger to back away. Suddenly, Eubank stormed back and sent Benn reeling towards the ropes. This was war in the trenches and by the fourth round Benn's left eye was closing, leaving him vulnerable to Eubank's right-hand punches. Benn was guilty of low blows and rabbit punches throughout and a clubbing right behind the ear in a thrilling eighth round sent Eubank to the boards for a mandatory eight count. Eubank insisted it was a slip.

Going out for the ninth round, Benn was in front on two of the three American judges' scorecards, but his left eye was now completely closed and Eubank took full advantage of it. Long lefts and rights landed on target and as Benn tried to counter-attack, Eubank got home with two powerful rights that sent Benn wobbling unsteadily into the ropes. The champion tried desperately to duck and roll out of danger. He escaped momentarily but Eubank was on him like a jungle cat, ripping in blows with both hands before referee Steele jumped between them and called it off. The time was 2:55 of round nine. It was a contest that Harry Mullan, then editor of *Boxing News*, described as the most thrilling he had ever witnessed in a British ring.

Referee Steele said at the post-fight conference, 'I've handled 79 world title fights and this one was in the very top category. It was too bad one had to lose. They are both champions in my book but it was my duty to stop it, so Benn can come back and win that title again. Benn was really gallant but just could not see out of his left eye.'

When Eubank was in Dublin in 2003 to promote his autobiography, he told this writer, 'I can tell you, Thomas, that the win over Benn was the culmination of everything I had sacrificed for boxing. I was champion of the world and it was a tremendous feeling, believe me. Watching the fight today, 13 years later, I thought of the words of Rudyard Kipling, "Force your heart and nerve and sinew to serve your turn long after they are gone and do hold on when there is nothing in you, except the will which says to them, 'hold on.' It was as though he was commentating on the fight. The poem goes on to say that if you can do all these things, then "Yours is the earth and everything that is in it." I was to hold the world title for five years.'

Benn remembered years later, 'Losing my title to Eubank was gutting but, looking back, he beat me fair and square, and I boxed well too. I was practically blind in one eye for most of the match and I pushed Eubank like he had never been pushed before. I fought until I had nothing left to offer and the referee called it a day. Eubank became more respectful to me after the fight but I was gutted. He damaged my eye and broke my heart but we're good friends today. I can't knock a guy who defeated me, though I still think he's a bit weird!'

Eubank defended his title three times in four months, the third time against Michael Watson, a fellow-Londoner who would play a significant and tragic role in Chris's career. The match was signed for 22 June 1991 at Earls Court, the first fight to be held at the London venue since July 1973 when Joe Frazier, who had lost his world heavyweight title to George Foreman six months earlier, outpointed Joe Bugner over 12 rounds.

Eubank struggled to get inside the 160lb weight limit and just made it with ounces to spare. It was clear that he would soon have to relinquish the title and move up to the super-middleweight division. Super-middleweight had been set up in 1984 to bridge the gap between the 160lb middleweight class and the 175lb light-heavyweight division, the widest gulf in boxing. In any event, Eubank's promoter Barry Hearn said there was more money to be made with fights against several high-profile super-middles.

Eubank made his usual grand entrance, strutting down the aisle as his theme music 'Simply the Best' blared out, though it was almost drowned out by a storm of booing from the large anti-Eubank crowd. It was clear that many had turned out to see him beaten. With the optimism of the yuppie era well and truly over, a growing sense of frustration, restlessness and general unrest had gripped the country. Already in a recession under

Margaret Thatcher, and not helped by Britain joining the US in the unpopular Gulf War, Eubank's rags to riches story did not inspire – it just seemed to irritate. 'A young man wearing jodhpurs and a monocle was an unpalatable sight for many,' boxing writer Sanjeev Shetty noted in his 2015 book *No Middle Ground*. 'It mattered not a jot that he did plenty of charity work, was involved in helping homeless people in Brighton and had strong anti-war feelings that would lead him to be arrested years after he finished boxing. Eubank had made himself a figure of hate. First the fans had put their trust in Benn to silence him. Now they were trusting in Watson.'

Touching his gloves together tentatively at chest level until he reached the ring, Eubank then hopped over the top rope and adopted his usual statuesque posture as the MC went through the formalities. As the first bell sounded, there was still no movement from the champion as Watson advanced to the centre of the ring. Eubank stared at the canvas for four or five seconds before launching a wild right that Watson easily avoided.

There was nothing between the fighters in the opening round, with Watson flicking out light left jabs as Eubank kept it mainly at long range, deftly slipping in and out when he decided to go to work and make an impression on the judges. As the fight progressed, it was not an easy one to score as so many of the rounds could have gone either way. Watson, who was the busier throughout, was also made to miss with a large percentage of his jabs which, from the back of the hall, appeared to be landing.

The significant punches were coming from Eubank, although there was never a sustained attack from either boxer at any stage. Both fighters were known for their resilience and never looked like being floored, although Eubank did appear unsteady in the last three sessions. In the 11th round, Watson missed with a right cross and Eubank slipped on to his back. The crowd roared, thinking that the champion had been floored, but referee Frank Cappuccino correctly waved it no knockdown. It was anybody's fight coming up to the last round, or so it appeared, but Eubank showed plenty of movement and often punched desperately at times. He managed a sustained barrage of lefts and rights but Watson retaliated, though not with quite the same force.

Finally, the bell and the announcements. Judge Carlos Colon of Puerto Rico had it 116-113 for Eubank. The score of Florida's John Rupert was announced as 114-114. By that time, Watson looked disgusted, shaking his head knowing that Eubank had retained his title with a draw at least. Finally, Las Vegas judge Art Lurie scored the fight 115-113, allowing Eubank to hang on to his title narrowly and prompting prolonged booing from the large contingent of Watson fans. As Eubank made his way to the dressing room, furious Watson supporters lobbed cans and tossed coins and crumpled newspapers at him in protest at the decision. Cries of 'we were robbed', 'scandal', 'shame' and 'rematch' could be heard.

'I deserved to win because there was no way he was ever in front of me,' said Eubank. 'I stayed with him and looked more classy than he did.' In his autobiography, he recalled, 'At the end of the final round, Watson actually jumped in the air in anticipation of triumph. However, if he had been given the decision, it would have been wrong. Many people felt he had won the fight. I didn't agree with that and watching the fight now, you cannot give him the title. He did not do enough to take that belt from me. I was running on empty by the tenth round but he still did not do enough. It was the right result, despite the uproar.'

A phone-in survey in the *Daily Mirror* found that almost 90 per cent of those who watched the fight felt the wrong man won. On ITV, boxing analyst Jim Watt, the former world lightweight champion, told an audience of over 10 million that Watson dominated the second half of the fight and should have won. Hugh McIlvanney of *The Observer* said Watson's performance was 'a triumph for honest orthodoxy over imaginative bombast … the scorecards came as a shock.'

A return match was inevitable and this time it was for the vacant World Boxing Organisation super-middleweight championship. Both men had been drained in making the middleweight limit and the obvious decision was to move up. The rematch was set, again for London, this time at White Hart Lane, home of Tottenham Hotspur football club. The date was 21 September 1991. Eubank was his usual cocky self in the months and weeks leading up to the fight, confident that he could add a second world title to his portfolio. Watson was equally sure that as he felt robbed in the first match, he would make no mistake second time around. Big-fight time quickly rolled around. With the weight limit at 168lbs, Eubank scaled 167lbs and Watson 16 ounces lighter.

It turned out to be a gruelling encounter, a night of triumph and tragedy. Watson was on the attack from the opening bell, possibly hurt by criticism that he had not forced the pace enough at Earls Court three months earlier. He landed a solid right cross, the first punch of the fight, only for Eubank to counter with a three-punch volley. Watson was doing all the forcing in this opening session, although many of his shots missed or were taken on the Brighton man's gloves. Eubank's more sparing blows had greater accuracy but it was Watson's punches that were enough to win him the round. It was a good start for the Islington boxer but could he maintain that form, or would his rival come on strong?

By the end of the second round, Eubank had a swelling on his right cheek and even if he did take a substantial number of blows on his arms, his workrate was noticeably inferior. By round five, with one and then the other gaining the advantage, the bout had all the makings of another close affair. In the sixth Eubank pushed his man over and, on rising, Watson was forced back by a body barrage before landing a solid right that had the dazed Eubank wandering around the ring. Watson had particularly good seventh and eighth rounds, pounding the Brighton fighter with an array of jabs and hooks. In the eighth,

Eubank seemed to be feeling the pace more but nailed his rival with a good right hook to the head.

Chris was looking tired and old in the ninth and Watson was making him work, but there was blood coming from Watson's nose and his mouth was open. The fast pace was beginning to tell on both boxers and the action slowed down – only for the bout to liven up near the end of the 11th round, when Eubank landed a thumping right that forced his opponent back to the ropes. Watson was ready and two smashing rights sent the Brighton fighter reeling and exhausted to the canvas, taking some of the mandatory eight count on one knee as pandemonium broke out in the big arena.

With about 20 seconds remaining in the round, the fight seemed to have only one possible outcome. Watson only had to survive a little over three minutes and the World Boxing Organisation super-middleweight title would be his. It would be sweet revenge for the injustice of his loss on points to Eubank three months earlier. Eubank was already behind on all three scorecards by six, three and one round and needed a knockout or stoppage to win.

'Eubank stood, wiped his gloves on the referee's shirt, stepped forward and threw one punch,' wrote Steve Bunce of *The Independent*. 'It was all it took. Watson also walked forward, his chin neatly hidden between his blood and sweat-coated gloves, but Eubank's punch, a simple right uppercut, picked the direct route and slid between the gloves to connect cleanly with the point of Watson's chin. He went over, his legs stiff, and his head snapped off the second rope. The bell sounded. It remains, even after all these years, a moment that never fades.

'His trainer Jimmy Tibbs and Dean Powell, his assistant on the night, were quick to assist their boxer back to his corner. It's the hurt business, a brutal game, so don't ask questions of men that act and fight with their hearts in truly desperate moments. The bell sounded and 29 seconds later it was over. Watson was not throwing punches and Eubank was throwing too many.

Referee Roy Francis, his hair flying in the outdoor breeze of a cooling autumn night, jumped between them.'

Watson was placed on a stretcher from the ringside area and rushed to North Middlesex University Hospital. The problem was that they did not have the facilities to perform the operations he needed on his brain and Watson was put back into the ambulance and transferred to St Bartholomew's Hospital in central London, where it was confirmed that he had a blood clot on the brain, necessitating a 90-minute emergency operation, the first of four.

The boxer would subsequently sue the British Boxing Board of Control for negligence for around £1m, eventually settling for £400,000 when they contested the action vigorously. Watson's claim was that there was no ambulance or paramedic at White Hart Lane. Doctors wearing dinner jackets arrived after some eight minutes, during which time the fallen boxer had received no oxygen. A total of 28 minutes elapsed before Watson received treatment in St Bart's neurosurgical unit, and he spent 40 days in a coma. Medical regulations at boxing tournaments have since been changed.

After regaining consciousness, Watson spent over a year in intensive care and rehabilitation and six more years in a wheelchair while he slowly recovered some movement and regained the ability to speak and write. In April 2003, Watson made headlines when he completed the London Marathon, walking two hours each morning and afternoon for six days.

Eubank contemplated retirement after the Watson fight. 'It was only natural, I suppose,' he remembered. 'I never wanted to be put in that position ever again. If I didn't fight, that would eliminate that possibility of it happening inside the ring. The buzz of boxing had gone. However, I didn't retire. Why? It was a simple equation, a matter of money. I couldn't quit because of money and I said this loud and clear to the press at the time. I needed money for my family. My objective was still to raise my standard of living and my profile. I was champion of the world.

I had beaten fighters who no one believed I would. To many, I was invincible. One has to be willing to give his life in this sport.'

Five months after the Watson fight, Eubank was back in the ring when he defended his world title against Thulani Malinga, a South African Zulu warrior known as 'Sugar Boy,' at the National Exhibition Centre, Birmingham on 1 February 1992. Eubank was going for his 32nd consecutive victory while Malinga had a 33-6 tally. With both boxers keeping their defences tight, it turned out to be a safety-first affair, and the most prominent feature of the fight was the number of misses on both sides. Eubank's were the more highlighted if only because of the added power that his punches carried. It was that power that almost terminated the fight in a sensational final few seconds in round five, when he caught Malinga with a smashing right to the jaw. The South African wobbled at first then crumbled to the canvas, his legs spread apart as his back hit the deck.

He watched Atlantic City referee Steve Smoger counting off the seconds and was up at eight before wobbling back to the ropes. With little more than ten seconds to go, Eubank went in for the finish, crashing in lefts and rights as Malinga defended, with his gloves up and lying against the ropes. He tried to rally but walked into a strong left hook and fell against the ropes once more. The bell rang but it was drowned out by the crowd, who were getting some action at last. Smoger moved between them and for a moment it looked as if he was stopping the fight, until it was realised that the challenger had been saved by the bell.

Eubank never got another good shot at his opponent. Malinga made a good recovery with smart defensive work and neat counter shots, often wobbling Eubank with head shots. By the eighth round, Eubank was clearly taking no unnecessary chances in this 12-rounder but he was looking fatigued. Still, he was able to outbox and outfight the Zulu boxer, who was having trouble connecting with meaningful shots. Over the final four rounds and up the last bell, Eubank had the better of the exchanges, in spite of a spirited showing by the South

African. It was a split decision. Canadian judge Harry Davis gave it to Malinga by 115-112 while the American pair Mike Glienna and Andre Van Grootenbruel marked their cards 116-113 and 115-113 respectively in the champion's favour.

Harry Mullan of *Boxing News* felt that Eubank now needed a rest from his busy schedule. 'Eubank's physical condition was as good as ever, and I have no doubt that he pushed himself as hard in training for this defence,' he wrote. 'But he had the look of a man who has asked too much of himself, who has crammed too many tough battles into too short a span and has additionally to cope with the unimaginable psychological pressures of returning to action after the Michael Watson catastrophe. I find it impossible to believe that the man who broke up Nigel Benn and who twice beat a quality boxer like Michael Watson would have had such difficulty with the relatively limited South African. I believe he is in real danger of burning out. He is not a "shot" fighter, as I heard someone suggest, just a very jaded one. Take five, Chris.'

Eubank read the report but, being Eubank, he ignored it. The boxing buzz and the thrill of the square ring were too great, as had been the case with boxers before and since. Over the next three years, he would make 14 further defences of his title, even if some of his challengers were not fully deserving of the opportunity. It was noticeable too that with the Watson tragedy embedded in his mind, Eubank never showed any desire to knock an opponent out, preferring to do enough to win on points, even risking a draw.

Seven fights after the Malinga victory, Eubank found himself back in the ring with his old rival Nigel Benn, who had also moved up to super-middleweight and won the world title as recognised by the World Boxing Council. With Eubank holding the World Boxing Organisation belt, they came together in a unification fight at Old Trafford, Manchester United's football ground, on 9 October 1993 before a crowd of 43,000 and a TV audience of over 100 million. It was billed as 'Judgement Day'.

'Walking out before such an audience was absolutely overwhelming,' Eubank remembered. 'It was just a seething mass of faces – they had all come to watch me and Benn. They took my focus away, probably the only time in my career that I really didn't have my focus intact. Normally I was totally tunnel-visioned but for this fight my heart wasn't pounding. I was distracted by the sheer volume of spectators. Also, as champion in my own right, I knew I was more emotionally intelligent than Benn, but what I couldn't have known was just how fused he was. He was wired. Benn was up for the bout but I still felt victory for me was a foregone conclusion.'

It seemed a new and gentler Chris Eubank who left the dressing room. He smiled and nodded his way through the crowd on the way to the ring, whereas before he would be cocooned in concentration. Perhaps he was trying to remake his image, and almost succeeding. But he was soon up to his old tricks. The showmanship and histrionics were returned as he jumped over the top rope and into the ring, where he went into his usual posturing. Yet it was Benn, close-cropped and deadly serious and threatening, who won the mind games before the bell. He stole his rival's thunder by inflating his chest in a parody of Eubank's style while the Brighton boxer, eyes closed, hugged trainer Ronnie Davies as Benn was introduced. *Boxing News* noted that Benn, one pound lighter than his 168lb opponent, 'was like a dog straining at the leash, and grinned and nodded at Eubank when referee Larry O'Connell ordered them to touch gloves'.

Benn tried to hustle Eubank out of his rhythm early in the opening round but the WBO champion quickly found the range for hard and accurate left jabs, shooting over countering rights as Benn came on to them. Late in the round, Benn landed two hard left hooks before being cautioned for a low blow, which he acknowledged. Eubank, as he did in the first fight, stood in mid-ring for fully 40 seconds at the interval before strolling unconcernedly to his corner with the air of a man who had just completed a round of routine sparring in the gym. A new Eubank? No, the old one was back.

The contest ebbed and flowed, with first one and then the other gaining an advantage. Round three was a particularly blistering one and was perhaps the best action round of the fight. Benn launched a strong attack that Eubank smothered before rocking the ex-soldier with a combination. Benn was warned several times in the ensuing rounds for hitting low but always reached out his glove in apology. It was as clear as a newly washed window that this rematch was being fought without the hate that made their first fight so draining for spectators as well as the protagonists.

Eubank seemed to be fading by the eighth round and at the bell he ignored his corner and walked to a neutral corner, where he stared out at the crowd until the final 20 seconds or so of the interval. It may have been designed to fool Benn that he had not been troubled by the course the fight was taking, but it did not work. Benn won the ninth and tenth rounds on the scorecards of two of the three judges. It was now all down to the final two rounds. Eubank stormed back in the 11th with a blistering attack that drove Benn back, looking disorganised, and at the bell Eubank held both arms aloft. The last round was a thriller, with both boxers determined to dominate the final three minutes. Late in the round, Eubank battered his man with an assortment of jabs, hooks and uppercuts, only for Benn to storm back with counterpunches.

The bell rang. The feud that had so intrigued British boxing since the first epic encounter in 1990 was over – and it was going to be a desperately close call for the judges. Britain's Harry Gibbs had it 115-113 for Eubank, Carol Castellano of the US made it 114-113 for Benn and fellow-American Chuck Hassett called it a draw on 114-114. The drawn decision drew howls of protest from the Benn camp while there was a philosophical shrug of the shoulders from Eubank. There were boos and cheers from the crowd, and opinions were divided around the ringside.

Perhaps the real loser was US promoter Don King, who staged the fight jointly with Barry Hearn. Under the terms of the contract signed by both boxers and negotiated by King, the winner and loser would have had to have signed with King for each of their next three fights. There was no agreement on a draw, so Eubank and Benn were still free agents.

Eubank was a fighting champion, successfully defending his WBO title a further six times before losing it to Steve Collins, a rugged Dubliner and former world middleweight champion. They met at the Green Glens Arena, an equestrian venue in Cork, on 18 March 1995.

Collins, known as the 'Celtic Warrior,' was a gritty fighter with a burning desire to win. He had a shamrock cut into his hair above his left ear and it was said that a concrete company had sponsored his chin. The Irishman had started his career in the US, where he won 19 fights, his lone loss being a points decision over 12 rounds in a WBA world middleweight title fight with the respected Jamaican, Mike McCallum, known as the 'Bodysnatcher' because of his ferocious body punching. McCallum had earlier knocked out Eubank's old rival Michael Watson in 11 rounds.

Collins was fully expected to give the Brighton boxer a tough night. 'Until you fight in the tough US school, nobody can call you a real fighter,' boasted Collins, who referred to his rival as the 'Brighton Dandy'. 'Eubank never fought there as a pro [he actually fought five times in New Jersey]. Important too is that I'll have home advantage, with the crowd yelling for me.'

Irish fans were unused to seeing such a spectacle as happened on fight night. As fireworks exploded high up at the back of the arena to spell out Eubank's name, Chris was raised on a hoist while sitting on a glistening Harley-Davidson motorcycle and revving up the engine with the lights flashing. After being lowered into the ring, he dismounted to a mixture of cheers and boos as his anthem 'Simply the Best' blared out from the public address system. Local sportswriters described the bout as being between the 'goodie' and the 'baddie'. Paul Howard of Ireland's *Sunday Tribune* referred to Eubank as 'the pantomime villain'. Meanwhile, Collins sat on his stool, head down and eyes closed as though he was in a trance, seemingly oblivious to what was going on. He wore headphones under his dressing gown hood, listening to tapes given to him by the sports psychologist Tony Quinn.

At the media conference to announce the fight, Collins had led Eubank to believe that he had undergone hypnosis and been programmed to fire two punches for every one thrown by Eubank. The Irishman let out the story that when the fight got under way, he would feel no pain. Collins was simply playing mind games and the alleged hypnotism was nothing more than relaxation. This was his big chance to become the first Irishman to win two world titles and he was not going to let it slip. Eubank was even more convinced of the hypnotism story when he saw Collins and Quinn in deep conversation at the weigh-in, where the Dubliner gave him a long, cold stare. Eubank even threatened to call off the fight on the basis that 'Collins will have an unfair advantage over me'.

It was only when his handlers convinced him to get the fight over quickly and leave no doubts as to who was the better man that he reluctantly agreed to go ahead. Still, he was desperately worried right up to fight time. Collins would admit to this writer in later years, 'Tony Quinn was just a sports psychologist rather than a hypnotist and was one of four that I used during my career to help me blank out any upsetting distractions. [He was] nothing more but Eubank was not to know that.'

During the preliminary announcements Eubank refused to look at Collins, keeping his head down until the bell rang. The 12-rounder began at such a fast pace that the US referee Ron Lipton had to caution both men for infringements, warning them 'to keep it strictly professional, boys'. Collins's plan was to keep the pressure on his opponent and Eubank's aim was to seek that moment to open up, and end it. The Irishman was not giving him that opportunity. It was anybody's fight after six rounds, with one and then the other getting through with stinging jabs and clusters of punches. But it was becoming clear from the seventh that Collins was scoring more effectively.

Both men visited the canvas, Eubank from a sharp right hook to the body in the eighth round and Collins from a big right to the point of the chin in the tenth. The Britisher beckoned Collins on for a grandstand finish when he could find the range for his big shots, but Collins wasn't having any, preferring to coast his way to the final bell. The decision was unanimous, with all three judges voting for Collins. Londoner Roy Francis called it 116-114, Cesar Ramos of Puerto Rico had it 115-111 and Florida's Ismael Fernandez had it 114-113. It was a first defeat for Eubank after 44 fights. Sportingly, he said the better man had won and had no excuses, even on being told that the Collins 'hypnotism act' was a trick.

Eubank had two easy wins before issuing a challenge for a return fight with Collins, feeling that he could do better next time. Six months after the initial encounter, the return was held in Cork again, this time at Pairc Ui Chaoimh, pronounced O'Keeve, the Gaelic for O'Keefe. A party of Eubank supporters travelled over for the fight, described by the *Sunday Independent* as 'a battle that paid scant homage to the niceties of boxing but was absorbing in its intensity'. Collins came out of his corner for the first round like a raging bull and nearly went through the ropes as Eubank sidestepped. Collins composed himself after that as both men traded blows with little regard for defence.

Ronnie Davies, Eubank's long-time trainer, recalled, 'I told Chris after every round from the fourth that he was heading for defeat but I couldn't get it through to him. He just wouldn't do anything about it, although in fairness, the aggressive Collins wouldn't *let* him do anything. Going out for the fifth, I told him he was losing it and I kept saying the same thing to him round after round. I kept telling him he had to go forward all the time and trade punches, but he said he was too weak. He had been struggling at 168lbs for a couple of years now and I used to urge him to go up to light-heavyweight at 175lbs. I had always rated Collins very highly and I told him never to underestimate him. He beat Chris in the first fight and here he was set for a second win.'

At the final bell, Eubank rejected Collins's attempt to embrace. Instead he turned his back and went to his corner to await the decision. The judges were divided. Genaro Rodriguez of Chicago surprisingly called it 115-114 for Eubank, which was soundly booed, while Aaron Kizer from Florida and Arizona's Paul Herman marked it 115-113 for the home boxer, creating the inevitable cheers. A poll of seven British writers at ringside revealed a wide winning margin for Collins.

Eubank's solitary comment to pressmen waiting outside his dressing room was, 'He gave me a good fight and I have no excuses. He won fairly.' In his autobiography eight years later, he disagreed with his trainer's assessment that he would not listen to advice between rounds. He stressed that Collins's motivation was so intense that he was taken aback. 'His resolve was maniacal and despite my best intentions and meticulous preparations, I could not wrestle the crown away from him,' he wrote. 'I was understanding of the events of life. It was due to happen again after so many title defences, having been a professional boxer for 11 years. Winning and losing is just part of life. I just lost.'

Eubank announced his retirement after the fight but just over a year later he was back in the ring after admitting on a Channel 5 phone-in programme that he needed 'a platform' and missed the limelight. His comeback was in Egypt of all places, a country with no tradition of boxing whatsoever, then and now. The location would be the National Sports Stadium in Cairo, a city with a population of 16 million but clearly designed for less than half that amount. Eubank would find the streets were jammed, the driving chaotic, the pollution choking 'and a noise that never dies'. Reporters would remember that cars tooted their horns day and night and people lived in squalor. Eubank's 16-day visit to the capital aroused curiosity but nothing like the glowing attention to which he had been accustomed during his five years at the top.

It was a self-promotion, with Eubank's opponent, Luis Dionisio Barrera, a short, stumpy, one-time welterweight, billed as the best fighter in South America. The Brighton boxer walked to the ring and jumped over the top rope, much to the crowd's amusement. The highlight for the fans was the attractive round card girl who drew cheers and whistles, though there was little to cheer about in the opening rounds, with Eubank merely jabbing with his left and tossing the occasional right with more serious intent. In a rare moment of aggression, Barrera landed a combination right-left to the body but Eubank seemed unperturbed. It was all over in the fifth when the Englishman dropped his man with a body shot. Barrera took the full count of Midlands referee John Coyle on one knee, with 42 seconds on the clock.

After another victory in Dubai, Eubank continued his comeback on British soil with a bout against newcomer Joe Calzaghe, born in London but raised in Newbridge, South Wales. They fought for the vacant WBO world super-middleweight title in Sheffield on 11 October 1997. There was to be no joy for the man from Brighton as he lost a unanimous decision after being on the canvas twice. Eubank's career ended in 1998 after he twice unsuccessfully challenged Manchester's Carl 'The Cat' Thompson for the WBO world cruiserweight title. In their first meeting in April, Eubank lost a decision over 12 rounds and three months later he was beaten inside the distance for the first time in his career when a badly swollen and closed left eye prevented him from going out for the tenth round.

At the time of the finish, Eubank was ahead on two of the three scorecards. Ironically, he enjoyed vociferous support from the crowd at the finish, a pleasant change from the past. The fans were finally on his side and he appreciated it. 'In the wake of the second Thompson fight, the British public warmed to me in a way they had never done when I was champion for five years,' he recalled.

In his retirement, Eubank purchased the lord of the manor rights in Brighton and used the ancient right of this position to appoint a town crier in addition to the one employed by the local authority. He took over a prime site in the city, called it Buckingham Place and had 69 flats built for the homeless. A regular on television shows including *Top of the Pops*, *Celebrity Big Brother* and *I'm A Celebrity, Get Me Out Of Here*, Eubank was caricatured as a puppet on *Spitting Image*. Trouble was never far away, however, and he was once arrested while driving around Parliament Square in his massive truck in protest over Prime Minister Tony Blair's involvement in the Iraq war.

Eubank's 15-year marriage, already hit by allegations of cheating with other women, ended in 2005 when his wife Karron filed for divorce. 'Fame made Chris feel invincible and it ended up driving me nuts,' she recalled. 'I simply couldn't live that life any more. Like so many fighters before him, Chris could go nowhere unless he was surrounded by an entourage of curious, and, sometimes dubious, hangers-on. He needed to be loved and adored every day. You see him on *I'm A Celebrity* when he demands hugs. One day Chris saw this tramp on the streets and decided to bring him home to live with us. It was like something out of the movie *Down and Out in Beverly Hills*. He just came in with this guy without any warning and said, "This is Max and he'll be living with us."

'When I asked him what Max was going to do all the time, Chris said he'd get him to shine his shoes. He stayed with us for months until even Max decided he needed to get away. One day, he suddenly ran off. Somehow Chris managed to track him down and asked why he had left. Max said to him, "Chris, I'm happier on the streets and I just want to have my old life back." That's how it was.

'Chris liked the idea of a world where the men retired to the billiards room after dinner. His drug was shoes, clothes and cars. He was like Imelda Marcos. Every day he seemed to be wearing a new pair of shoes. It seemed like he had thousands of them. He'd change his outfit three or four times a day. Every week, the dry cleaners would send a big van to pick up all his stuff. He had outfits for riding his motorbikes, outfits for driving, outfits for taking a walk, outfits for interviews.'

Eubank, who remarried in 2014, says today that he would like to be remembered as a boxer who brought integrity to the sport, 'So often, people have agendas but I possess this quality of integrity.' Reflecting on the negative press coverage he received during his career, he says, 'They had a job to do, and I would like to thank them for making me more famous. I think it's great what I've done in creating this character who is supposedly arrogant, aloof, enigmatic and strange. It makes life more interesting because of it.'

Chapter 4

Mammy's boy lived and died by the gun

F OR someone who did not fear anybody, Stanley Ketchel always carried a six-shooter in his jacket pocket. A charismatic individual with piercing grey eyes and chestnut hair hanging low over his brow, he was undisputed middleweight champion of the world in an era of great 160-pounders shortly after the turn of the 20th century. Known as the 'Michigan Assassin', Ketchel was one of the most powerful hitters boxing has ever known – whether throwing a left or right hook, a body shot, an uppercut with either glove or a swing. Yet he would eventually meet a violent death at the hands of a jealous farm worker at the age of 24.

Over 100 years have passed since his untimely end yet Ketchel is still rated among the greatest middleweights by ring experts around the world. In 2004, *Ring* magazine had him the eighth-best 160-pounder and in the recent *Boxing News 100 Greatest Boxers of All Time*, he is listed at 16 , in front of greats like Gene Tunney, Jack Dempsey, Rocky Marciano, Mickey Walker, Thomas Hearns and many others. When Sugar Ray Robinson, universally acknowledged as the best middleweight ever, was asked how he might have fared against Ketchel, he rubbed his chin reflectively and said, 'Hell, I'm glad I wasn't around in Stanley's day!'

A legitimate middleweight rarely weighing over 160lbs, Ketchel regularly took on light-heavyweights and even heavyweights. In 1909, he dumped the great world heavyweight champion Jack Johnson on the canvas at a time when the Texan, heavier by 35lbs, was in his prime. That same year, Stanley was deprived of a certain knockout when the bell saved another great, Philadelphia Jack O'Brien, who was world light-heavyweight champion at the time. Stanley never learned how to box and nobody ever explained the rudiments of the game to him. He did not need the fancy stuff anyhow as few could stand up to his powerful punching and constant aggression.

'Ketchel punched out heavyweights as easily as middleweights,' reports the *Cyber Boxing Zone* website. 'He put tremendous pressure on his opponents and could land knockout punches from either hand.'

Stanley used a very unusual method going into his fights. He claimed he had a very close and loving relationship with his mother. It is rumoured that before each of his fights, he would imagine that his opponent had insulted his mother. Thus, he would be fighting with almost insane fury. Ketchel would most definitely come into the wildcard category.

Ketchel was as cocky as they come and genuinely believed he was unbeatable. His confidence was based on accurate knowledge of what he could do in the ring, just as it should be. Before a fight, he would send a telegram to his father telling him he had won – and he was only beaten four times in 60 fights. He liked his 'Michigan Assassin' nickname and always tried to live up to it. Stanley genuinely believed he was an assassin, an assassin with gloves, and it did not take much for him to live up to it. Once he made up his mind to wade into his opponent, whether a middleweight, a light-heavyweight or a heavyweight, there was no stopping him.

'Ketchel was utterly fearless,' said his biographer Wilfrid Diamond. 'He could deliver a blow with either hand and if he missed with one hand, he could deliver with the other. His fists were always ready to shoot and he could weave, dodge and roll with punches whenever the occasion called for such tactics. I have no hesitation in saying that there never was a more vicious puncher in boxing history than Stanley Ketchel, and that's saying something.'

Ketchel was born in Grand Rapids, Michigan on 14 September 1886 to a Russian father and a Polish mother. When Stanislaw Kiecal arrived, his mother was only 14. The subsequent tragic deaths of his parents should have been an indication of the fate that would befall Ketchel. His father was found in a hayloft on the family farm, his throat cut from ear to ear. His mother was also found dead on the farm and three examinations failed to determine whether the cause of death was murder or suicide.

Ketchel was adopted by a neighbouring family but with no interest in schooling and without any proper parental guidance, he got into lots of street fights. When he was 14, he ran away from home and lived as a hobo, hitching on to freight trains, or 'riding the rods', as it was called. He travelled across America and even into Canada, finishing up in Butte, a tough mining town in Montana in the Rocky Mountains. Stanley found plenty of work there as a hotel bellhop, a bouncer in local dance halls, digging in fields and checking livestock in a yard. Hot headed, he found himself involved in skirmishes and his reputation as the best scrapper in town grew fast.

Ketchel was ruggedly handsome and strong, and naturally a big hit with the ladies. 'The dance hall girls took a shine to him and after working hours, he would dress up to the nines and he would be the best-dressed guy in the halls and saloons,' wrote Stanley Weston in *Boxing and Wrestling*. 'Packs of girls would cluster around him, begging for his attention. There was no doubt that while he was best fighter in town, he was also the most popular with the fair sex.'

In later years, Ketchel told Nat Fleischer, editor and publisher of *Ring* magazine, 'I loved the attention of the ladies but I was also conscious that I would have to get a steady job. My first thoughts were to become a boxer and instead of getting a few dollars and cents from customers in the various establishments around town, I could make good money in the boxing ring, maybe even become a champion. I thought the prospects were pretty good.'

Though he fought in what he called backroom matches against all-comers in Butte, the manager of the local Casino Theatre often paid him $20 a fight to meet visiting cattlemen who fancied themselves as fighters. These fights never got into Richard K Fox's record book and Stanley reckoned he had over 200 of them. His first officially recorded professional bout was on 2 May 1903 in Butte against Jack 'Kid' Tracy, a popular local. Tracy was knocking out all his opponents but he didn't knock out Ketchel, at least not officially.

Tracy had a thin curtain at the back of the stage and when an opponent's head hit this, a man behind the curtain hit the bulging spot with a bag of sand and Tracy would take credit for the knockout. On this occasion, following a long right from Ketchel, it was Tracy's head that bulged the curtain, and the bag struck the wrong man – with Stanley getting full credit for knocking out the 'Kid'. He was out cold for ten minutes.

At 17 years of age, Ketchel was now raring to go, like a fidgety racehorse waiting for the off at the starting gate. For his next few fights, he would stay in local rings. In his second appearance he had another knockout win, this time in 24 rounds over Mose Lafontise. In fight number three, Stanley was held to a 20-round draw against Rudolph Hinz before facing another local favourite, Maurice Thompson.

The fight started with great excitement, with both boxers slugging away before there was a mighty crash on one side of the makeshift arena as the seats collapsed and dropped several hundred spectators to the floor. Thompson laughed and pointed with his glove to the struggling fans on the ground. When Ketchel turned his head to look, Thompson landed a vicious blow to the back of the neck and Stanley went down.

He managed to get to his feet at the count of nine, still dazed by the illegal rabbit punch, his hands dangling limply by his sides.

There Ketchel was – wide open as a gate in a storm. Thompson measured him for the kill and landed a thumping right to the chin. Ketchel went down again and it looked like the end, but it wasn't. He managed to get to his feet at seven and fell into a clinch before the bell clanged. What a round. For the next three sessions, Thompson had him down three more times but Stanley was still in there battling away. By the sixth and final round, he was still exchanging punch for punch but it was Thompson who was deservedly awarded the decision. 'That guy ain't human,' said Thompson on leaving the ring. 'He's made of pig-iron.'

The pair would meet each other again on two occasions in 1904, with Ketchel losing a decision and being held to a draw, both over ten rounds and in Butte. After the drawn verdict, Thompson became Ketchel's manager. 'It's easier looking after him than fighting him,' he said. It is worth noting that in Ketchel's 15 fights that year, including two losses and two draws, 11 ended in knockout victories, an indication of his hitting power.

What Stanley realised now was that he needed experience against different types of opponents – sluggers, hard hitters, skilful boxers, shifty movers, anyone he could learn from. But his reputation across Montana was spreading like wildfire as he took on anybody willing to share a ring with him. At the end of 1905, his impressive record read 34 wins, two losses and five draws, or 34-2-5, as modern record compilers would have it. Of his 34 victories, all had ended inside the distance, the vast majority by clean knockouts, the rest on stoppages by merciful referees.

Ketchel and Thompson realised they would have to get out of Butte and neighbouring towns and cities and show their wares nationwide. In any event, Stanley's prowess had reached California, where boxing was in a healthy state. Packing their bags, they found themselves in the Orange State in early 1907 and got to know influential people in the boxing game. In Sacramento, fighter and manager had a disagreement over the financial arrangements and parted company.

Anxious to get some important matches, Ketchel linked up with a local and important manager named Willus Britt, who boasted that he knew everybody who was anybody in boxing and would prove it by issuing challenges to the top middleweights, including the three men who were laying claim to the vacant world title, Hugo Kelly, Jack 'Twin' Sullivan and Billy Papke.

Willus had managed his brother, Jimmy Britt, a prominent lightweight in his day. But Jimmy was now getting older and was on the cusp of retirement, especially after Chicago's Packey McFarland, one of the best boxers who never won a world title, whacked him on the chin one night and Britt took the full count. Exit Jimmy Britt and enter Stanley Ketchel.

On American Independence day, 4 July 1907, Ketchel forced a draw over 20 rounds with Joe Thomas, who was claiming the world middeweight title following the reign of Tommy Ryan, who had retired as undefeated champion. Thomas argued he was not fully fit for the fight and deserved a return.

They had two successive bouts before the end of the year, which Ketchel won, knocking out Thomas in 32 rounds and winning a decision over 20. They would meet again a year later, when Stanley finished off Thomas in two rounds. When Thomas got to his feet, he went over to Ketchel's corner, put his gloved hand on his conqueror's shoulder and said, 'I guess you have my number now, Stanley.'

After that fight in San Francisco, Britt threw out a bold challenge on behalf of Ketchel for a world middleweight championship fight with Jack 'Twin' Sullivan, one of several boxers who were claiming the title that was officially vacant. Sullivan said he would take on Ketchel if Stanley fought and beat his brother Mike. The match was set for 22 February 1908 in Colma, California. Scheduled for 25 rounds, it lasted only one. Four smashing punches decided it – all from Ketchel. A left hook to the head dropped Sullivan for a count of eight. On rising, an overhand right body-shot put him down again for six.

Another left hook to the head staggered Sullivan before a solid right, again to the body, left him motionless on the canvas as he was counted out. Sullivan seemed to have stopped breathing and referee Billy Roche exclaimed, 'My god, he's dead!' But after his seconds raised him from the canvas and gave him some attention, he thankfully recovered.

At ringside, Mike told newspapermen, 'Ketchel is a pretty good fighter but he still has to fight and beat my brother Jack. If and when that happens – and I really can't see it happening to be honest – Ketchel can call himself a contender. Not before.'

Ketchel and Jack 'Twin' Sullivan squared off in the same ring just 11 weeks later and the authorities agreed to officially sanction the 35-rounder as being for the world middleweight championship. The only condition set for the fight was that the winner would have to defend the title against two other deserving contenders, Billy Papke and Hugo Kelly, inside 12 months. Both Papke and Kelly were peeved that they were being overlooked for a title fight in the first place, but the winner of the Ketchel-Sullivan bout agreed to accommodate them.

Britt warned Ketchel that Sullivan was a tricky fighter who would claim foul at any given moment, even if no illegal punch had landed. There was no shortage of action in the first round, with both fighters anxious to score an early knockout. Ketchel was scoring with his vaunted right hand but Sullivan was sharp on the counter and nullified many of Stanley's shots. The early rounds were fairly even, with one and then the other dominating the action, but it was noticeable that Ketchel was the heavier hitter. In the sixth round, a terrific body punch staggered Sullivan but he stayed on his feet to go blow for blow with the Michigan fighter. There was too much at stake here.

As Willus had accurately predicted, Sullivan went down in the seventh round from a perfect body shot and claimed a foul, his face grimacing in fake pain. But referee Billy Roche did not see any foul and neither did anybody else. He ordered Sullivan to get up or be counted out there and then. Sullivan got to his feet at the count of nine and retreated in the face of the Michigan boxer's constant aggression.

By the eighth round, Sullivan was beginning to weaken and was definitely slowing down. He made a strong burst in the ninth but it was his last stand. From the tenth onwards, Ketchel punished Sullivan to head and body with an assortment of blows from all angles.

Only the gameness of the 'Twin' kept him on his feet. In the 15th round Ketchel seemed to ease up, knowing that he had the fight won, but he resumed his attacks in the closing stages with bursts of two-handed fighting.

At the beginning of the 20th round, Sullivan made a final stand with several punches to the head and body. But a minute or so from the last bell, Ketchel caught his man with a terrific right uppercut to the chin near the ropes before following through with a mighty left hook to the stomach. Sullivan sank to the canvas and was counted out. Stanley Ketchel was middleweight champion of the world.

'I'm now calling on the heavyweight champion, Tommy Burns, to put his title up,' said a jubilant Ketchel in the dressing room. As it happened, Burns, a native Canadian, was too busy barnstorming his way around the world in title defences and paid little or no attention 'to a middleweight trying to overreach himself and aiming for the heavyweight title', as he put it. In any event, under the agreement signed before the Sullivan fight, Ketchel had to give first consideration to the two leading middleweight contenders Billy Papke and Hugo Kelly. Papke, the son of German immigrants, came from Spring Valley, Illinois and Hugo Kelly, born Ugo Micheli in Florence, Italy, emigrated to the USA and settled in Chicago.

The problem of who to fight first was solved when Papke and Kelly fought each other twice, resulting in a draw and a decisive points win for Papke, who would be the official challenger. Billy started his working life as a miner like his father but gradually got tired of the hard, relentless and dangerous work, and yearned to be a boxer. The miners often staged impromptu boxing matches at a local recreation hall and Papke enjoyed the thrill of matching their wits and skills against others. He also loved the camaraderie among the workers.

Dubbed by a newspaper reporter as the 'Illinois Thunderbolt,' the nickname stuck. A good puncher with a solid defence, Papke built up a solid record of knockout victories and looked like being a worthy challenger. He would meet Ketchel four times in all, and each match was a thriller, with neither boxer taking a backward step. Their first bout, in Milwaukee on 4 June 1908, was Stanley's first defence of his world middleweight title and, not unexpectedly, it turned out to be a real slugfest.

Both were looking for the knockout but it never came despite some fierce exchanges. It looked all over seconds after the sound of the first bell when Ketchel knocked his rival down with a smashing left hook to the midriff. Papke shook his head and jumped up before a count could start, and straight away sailed into the champion, who had expected the Illinois battler to stay down. But Papke was a true warrior and this was going to be a war – a war that he planned to win.

As the rounds went by, and with the crowd on their feet throughout, both fighters landed big punches that would have dumped heavyweights on the boards, probably for keeps. In the fifth round, Papke found an opening and dropped Ketchel to one knee with a hard right uppercut delivered with terrific force. He was up at the count of two and immediately sailed in. In the sixth it was Papke who went down, this time from a looping left hook. When Billy arose, Ketchel moved in for the kill and sent his man staggering back to the ropes with several powerful body blows. As the 'Assassin' moved in to finish the job, the bell rang, his big chance lost.

Papke never fully recovered from those heavy body punches and although he fought back magnificently in the remaining four rounds, it was always going to be Ketchel's fight. Papke hurt Stanley in the ninth with a ripping right to the head but the champion was resilient and took Papke's best punches to wrap up the tenth and last round with a blistering attack. At the final bell, Billy knew he had lost. Stanley Ketchel was announced as winner and still middleweight champion of the world.

With Hugo Kelly now demanding a title fight, Ketchel obliged. The bout was set for 31 July, four weeks after the Papke match, with San Francisco selected as the venue. It was all over in three rounds, with two left hooks to the jaw and a right to the body finishing off the Italian. Eighteen days later and still in San Francisco, Ketchel made his third title defence an even quicker one when disposing of the local hope Joe Thomas in two rounds.

By now Papke was calling for a return fight with Ketchel, claiming he was not fully prepared for their first meeting. Ketchel had no hesitation in agreeing to it. The match was set for 7 September 1908 in a ring pitched in Vernon, just outside downtown Los Angeles. Amazingly, it would be Stanley's sixth world title fight in seven months.

The referee for the big fight would be the former world heavyweight champion James J Jeffries. Big Jim announced that he would take no nonsense from the contestants and wanted a clean, fair fight, two attributes that were foreign to champion and challenger.

After the preliminary instructions, both boxers returned to their corners to await the first bell. As was the custom, a practice still in use today, Ketchel extended his gloves in a gesture of good luck. As far as Papke was concerned, the niceties were over and now it was time to fight – and for real. Instead of tapping Ketchel's extended gloves, he slammed Stanley heavily on the jaw with a hard right hand and immediately followed with another jolting right to the face.

Instead of disqualifying Papke there and then, Jeffries merely reprimanded him but those two unexpected and sly blows would have a major bearing on the result. They became one of boxing history's most notable 'sucker punches'. As Ketchel rubbed his eyes with the front of his glove, Papke moved in fast with lefts and rights that drove the 'Assassin' back to the ropes. Moving away, Ketchel landed two hard rights to Billy's head but Papke, living up to his 'Illinois Thunderbolt' nickname, retaliated with two of his own pet punches, a short left hook and right uppercut that dropped the champion to the boards.

Struggling to his feet at the count of nine, Ketchel held on but Papke would not be denied and floored Stanley for a second count of nine. He took a third count of nine shortly before the bell rang and made his way to his corner, his eyes swollen and his confidence shattered by that first illegal blow. As the rounds went by, with Papke well ahead, it did not look likely that Ketchel would survive. All that was keeping him in the fight was his indomitable spirit and toughness. 'If it hadn't been Stanley Ketchel in there, the end would have come by now,' wrote Wilfrid Diamond. 'Stanley couldn't see what was happening to him. All he could do was to feel, grin and bear it.'

Papke's flaying fists knocked Ketchel out of the ring and into the press seats in the 11th round, but Stanley was no quitter. Several writers pushed him back into the ring and he vowed to himself he would fight to the bitter end. It came in the 12th round. Papke caught Ketchel with a powerful left hook that sent him down for a count of eight. Immediately, Papke floored him again. As he was struggling to his feet as the count reached nine, referee Jeffries waved his hands wide and motioned to the champion's seconds to look after him. It was finally over and Billy Papke was the new middleweight champion of the world. The 'Thunderbolt' had destroyed the 'Assassin'.

Papke was booed as he left the ring, head bowed, and made his way to the dressing room with his handlers. 'Ketchel was really game out there,' he said. 'I was really surprised the way he stood up to my best punches. Asked why he took advantage of the unsuspecting Ketchel with those sneak punches before the first, he said, 'Listen, you should protect yourself at all times and Ketchel did not do that.'

Ketchel told reporters, 'I never fully recovered from those foul blows. Most of the time I could hardly see him. But I want a return match and you will find I will do better next time. My manager here will demand a second fight and if Papke wants to prove himself the true champion, he will give me first crack. At least I deserve that. I'm ready for him and he had better get ready for me.'

The following day's newspapers heaped criticism on Papke's unsporting behaviour, calling for an immediate return match. The reporters pointed out that as well as providing Ketchel with the opportunity to get revenge, the fight would give Ketchel the chance to become the first boxer to win back a world title, even though history would be against him achieving that feat. It was a kind of jinx.

In the heavyweight division alone, two world champions had already failed to regain their titles in return matches. James J Corbett had lost his crown when he was knocked out by the Cornishman Bob Fitzsimmons in 1897 and failed to regain it in two subsequent challenges against James J Jeffries in 1900 and 1903. Fitzsimmons, too, came out a loser, also against Jeffries, in 1902.

But Ketchel felt he could pull it off. The only problem was that Papke was reluctant to agree to a rematch, claiming that he wanted to give other deserving contenders a chance. Was Billy running from Ketchel, knowing that he would be facing a fully fit contender grimly determined to win back his old title? Everybody thought so, including America's most influential newspapers, whose sports editors and boxing writers were demanding that Papke face his most deserving contender sooner rather than later, or have the title taken from him.

Ketchel's manager Willus Britt hit on a plan. Stanley would disappear from the scene and spread reports that he was remorseful about losing the championship and had taken to drink to drown his troubles. They would spread reports, too, that he was abusing his physical well-being and considering giving up boxing altogether. 'Stanley is simply fed up with boxing and is considering retiring,' Britt told newspapermen. 'In simple terms, he's just had it, and just wants one more fight, against Papke or anybody else, before calling it a day.'

Meanwhile, the newspapers continued to blast away at Papke, accusing him of being scared of his rival. Finally, Billy and his team bowed to mounting public opinion and the match was arranged for Colma, in the San Francisco bay area, for 26 November 1908, two months after their first meeting. Ketchel entered the ring as a 10/6 favourite in spite of widespread reports that he had neglected his training. But there was some strong support, certainly among Papke's own following, for the champion to repeat his stunning victory.

This time, Ketchel and Britt had a clause in their contract that they would have a choice in naming the referee. James J Jeffries was definitely out after allowing Papke to get away with those two foul punches last time. Promoter Jim Coffroth suggested Jack Welsh, one of America's most prominent referees, who had a reputation for being honest and fair. Ketchel and Willus agreed. Welsh is best remembered from the famous 1915 photograph showing him counting out Jack Johnson, who is shielding his eyes from the blazing sun as Jess Willard walks away, the new heavyweight champion of the world.

Ketchel stepped between the ropes with a 43-3-4 record, which included 41 wins by clean knockout or stoppage. Papke's record was 26-1-5, with one no-decision, 20 of his victories coming by the short route. As with tradition, Ketchel entered the ring first as the challenger. When Papke climbed between the ropes, he was surprised at Stanley's physical condition, seeing that he had been led to believe that Ketchel had not been well and was just taking the fight as a swansong before hanging up the gloves.

The ex-champion certainly looked in prime condition, appearing lean and fit. Even before going to his own corner, Ketchel went over to Papke and, in sombre mood, said, 'There will be no handshake this time. It took you 12 rounds to beat a blind man last time. This time it won't take me 12 rounds to get my revenge. You'll see.' Papke retorted, 'You're so wrong, Stanley. What I did before, I can do again.'

Ketchel had committed himself to winning in 11 rounds at the latest and told his manager as much. Willus advised him to be careful. 'This guy will try anything to win, legally or illegally,' he warned. 'Get out there and show him who's boss, show him who the real champion is. You know you can do it and I know you can do it,' he said.

At the bell, Papke was first into action, landing a light left jab to Ketchel's face. Stanley replied with a long left hook that grazed the champion's jaw. As they came out of a clinch, Ketchel connected with a stiff left hook to the body and followed through with two hard rights to the head that drove the Illinois boxer back against the ropes. This was a different Ketchel than before. Now he was a man out for revenge after being illegally shorn of his prized title.

The first round was Stanley's and so was the second as he kept on the attack, relentlessly driving Papke before him with smashing left hooks, right crosses and uppercuts. Papke did connect with some solid blows to the head and body, notably in the third round, but they did not seem to have any effect on the aggressive challenger, who was superbly fit this time.

From the fourth round on, Papke fought when he could and held on when he could. Occasionally, he landed to the face with long rights but his blows carried far less impact than those of Ketchel. In the fifth, Papke fell through the ropes as a result of a punch and the fall did his confidence no good. After being pushed back into the ring, he retreated under Ketchel's pressurised attack and there was a chant from Stanley's fans to finish his man. But Ketchel was biding his time. .

Stanley slowed up in the eighth after the fast, aggressive pace he had been setting, but he more than held his own and roughed Papke about the ring. Remarkably, Papke looked fresher by the 11th than he had in the first round, but it was still Ketchel's fight by far. Ringsiders had him well ahead on his sharper punching and ring generalship. Midway through the 11th, Ketchel landed a powerful left-hand swing to the jaw that had all his power and strength behind it and the champion fell forward on his face.

Rolling over, Papke managed to get to one knee but fell over. As he struggled upright, the timekeeper's count had already reached 11 seconds. Referee Welsh waved his hands wide. It was all over. Ketchel did what he said he would do – knock out the champion in faster time than Papke had accomplished it. He was once again middleweight champion of the world.

'I knew I had him as early as the second round,' said Ketchel in the dressing room. 'Sure, he was strong and tough but I can tell you, boys, that nothing in the world would have stopped me from winning back the title, *my* title. He stole it from me last time and now it was my chance of revenge. Somebody told me as I left the ring that all the excitement was too much for one spectator and he keeled over and died. I'm very sorry about that. I'm very happy that I did not let down my faithful supporters and I'm prepared to defend my title against any deserving challengers.'

Papke, comforted by his manager ,Tom Jones, and handlers, said, 'I don't know what was the matter with me today but I just wasn't myself out there. I just couldn't get started. I never fought such a poor fight in all my life. I couldn't say that Ketchel was any better than he was in the last fight but I guess you guys might dispute that. I would certainly like another fight with Ketchel and I hope he will give it to me, as I did with him.'

The fight made headlines the next day and all the reporters agreed that Ketchel was a worthy winner and new champion. Harry S Smith of the *San Francisco Chronicle* wrote, 'It was a spectacular triumph by Ketchel. Manifestly the better of the two, he was a fighting demon and there was no round of the 11 in which it could be said that Papke had more than an even break. The winner fought the best fight of his career, boxing well, blocking in a way that at times made Papke appear a beginner at the game. He landed stiff punches to the body that hurt Papke from the outset and in no way suffered himself. Papke was beaten by a better man.'

W O McGeehan of the *San Francisco Bulletin,* and later editor of the *New York Times,* wrote in his familiar descriptive style, 'Never since the days when the gladiators fought for their lives with the celsus was there such a fight as yesterday's title fight. It was the sort of fight that had the crowd gripping their seats and howling like wild beasts that hover around a battle between other animals in the jungle. They fought because they hated each other bitterly.'

Ketchel and Britt were now casting their eyes on the heavyweight division ruled by Jack Johnson. Stanley felt he possessed the big punches to bring down Johnson and keep him there. When Britt issued an open challenge through the newspapers, Johnson proclaimed, 'I don't normally fight little guys but if this fellow Stanley Ketchel wants to fight me, I'll take him on. But let him prove himself by taking on a heavyweight, or even a light-heavyweight. Then we might be able to talk business.'

Privately, however, Johnson had little if any interest in taking on the dangerous Ketchel – at least not yet. Meanwhile, to keep busy, Britt decided to pit Ketchel against a leading light-heavyweight in New York, where he had never boxed. 'Back East, they've never seen Stanley,' said Britt. 'They would know of him, sure, but seeing him in the flesh was another matter. They will love him.'

Making inquiries as to what big names were available, they opted for Philadelphia Jack O'Brien, a master boxer with a strong left jab and a solid right, and a master at defence. He was adept at blocking punches and countering fast. Not a particularly hard hitter, O'Brien depended on his skill and agility to win fights. Often he would step into the heavyweight division, even though he rarely scaled more than 165lbs, five pounds over the middleweight limit and ten pounds inside the light-heavyweight boundary.

Born Joseph Francis Hagen, he turned professional in January 1896, a month short of his 18th birthday, in his native Philadelphia. On the advice of a friend, he changed his name to Philadelphia Jack O'Brien on the grounds that Irish boxers, or boxers with Irish names, were very popular in the US – and O'Brien was a very common Irish name. He was a shrewd publicist who valued good publicity in whatever form as long as it was associated with himself.

A virtuoso on the violin in his spare time, O'Brien started his career as a lightweight and matured fast, developing into a welterweight and then into a middleweight before his regular and more comfortable spot as a light-heavyweight. He built up a good record over the next few years but it was not until he decided to make what turned out to be a successful English tour in February 1901 that he started to attract attention. He won all his 19 fights, 15 inside the distance, in towns and cities all over the UK. Not all his opponents were of top quality but the main point was that he had emerged victorious. He was canny enough as well to send reports of his victories to the Associated Press news agency, which alerted fans and sports editors to his success.

Returning to the US in glory, and reportedly with 18 trunks of new clothes, O'Brien was greeted at the dock by the mayor of Philadelphia and a crowd of 10,000 fans. He soon hit the lecture circuit with Major Anthony J Drexel Biddle, a prominent Philadelphian and avid boxing fan who encouraged Jack to go after the big guns in the sport.

Inside four years, he had built up such an impressive record, mainly in no-decision bouts, that he was accepted as a challenger for Bob Fitzsimmons, the veteran Englishman who held the world light-heavyweight title at the time. They met in San Francisco on 20 December 1905. After 11 rounds, with one and then the other gaining the initiative, O'Brien opened up in the 12th round with an all-out attack shortly after the bell sounded.

Zig-zagging his way to his corner, the 42-year-old Fitzsimmons slumped on his stool before slipping to his knees from sheer exhaustion. His seconds picked him up but Fitz mumbled he could not carry on and told referee Eddie Graney he was through. O'Brien was the new light-heavyweight champion of the world.

Flushed with success, O'Brien went on a six-month vaudeville tour to capitalise on his fame. Resuming his ring activity in July 1906, he took on world heavyweight champion Tommy Burns in a title fight four months later and held the Canadian to a draw over 20 rounds. O'Brien demanded a return match and got it in May 1907 but lost the decision, again over 20 rounds. On the advice of close friends, he decided to stay in the light-heavyweight division at least for the time being.

O'Brien agreed to face Ketchel at the National Athletic Club on East 24th Street but his title would not be on the line. It would be a no-decision match over ten rounds. Stanley and Britt would naturally have preferred it if O'Brien had put his title on the line for their New York debut, but the canny light-heavyweight champion insisted no-decision or no fight. In any event, a good performance by Ketchel would impress the New York reporters and fans, and perhaps force the Philadelphian into a championship fight.

From the first clang of the bell, the action was fast and furious. Both boxers liked it that way. O'Brien displayed his customary scientific boxing and good footwork as he moved around the ring like an expert ice skater, while Ketchel was constantly aggressive, hooking, uppercutting and swinging in an attempt to bring down the fleet-footed 175lb champion. But O'Brien, one of boxing's great thinkers, kept his cool, watching Ketchel's every move, every moment. Towards the end of the opening round Ketchel landed a solid right that O'Brien claimed was low, but referee Tim Hurst did not agree and waved the fighters on. Ketchel went back to his corner at the bell with a lump over his left eye, the result of a stinging right cross midway through the session.

O'Brien easily won the second round on his sharper boxing and ring generalship and it was looking anything but good for the middleweight champion. Stanley could make little impression on this boxing master, who always seemed to be one punch ahead, though he managed to cut the Philadelphian's right eye with a right-hand swing in the second round.

The next three rounds were packed with action as O'Brien moved swiftly around the ring and kept up a rat-tat-tat with his fine left jab. The punch was rarely out of the Michigan boxer's face, which was speckled with blood from a cut right eye. Kid McCoy, the former world middleweight champion, who was in O'Brien's corner, told Jack after the sixth round that the fight was his but to watch out for Ketchel's long-range shots and to keep something in reserve for the rest of the fight.

O'Brien recalled in later years, 'Early in the seventh round, I was wondering how Ketchel was able to absorb my Sunday punches but he was a pretty tough guy. Near the end of the round, Ketchel shot a solid right and while I saw it coming, somehow my brain didn't function. I failed to sidestep and the blow caught me flush in the face. It was hell on earth as I saw him do his awkward shuffle and then threw his roundhouse right, which missed. He then stepped forward with his right foot and brought his left around. It connected and I was pretty shaky when the bell sounded.'

O'Brien was more than shaky. Both his eyes were cut and there were red welts across his body from Ketchel's constant battering. By the eighth round, O'Brien looked a well-beaten man. His strength was fading. He clinched and hung on, but Ketchel was always coming in, hooking, uppercutting, swinging. There was no respite. It was the same in the ninth. A powerful left hook to the stomach sent the Philadelphian staggering against the ropes. His legs gave way and he slumped to the canvas. He rose on rubbery legs at nine and immediately fell into a clinch. It looked as though O'Brien would never last the round, but he did. Had his seconds thrown in the towel, nobody could have complained. It would have been the wise thing to do.

This is how Ketchel's biographer Wilfrid Diamond graphically described the tenth and final round, 'The savage, snarling, snorting Stanley came tearing out of his corner and a left and right swing to the jaw sent O'Brien down. He took advantage of a nine count and tried to keep Ketchel off with lefts as he had done in the earlier rounds but Stanley just brushed them aside and came in. A right to the body, another right to the jaw and the Philadelphian was on his back again. The Assassin was showing no mercy. He never could. He never would.

'Jack had no way of stopping this wildcat who was forever punching with relentless fury. O'Brien wanted to last out the round, wanted it very much. All he could do was hang on, and hope for the best. But hope is a poor defence when somebody is murdering you. A left to the body and a right to the jaw sent O'Brien reeling backwards and he fell to the canvas, his head resting in the sawdust box in Ketchel's corner. Referee Hurst started to count but by the time he reached four, the bell sounded and saved O'Brien from an official knockout. It was a glorious defeat for Jack, and a great victory for Stanley.'

Ketchel could have legitimately claimed the world light-heavyweight title, even though it was only a no-decision bout. O'Brien had not defended the title since winning it four years earlier. But the 175lb division had become something of a nonentity, a forgotten class, and nobody even talked about it. The class would continue to lay dormant for another three years until Jack Dillon became the legitimate champion by defeating one of Ketchel's old rivals, Hugo Kelly. Dillon would be known as 'Jack the Giant Killer' for his ability to handle the most unstoppable heavyweights of his day.

Meanwhile, Ketchel told the press that he was not satisfied it had taken him so long to knock out O'Brien and sought a return. O'Brien agreed that a return fight would settle things once and for all, especially as he felt he had not trained hard enough for such a formidable rival. This time he wanted the fight in his hometown of Philadelphia before his own faithful followers, but it would still be another no-decision contest. Ketchel went along with O'Brien's request and the match was set for the Sporting Club on 9 June 1909, just ten weeks after the first bout, a clear indication of the speed with which important fights were arranged in those days.

In between the two fights, O'Brien even managed to box a six-round exhibition with the world heavyweight champion Jack Johnson in Philadelphia. According to contemporary reports, Johnson found it hard to break through the Philadelphian's tight defence. Johnson would go on record as saying that O'Brien could outfox the middleweight champion on his sharper boxing and accurate punching, as long as he kept his chin well guarded from Ketchel's constant attacks.

When the bell clanged, Stanley was the first to score when he reached O'Brien's face with a looping left hook. Jack grimaced but fought his man off with left jabs and straight rights. It was clear that the middleweight champion was out for the kill, and O'Brien knew it. A swinging left caused a cut over the heavier man's right eye and he went straight into a clinch. His seconds were looking very worried at this stage and shouted 'Move, move', as Ketchel shook himself free and continued his two-handed onslaught. It did not make any difference whether there was an opening or not, Stanley just bored in, determined to put O'Brien on the boards and keep him there.

A terrific right to the jaw in the second round sent the game Philadelphian to the floor. He hauled himself to his feet at the count of nine to face his tormentor, but Ketchel would not be put off. Flushed with success, the 'Assassin' tore in again and dropped O'Brien for the second time with a similar blow. As the count proceeded, he struggled to get upright and looked like falling over when the bell rang at four. His seconds had to rush into the ring and bring him to his corner. They shoved smelling salts under his nose and doused him with water, but why they did not do the sensible thing and throw in the towel remains a mystery to this day.

Ketchel bounded out of his corner for the third round and rushed the weakened O'Brien to the ropes. The Philadelphian managed to get out of immediate danger by moving to the centre of the ring in an attempt to use his jab to keep Ketchel off.

Ben Weider described the action as follows in *Boxing and Wrestling* magazine, 'O'Brien had hobbled his way to his corner at the end of the second round like a man with rheumatic legs. By the third, the terrific smashes to O'Brien's jaw had dulled his brain and the ripping uppercuts to his stomach had stolen his wind. This was no longer Jack O'Brien, the world's greatest boxer. This was just a battered hulk unable to hold up his hands or even take his hand off the ropes which held him up. Referee Jack McGuigan took one look, grabbed Ketchel by the hand and led him to his corner. Ketchel then went over to O'Brien's corner and shook his hand warmly. They stood there together exchanging a few words of mutual admiration as the crowd went wild.'

Ketchel had proven his mastery over the world's best light-heavyweight and was unofficially the champion in that division. But Stanley and his manager were not interested in a crown nobody seemed to care about, as noted earlier. In any event, they were still looking to the heavyweight championship, which was in the capable hands of Jack Johnson. If a Ketchel-Johnson fight could be made, what an attraction it would be

– the world's best middleweight and technically the number one light-heavyweight against the top heavyweight. Moreover, Stanley fancied his chances against Jack, even though there would be a considerable difference in their respective weights.

The son of a former slave, Johnson grew up in a rundown area of Galveston, Texas at a time when blacks were forbidden to use the same pathways as whites. In boxing, black fighters were regarded as inferior to their white counterparts, both mentally and physically. The white boxers could draw what was called 'the colour line' if they wanted to avoid a dangerous black boxer.

This was why the blacks were forced to meet each other time and again, and if they wanted to earn big money with their fists, they were tossed into a ring, often a dozen at a time, and left to eliminate themselves to the amusement of the white spectators. These multiple bouts were known as 'battle royals'. Johnson began his career this way but his all-round cleverness and strong punching power allowed him to emerge as the winner so frequently that before long he was able to forge a reputation for himself as a formidable boxer.

It took Johnson some ten years to reach the position of number one challenger for the heavyweight title, and when he got the chance he was fully ready, even if had to travel to Australia for it. On the afternoon of 26 December 1908, in a Sydney ring, he stopped the Canadian Tommy Burns in 14 one-sided rounds to become the first African-American to capture the world heavyweight title. But it was the manner in which Johnson behaved during the fight, taunting Burns with remarks like 'Is that the best you can do, Tommy?' and 'You'll have to do better than that' which made him unpopular. When he returned to the US, he lived the high life, driving fast cars and regularly breaking the speed limit, as well as hanging around with white hookers.

Soon there were calls for a 'Great White Hope' to topple Johnson, and in the first of such fights, and Johnson's initial defence, promoter Jim Coffroth selected Ketchel, who had been challenging Johnson in any event. Johnson agreed and the 20-rounder was set for Colma on 16 October 1909. Ketchel had boxed in the Californian town before and had a big following there. Although Stanley would be conceding some 25lbs in weight and four inches in height, he felt confident he could not only beat the heavyweight champion, but knock him out.

In the weeks leading up to the fight, rumours abounded that the bout had been fixed and that Johnson would carry Ketchel to the end for the benefit of the movie cameras. By allowing the fight to go the full distance and give cinemagoers good value, it was claimed that Jack could pocket a percentage of the revenue and still come away with his title. Johnson always strongly denied any agreement was made. 'I didn't need any deal with Ketchel,' he said.

Hissed as he climbed into the ring, Johnson coolly smiled. Not even the American flag draped around his waist won him any new friends. Ketchel entered the ring to wild cheers and shouts of 'Go get him, Stanley' and 'Finish him quickly, Stanley'. The fight started like so many other Johnson matches. Jack toyed with his opponent through the early rounds, using his wide range of punches to head and body as Ketchel's hooks and swings either missed their target or glanced off Johnson's body. Stanley could not reach the heavyweight champion with any effective blows.

As the rounds went by, Ketchel continually attacked but Johnson either ducked or slipped away out of danger. This was a classic example of the boxer against the puncher. A right hook caught Johnson on the side of the head in the tenth round but Jack was moving and by the time Ketchel could follow through, Johnson was back in the centre of the ring, controlling the action at long range. If the fight was fixed to go the distance, then Johnson was cooperating fully. He did not appear to be extending himself. Or else, he wanted to conserve his energy against an opponent who was continually charging forward.

Although Ketchel's mouth and nose bled freely, he did not seem to be seriously hurt.

The 12th round began like the rest. Johnson stepped briskly from his corner and met Ketchel's attack with a strong left jab followed by a right uppercut, but eased off quickly. Suddenly, like the car you never see on a dark road, everything changed dramatically. A roundhouse right swing caught Johnson just behind the left ear and the heavier man fell clumsily to the canvas, partially stopping his fall with his right hand. Grinning, he was up before referee Jack Welsh could begin a count. Ketchel, sensing the kill, rushed Johnson but was met by a volley of punches. Because Stanley was moving forward, the power of the blows was increased.

One tremendous punch, a right uppercut, landed on Ketchel's open mouth and the leather on Johnson's glove was torn on the challenger's teeth. The middleweight champion fell as though he had been shot and was stretched flat out like a starfish as Welsh tolled 'ten and out'. Ketchel's cornermen rushed into the ring and carried him to his stool. Johnson seemed worried that he might have killed his man but smiled with relief when Stanley regained consciousness. A great heavyweight had defeated an equally great middleweight.

There was no more talk of the alleged fix until 1944, 35 years after the famous fight, when Johnson revealed what he claimed was the true story of the bout. 'My fight with Stanley Ketchel was not a fake or a fix,' he said. 'There was a deal, however. Rather there was an understanding to protect the much smaller man by the fight going the full 20 rounds. By the 12th round, I was well ahead when I heard Willus Britt, Ketchel's manager, crying out "Now Stan". I turned my head in Britt's direction. That was my big mistake. I didn't see Ketchel's right zooming out and before I realised what had happened I was on the floor.

'He caught me good, fair and square but I didn't take a count and leapt to my feet. Ketchel leaped at me, arms flying, the look of a cold killer in his eyes. I waited until he came close, took a quick step backward and drawing on every ounce in my body, exploded a short right uppercut in his face. I can never remember hitting a man harder. Ketchel's body went limp and he dropped to the floor like a man who had been hit in the head by a shotgun blast. He didn't move a muscle as he was counted out. In the dressing room, my sparring partner Bob Armstrong found three of Stanley's teeth embedded in my right glove.

'Despite Ketchel's obvious attempt to double-cross me, I always respected him as one of the greatest fighters that ever lived. As the years passed, my respect for him increased. I didn't blame Ketchel for taking a long shot with the heavyweight championship of the world as the prize. I told Bob Armstrong I think I might have done the same thing myself.'

The Johnson fight was the last one Ketchel ever lost. He boxed only five more times. One day short of a year later, he went to a ranch in Conway, Missouri to train. In this remote locale, the melodrama of Ketchel's life finally caught up with him. He was shot in the back by the jealous boyfriend of a girl with whom Stanley had been sleeping. The bullet, fired from a Springfield rifle, entered Ketchel's back and cleaved the main artery of his heart, and he died as violently as he had lived. The killer, Walter Dipley, was convicted of first-degree murder and served 23 years in prison.

'Had Ketchel not died at 24 years of age, he might have accomplished much more,' said Edward Brophy, executive director of the International Boxing Hall of Fame in New York when Stanley was inducted in 1990. 'Perhaps even winning the heavyweight championship of the world.'

Chapter 5

The man they loved to hate

IT was Christmas Eve 1970 and Geraldine Liston was in St Louis to visit her mother for the holiday season. She was accompanied by her adopted son, a Swede named Danielle. As she had not heard from her husband Sonny in Las Vegas for several hours, she called home several times but got no answer. She assumed he was out, 'more than likely painting the town red with his lady friends,' as she put it later.

Geraldine and Danielle returned around 9.30pm on 5 January. Her pink Cadillac was parked under the carport alongside Sonny's black Fleetwood, just as it should be. Next to the vehicles lay an unusually large number of copies of the *Las Vegas Sun*, a good few days' worth. When she entered the house, the lights were all on, the doors unlocked and the window flung wide. The only noise came from the master bedroom as the television crackled away. She headed for the patio at the back of the house, only to change direction when she detected a pungent, unpleasant odour.

Thinking that Sonny might have left out some food that was beginning to rot, she walked up the three steps leading from the den to the kitchen. There was nothing amiss. Finally, she went upstairs to the master bedroom. At the foot of the bed lay a smashed chair. Propped up against it, she saw the rigid, inert figure of her husband wearing a shirt smeared with dried blood, head slumped to one side. The mystery of Sonny Liston was only just beginning.

Recognised as the most terrifying heavyweight of his generation, Liston won and lost his world title in equally dramatic fashion. Throughout his career, he was never allowed to forget his delinquent teenage years or his underworld connections as he strove to establish himself on the world boxing stage. He was arrested 19 times and served two prison terms. Liston would remain a mystery and an enigma throughout his life. To the public he was a brooding, menacing figure who, in his day, was the most frightening figure in the heavyweight division. They called him 'Old Stone Face'.

Liston often tried to explain his bad-guy image when he became established as a contender. 'I tried to look tough because I'm trying to scare the other guy,' he said. 'The way some of those suckers fight, they're scared. A boxing match is like a cowboy movie. There's got to be good guys and there's got to be bad guys. That's what the fans pay for – to see the bad guys get beat. So I'm a bad guy. But I change things around. I don't get beat.'

With arms outstretched, Liston's 84in reach was 16ins longer than Rocky Marciano's. His fists were 15ins in circumference, larger than any previous heavyweight champion, including big Primo Carnera. *Sports Illustrated* writer Mort Sharnik said his hands 'looked like cannonballs when he made them into fists'. Liston's noticeably more muscular left arm, crushing left jab and powerful left hook lent credence to the widely held belief that he was left handed but utilised an orthodox stance. Sonny strengthened the muscles in his 17ins neck by standing on his head for a couple of hours a day, listening to his favourite song 'Night Train'. A moody individual, at the weigh-in for one of his early contests, Liston's opponent said to him, 'Sonny, you can talk to me. I'm your friend. Why do you scowl so much at me?' 'You'll find out tonight,' Liston replied. The fellow lasted only 118 seconds after the opening bell rang when Sonny hit him with his ramrod left.

For all his raw power and size, Liston's biggest asset was more psychological than physical. 'Sonny made a science out of inspiring fear in the hearts and minds of his opponents, scoring knockouts or stoppages as if by will alone,' said author and broadcaster Bert Sugar. 'He sought to break opponents' wills with a stony glower during the referee's pre-fight instructions. His enormous physique made to look all the more awesome by the padding of towels stuffed beneath his robe. During a bout he would turn his icy, deep brown eyes on his opponents, looking through them rather than at them, almost as if his blink could cause seismic shock waves.' Yet those who knew him, including some of America's most prominent boxing writers and sports editors, recall a man who, once his surly protective shell was breached, was entertaining company with a sardonic wit.

Although Sonny got on with his boxing career, his shadowy past and dubious acquaintances meant that he was never given the full respect he deserved. He was regarded as the bad boy of boxing. In the Christmas 1963 edition of *Esquire*, the magazine described him as 'the last man America wants to see coming down the chimney'. But Sonny was a formidable fighter, a powerful puncher with sharp boxing skills.

Inducted into the International Boxing Hall of Fame in New York in 1991 with an impressive 50-4-0 record, Liston has been rated by *Ring* magazine as the seventh greatest heavyweight of all time. When the British and European heavyweight Henry Cooper was strolling down the Old Kent Road, London in January 1963 with his manager Jim Wicks, they saw Sonny, who was on an exhibition tour at the time, coming in the opposite direction and promptly crossed the road in case Liston came up with any crazy ideas of meeting Cooper in actual combat. Perish the thought.

The Sonny Liston mystery began the day he was born to Tobe Liston and Helen Baskin in St Francis County, Arkansas. They had 25 children, though only ten of their own as Tobe had been married before and was father of the remainder, including

Sonny. As nobody bothered about certificates for the children of poor black families on cotton plantations in those days, Sonny's birth was never officially registered. In later years, he claimed he was born on 8 May 1932 but there is strong evidence that he first saw the light of day much earlier. Liston's mother remembered a different date. 'I think it was 18 January 1932. It was very cold and I recall it well,' she said.

Years later, she dispensed with the memory of a chilly winter's night and confused matters by claiming Sonny had been born on 22 July 1927. Liston himself added to the puzzle by saying that his mother had carved the date of his birth on a tree but that the tree had since been cut down. As to the location of his birth, he would say he was actually born in Little Rock, Arkansas, while on one legal document he gave the place of his birth as Memphis, Tennessee. He also said that as a kid he was known as Charles L Liston but as time went on he became Sonny. He often said he never remembered who first gave him the nickname.

Although slavery had been outlawed by President Lincoln several generations before, for those poor blacks at the bottom of the heap grinding out a living was no less a cruel and binding master. By all accounts, Sonny was a quiet boy but never went to school. 'As far as my father was concerned, if the children were big enough to go to the dinner table they were big enough to go and work in the field,' Sonny would tell newspapermen in later years. 'We had practically no education. The only thing my old man gave me was a beating. He never cared for any of us. We grew up with few clothes, no shoes, little to eat. My dad worked me hard and whipped me hard. If he missed a day, I felt like saying, "How come you ain't whipped me today?" I've often wondered where were all those people we hear about who work with kids when I was growing up.'

When Sonny was 13, Tobe left the family threshold and Helen went on her own to St Louis, Missouri on the banks of the Mississippi. She would settle down in the busy city and worked at several jobs, mainly in a shoe factory. Soon, Sonny joined her after sneaking aboard a train and enrolled in the local school at first grade. But trouble soon loomed. The humiliation and taunts the illiterate, slow-speaking country boy had to take from the sharp city kids was painful, especially when his classmates learned that Sonny had never even owned a pair of shoes until he came to St Louis.

Liston left school one day and never went back. It was now the cold winter of 1949 and roaming the streets he got involved with gangs, soon taking part in a series of robberies and muggings. 'I just got caught up with a bad crowd,' said Sonny, who became known to the St Louis police as the 'Yellow Shirt Bandit' due to the shirt he always wore. 'I was 16 then and weighed over 200lbs. I was in a lot of street fights. I used to punch first and ask questions later. None of the other gangs would mess with me.'

In May 1950, Sonny was arrested with several companions and convicted of the armed robbery of a store, where their total haul turned out to be $37. Given a five-year sentence, Sonny was sent to Missouri State Penitentiary in Jefferson City. 'I was back there in 1957 after another robbery,' he said. 'I didn't mind prison. It was the first time in my life I got three square meals a day.' Inside a few short years, he would return to prison under totally different circumstances – as a special guest, heavyweight champion of the world.

The first person to show a particular interest in Liston was the prison chaplain, the Rev. Edward Schlattmann, and not his replacement, Father Stevens, as is generally believed. Father Schlattmann was the first to put boxing gloves on Sonny. There was a problem with the gloves, however, as they could not find a pair big enough. It meant he had to force his hands into the biggest gloves available and lace them loosely. In later years as a boxer, he had to have special gloves made. 'After four years in the gym, nobody in the penitentiary would get into the ring with Sonny,' recalled Schlattmann.

When Schlattmann was transferred to a parish, he was replaced by Father Stevens, whose official title would be Athletic Director. Even more than his predecessor, Stevens saw Sonny's antagonistic contempt towards the world and sought to channel those energies into boxing. 'Father Schlattmann told me about Sonny and I got to look at him in the gym one day,' he said. 'My first impression was the size of his fists and there was that cold, menacing look in his eyes. I felt he could well be a champion some day if handled right. I arranged with a trainer at the gym, Munroe Harrison, to bring in a fighter named Thurman Wilson to box him. Wilson was considered to be the best heavyweight in St Louis and he would test Sonny. Wilson came, climbed into the ring for a sparring session, but only did two rounds before getting out and complaining, "I'm quitting. I don't want any more of that guy." That's the kind of fighter Sonny was in those early years.'

Harrison went to Frank Mitchell, proprietor of the *St Louis Argus* and a man who already had a small stable of boxers. Together, they campaigned for Liston's release. On 30 October 1952, Sonny was paroled to Mitchell and Harrison. They found him a job at the local steelworks, a room at the YMCA and what turned out to be a new life. Liston was entered into the inter-city Golden Gloves tournament in St Louis in February 1953 and won all his three fights, two by knockout. In one tournament in 1953, he beat Ed Sanders, who had won gold for America at the Helsinki Olympics the year before. By now, Sonny was having serious thoughts about turning professional. After approaching two local promoters, Irving Schoenwald and Hans Bernstein, who often worked together on joint promotions, Harrison and Mitchell invited one of America's top trainers, Ray Arcel, to have a look at Sonny.

'I have to say I was extremely impressed,' said Arcel later. 'It wasn't Liston's magnificent body that captured my imagination. Nor was it his effortless agility or his obvious cold confidence. It was the way he used his left hand, jabbing and hooking with it, switching a jab into a hook and back into a jab again. I was amazed. No, it wasn't the first time I'd seen a left hand used so skilfully. The great world lightweight champion Benny Leonard was a past master at it and so was Billy Conn, the light-heavyweight champion who gave Joe Louis such a scare. But they were top professionals while Liston at this stage was only an inexperienced amateur.'

Liston signed professional contracts with Harrison and Mitchell, who handled his parole papers as well. They would get half of Sonny's purses and pay for all his expenses, including the hiring of sparring partners. Liston made his debut in a preliminary bout at the St Louis Arena on 2 September 1953, when he fought newcomer Don Smith in a scheduled four-rounder. Smith had won his two previous bouts by early knockouts but was swept away by Liston in 33 seconds. Smith was out cold for five minutes after taking a powerful right to the side of the head, the first punch Sonny threw. The purse, $199, was the most money Sonny had ever seen in his life.

Liston won two more fights in 1953, both wins coming on points, all in St Louis. In 1954, his winning run continued in Detroit. He made his debut in the Motor City on 29 June with an impressive points win over the highly touted Johnny Summerlin, who entered the ring before a near-capacity crowd of 1,200 as a heavy favourite. Liston soon changed all that by both outboxing and outfighting Summerlin to win the decision, proving to his handlers that he could also take a good punch. The victory drew critical acclaim in the newspapers and *Ring* magazine named Sonny its Prospect of the Month. They met in a return two months later, resulting in another points win for Liston.

Sonny's rising popularity in Detroit suffered a setback on 7 September, when he suffered his first loss, against the local Marty Marshall. According to Liston, 'I was told that Marshall was a clown, so I took it easy with him. My corner had told me to carry him a few rounds so as the fans could get their money's worth and then knock him out. In the second round, he was hopping up and down and I started laughing at his antics. Suddenly, he lets out a yell like the Red Indians used to do in the movies and with my mouth open, gaping at him, he whacks me on the jaw. It didn't hurt but I couldn't close my mouth. I had to fight the last six rounds with my mouth open. After a while, it hurt real bad and when I went to the hospital it was discovered my jaw was broken.'

Marshall, who subsequently became a stock checker for a paint company, was offended by Liston's version. 'It's not true that I jumped in the air and whooped, or that we were laughing all through the fight,' he claimed. 'I saw an opening in the second round and let him have it with a right to the jaw. That's all there was to it. I beat him fair and square and he knows it.'

Liston's handlers, Mitchell and Harrison, were not exactly pleased when Sonny gave them a dentist's bill for $40. The operation on the jaw cost $400, which the St Louis Athletic Commission agreed to pay. Liston was out of action for six months and under the agreement he signed, Mitchell and Harrison had to pay him $35 every week. With no prospect of anything in return during that period and the coffers running low, Mitchell bought out Harrison for $600 and sold his share to a local drugstore owner named Eddie Yawitz, who had strong connections in the fight business.

Liston began his comeback on 1 March 1955 with a eight-round points win over Neil Welch at the Masonic Temple in St Louis. A victory is a victory but the press was not satisfied. W J McGoogan of the St Louis Post-Dispatch reported, 'Despite the fact that Liston pounded Welch at will and the Toledo boxer's only defence was to wrap his arms around his head, Liston was unable to floor the visitor, let alone knock him out. On occasions, Welch managed to land a punch which momentarily stopped Liston, although Sonny wasn't hurt at any time while Welch appeared to be on his way out several times. He also managed to evade the kayo punch, or Liston didn't find the right way to land it.'

Liston's mind was now concentrated on the one man who had beaten him in 14 fights, Marty Marshall. 'I just had to wipe the slate clean,' he said. The return match was set for the Kiel Auditorium, St Louis on 21 April. For three rounds it was fairly even but in the fourth, the unthinkable happened. Sonny was knocked down for the first time in his professional career, a flash right to the head doing the damage. But he got up and in the sixth round sent Marshall reeling to the canvas four times before the fight ended on a stoppage. Sonny had been amply avenged. 'He hit me like no man should be hit,' Marshall told George Puscas of the *Detroit Free Press*. 'He's tough. That's one thing nobody can deny about that man. He hurts when he breathes on you.'

Liston always denied that Marshall put him down, a feat no other foe would manage until Muhammad Ali did it in 1965. 'I never understood why he always denied I floored him in the fourth round of our second fight,' Marshall would say. 'Everyone remembers. It was in the papers and it was a fact. It's the one thing that gets me about that fight.'

The defeat of Marshall was the first of six consecutive wins for Liston, including a third bout with Marshall on 6 March 1956, this time in Pittsburgh, which went the full ten rounds. Just prior to the fight, Mitchell talked to Tom Tannis, the erstwhile manager of the former world heavyweight champion Ezzard Charles, who was then nearing the end of his career. 'I've got the next heavyweight champion of the world,' Mitchell said. 'Can you move him for me?' Tannis wrote a letter to *Ring* magazine editor/publisher Nat Fleischer, who had apparently forgotten the Prospect of the Month tag he had put on Sonny two years earlier. Tannis agreed to take a 50 per cent stake in Liston's contract but changed his mind after hearing of Liston's close association with mobsters.

True to form, Mitchell and his new partner, Eddie Yawitz, found they were gradually losing control of Sonny's affairs. Moving in slowly but steadily, like a tide, was Frankie 'Blinky'

Palermo, an undercover boxing manager and associate of crime boss Frank Carbo. Palermo's assistant on record was Joseph 'Pep' Barone, who would soon become a major part of the Liston entourage. It is agreed in boxing circles that Sonny would have made it to the top anyhow on his natural ability, but having the right people behind you who would make the right connections was certainly no hindrance.

Trouble, however, was never too far from Liston. On 5 May 1956, Sonny and his girlfriend, Geraldine Chambers, attended a party thrown by some friends on North Taylor Avenue, St Louis. At the end of the night, or the early morning, Liston called a cab to take him and Geraldine to their homes. Sonny said that when he saw the cab pulling into an alleyway with its full lights on, they ran down and saw Patrolman Thomas Mellow on his rounds talking to the driver. When Sonny asked what was wrong, the cop said the cab was blocking the alleyway and would have to move further on. 'The cab stays right here,' said Liston defiantly.

When Mellow reached in his pocket to give the cab driver a ticket, Sonny lost his temper and pushed him to the pavement. Soon, two more cops arrived on the scene and Liston was given a summons. In court on 8 January 1956, Liston pleaded guilty to assaulting a police officer and was sentenced to nine months in the city workhouse. On his release after just seven months, he married Geraldine. He was 25 and she was 33. Geraldine had a 13-year-old daughter from a previous relationship and while Liston liked the company of children, they would never have any of their own.

Out of the workhouse but still in trouble, Sonny was arrested for speeding as well as being picked up as a suspected thief while carrying a loaded gun. In court on both occasions, the charges were struck out on condition that the boxer be of good behaviour. In court, Captain John Doherty, the chief of police in St Louis, made it clear that Liston should get out of town, and stay out. Sonny lamented in later years, 'There was nothing they didn't pick me up for. If I went into a store and asked for a stick of gum, they'd haul me in on a stick-up charge. I often wondered about black fighters like Joe Louis or Floyd Patterson. They never encountered such overt attention. Maybe I came from a worse environment than they did.'

Determined to stay out danger on the streets, Liston concentrated on his activities in the ring. On 1 January 1958, he made a New Year resolution to remain on the straight and narrow, with no distractions. He moved his base from St Louis to Denver, Colorado and was encouraged by the local Catholic priest, Father Edward Murphy, a boxing fan. Under Father Murphy's patient tuition, Liston mastered the rudiments of reading and writing, and began to enjoy life in his new home town. Relaunching his career on 29 January 1958, he finished off Billy Hunter in two rounds in Chicago. Since turning professional three years earlier, he had won 15 fights against just one loss, later reversed on two occasions. Eight of his wins had come inside the distance. The boxing world was finally beginning to take serious notice of this menacing fighter with fists of iron.

Liston won eight out of eight in 1958, including two decisions over the capable Bert Whitehurst in St Louis. Whitehurst was also an academic. He held a Bachelor of Science degree at Morgan State University and was studying for a Master's in biology at New York State University. An all-round athlete, he played football and tennis for recreation before concentrating on boxing.

In later years, Whitehurst remembered the first time he and Liston fought, 'In the first round I was unable to get past Sonny's long left jab. Every time he stuck out his left in the first round, it was as if he held a stick in his hand and the stick was telling me to stand back. His left stuns you and knocks you across the ring. My trainer, Charlie Brown, told me to slip the jab, step inside and work my own left. By doing that, I found not only a way to survive but I was able to work the body and tie Liston up. Over the second half of the fight, Liston re-established himself on the outside and got to me in the eighth.'

Remembering the second fight, Whitehurst said, 'My manager then, George Gainford, who guided Sugar Ray Robinson's career, told me to box on the outside. I ran for six rounds but took a good beating. By then, Sonny was too tired to run so I moved inside and survived the ten rounds, but it was like being in the eye of a hurricane. On the outside, it was hell but in close it was calm and I was safe. If I had listened to Charlie Brown in the first fight I might have beaten Liston, but that's an old story. Liston was an excellent fighter, a mean fighter, but if I had gotten another shot at him I would have gone into hard training, winner take all. It never happened.'

Liston's win over the Cuban Julio Mederos on 14 May 1958 was the first time he got national television exposure. The fight was broadcast from the Chicago Stadium as part of the Interntional Boxing Club's Wednesday night programme on the CBS network. Sonny was in a hurry and knocked out the Havana battler in the third round. Two months later, Sonny did a 56-second demolition job on Wayne Bethea, who was expected to provide stiff opposition but instead became another victim, losing seven teeth into the bargain.

If 1958 was a good year for Sonny, 1959 was even better. In his first fight of the year, on 18 February in Miami Beach, Florida, he went in against Mike DeJohn. Liston was now ranked seventh in *Ring* magazine's top ten monthly rankings and was out to show everybody what he could do. The aggressive DeJohn shook him a few times, noticeably in the third and fourth rounds, but Sonny ploughed on. In the sixth, a massive left hook to the head dropped the New York-based boxer for a count of eight and then a booming right to the chin finished him off. 'This was one of the most brutal outpourings of punishment in recent heavyweight history,' said the *Miami Herald*.

Rocky Marciano, who had retired as undefeated world heavyweight champion three years earlier, was at ringside.

'Liston is not too far away from the title,' he said. 'He has the best left jab I've seen since Joe Louis. He gets real force into his jabs, like Joe used to do, though he loops his punches more than he should. He should try and shorten them up more. Can he take a punch? I don't know. He didn't have to, fighting DeJohn. A couple of uppercuts shook him and his legs wobbled but he came right back. Would I like to make a comeback and fight Sonny? No thanks, I'm staying on this side of the ropes, the safe side.'

Truman Gibson of the International Boxing Club, the leading promotional body of the day, offered the reigning world heavyweight champion Floyd Patterson $250,000 to meet Liston, and while Floyd was keen to prove himself as the world's best man at his weight, his canny manager Cus D'Amato said 'No.' In any event, D'Amato was at loggerheads with the IBC, which he claimed, quite rightly as it happened, was monopolising the sport. Many suspected, though, that Cus was merely thinking of Patterson's health and that there were plenty of other less dangerous contenders around than Sonny Liston.

Cleveland Williams fancied his chances against Liston. Born on 30 June 1933 of African-American and Cherokee Indian heritage in Griffith, Georgia, Williams turned professional in 1951 at the age of 18 and inside three years was on the fringe of world class. One of the fiercest punchers of his generation, Williams's main problem was that his fragile temperament, not to mention suspect chin, often let him down when it mattered most.

Known as the 'Big Cat,' Williams lost fights he should have won. The big-hitting but erratic Bob Satterfield put him away in three rounds in June 1954. He clawed his way back and should have been given a title shot against Floyd Patterson in the late 1950s, but Floyd's manager Cus D'Amato didn't want to know. Instead, Patterson would defend against hand-picked opposition, notably the 1956 Olympic heavyweight champion Pete Rademacher, who had never fought professionally in his life. Though Patterson won on a stoppage in the sixth, he suffered the ignominy of being put down for a count in the second round.

Williams came to London on 25 March 1958 to meet Dick Richardson at the Empress Hall, Earls Court in what turned out to be a fiasco. After repeated warnings for fouling, the Welshman was finally disqualified in the fourth round. When a rematch was set up for later in the year, Williams claimed in his hotel room on the afternoon of the fight that he heard voices in his head telling him not to get into the ring. Packing his bags, he took the next flight back to his adopted hometown of Houston, Texas.

In early 1959, with Williams still seeking a deserved championship fight, he was matched with Liston in a bout to take place in Miami Beach, Florida on 15 April. Though hailed by Liston himself as the hardest hitter in the heavyweight division, Williams was finished off in three rounds. Nino Valdez, a 6ft 4ins Cuban who boxed exhibitions with Joe Louis in the post-war years and was now a formidable contender in his own right, took on Liston in Chicago four months later and went the same way – out in the third round. Continuing his 18-fight winning streak, with only four going the distance, Sonny stopped Germany's Willi Besmanoff in the seventh round on 9 December in Cleveland and celebrated Christmas early with a big party at his home.

By now, there had been a new world heavyweight champion. In a stunning upset in New York in June, Sweden's Ingemar Johansson had taken the title from Floyd Patterson in three rounds but had shown no interest in tackling Liston, mainly because he was technically obliged to give Patterson a return fight. The National Boxing Association, a forerunner of the World Boxing Association soon to be formed, now had Liston as its number three heavyweight behind Patterson and the skilful Zora Folley, from Arizona via Dallas, Texas. The December issue of *Boxing Illustrated* featured Sonny on the cover, with the headline 'Nobody Can Beat Sonny Liston'. Inside, the magazine said, 'Enormously powerful, terrific-hitting and well experienced, Liston is considered by the vast majority of experts to be the best heavyweight in the world.'

Liston continued his rampage through the heavyweight division in 1960. In a return with Cleveland Williams in Texas in March, the 'Big Cat' lasted under two rounds, a left-right finishing him off. Roy Harris, a farm boy from Cut and Shoot, Texas who had once floored Patterson, did not even last the first round, during which Sonny had him down three times before their fight in Houston in April was stopped at 2:35.

Three months later, Liston climbed into the ring in Denver to face his most searching test yet, against the number two contender Zora Folley, who had ten consecutive wins behind him. Though conceding 14lbs, Folley was known in the fight trade as a 'fancy dan' because of his skills. He went the same way. Liston caught up with Folley in the second round and had him down three times before the bell came to his rescue. At the start of the third, Folley came out on shaky legs, with his eyes as misty as a Loch Lomond dawn. Liston feinted with a left before landing a cracking right-left combination that rocked Folley on his heels before the fight was stopped.

The only contender now left for Liston was Eddie Machen, the fourth-ranked heavyweight from Redding, California. The son of a postman, Machen was a clever counter puncher with a strong, fast left jab and a good, solid right. They met in a 12-rounder in Seattle, Washington on 7 September 1960. In the opening two rounds, Machen moved smoothly around the ring as Liston put him under pressure. By the fifth, Liston was continuing to force the pace but Machen continued his hit-and-run tactics as the crowd started booing. 'Get off your bicycle, Machen,' yelled one wag during the seventh round. It was fairly close by now, and Liston's corner was telling him to 'go for the body'. In the 11th, Sonny was twice warned by referee Whitey Domstad for low blows before a solid right dropped Machen to his knees.

Domstad picked up the count, then unaccountably stopped to give Machen a rest in his corner. The 12th came and went, with Liston pressing forward against the retreating Californian and catching him with some strong rights to the head. The bell rang, with the unanimous decision going to Liston. For the first time in ten fights, he had been forced to go the distance.

Liston's opening fight in 1961 was in Miami against Howard 'Honey Boy' King of Texas on 8 March. Though he would never box for the heavyweight title, the 6ft 2ins battler kept busy and took on several top contenders of his era. British fans would come to remember him against Brian London at the outdoor Royal Showgrounds in Blackpool in August 1962. The fight was notable in that after a heavy shower of rain, the canvas was so wet and slippery that both men agreed to fight in their bare feet. After five rounds of action, London knocked out King in the sixth.

Peter Wilson of the *Daily Mirror* was at ringside for the Liston-King fight. 'In the first round after just three jabs with all his 214lbs behind them, which made King look as though he had been struck in the face by a sawn-off telegraph pole, Howard was bleeding from the face,' he reported. 'Liston looked cumbersome but deadly. In the second, King was down for eight after being damaged and dazed by a right to the jaw. He was wrestled down again in this session and you looked at Liston with some awe.

'There is something primitive or even primeval about Liston. Knit your defence as you may, there is no cover which cannot be pierced by the driving force of the man. The third did not last long. Liston set his man up with that tremendous left, pinned him on the ropes like a dusky butterfly quivering on a cork and then applied a killing right cross. King sprawled against the ropes, made a grab for one strand, fumbled it, fell further out of the ring and was counted out as he thrashed helplessly on the canvas like a man trying to swim through seaweed.'

With Liston already recognised universally as the number one contender, he still had to stand idly by as Patterson and

Johansson played a kind of ping pong game with the title. Johansson had won the first fight but lost the second and third. With Patterson now back as champion, Sonny called him out with no response. In the meantime he kept fighting and while several heavyweight contenders declined to take him on, particularly those who had already tasted Liston's power in previous fights, the unrated Albert Westphal bravely stepped forward. A two-time, 30-year-old former German champion, he thought he could surprise Liston. Wishful thinking or daydreaming? .

The fight would be part of a closed-circuit television card on 4 December 1961. Liston would meet Westphal in Philadelphia while Patterson defended against the equally unknown Tom McNeeley in Toronto. The twin bill was projected in 150 cinemas across the US and Canada, plus an additional 50,000 homes on a pay-per-view basis. But the local papers were rightly scathing of both mismatches, many refusing to even cover them. Liston only agreed to fight Westphal to put further pressure on Patterson. Sonny needed only two punches, a stabbing left jab and a booming right to the jaw, to flatten the German after 1:58 of the opening round.

The TV commentator asked Westphal the silliest question of the year, 'Would you like to fight Liston again?' The German shuddered and answered firmly, 'Oh god, no.' Westphal visited Liston's dressing room after the fight and asked him, 'I've no hard feelings about you knocking me out but why did you have to give me such a mean look when we were introduced in the ring? I'm your friend, you know that.' Liston replied, 'I came to fight, not make love.'

In the night's TV co-feature, Patterson was far from impressive. He dropped McNeeley, a former football player, seven times before finally knocking him out in the fourth round. The ever-vulnerable champion was on the canvas himself in the fourth and the odds against him standing up to Liston's heavy artillery shifted even wider as a result. Despite the one-sided nature of both fights, the twin bill had the desired effect from Sonny's point of view. The public would hardly stand for Patterson defending against another no-hoper like McNeeley, and President Kennedy let it be known that he believed Liston should be given his chance. Patterson later denied that JFK wanted the fight and was totally against it.

Cus D'Amato, Patterson's manager of record, continued to oppose Liston as a challenger but in the end Floyd sensed he would forfeit every ounce of self respect he had earned in the ring if he ducked his leading contender. With pressure coming from all sides, Patterson's advisers, including D'Amato, had no alternative but to agree to a defence against his most deserving and patient contender, Sonny Liston.

New York, the traditional home of boxing, was the obvious state in which to hold the fight but D'Amato had since lost his licence there because of his links with racketeers. Liston, too, had mob connections and had gone through a succession of managers, all with unsavoury backgrounds, including his latest, Joseph 'Pep' Barone. The message was clear. Liston was not welcome in New York. There was discontent, too, with civic leaders across the US and they made it clear with protests that Liston's unsavoury character would set a bad example to youth. He was a forgotten, unwanted man in his own land. The Illinois State Athletic Commission finally came up with an offer to stage the fight 'in late 1962' at Comiskey Park, where Joe Louis, admired by both Liston and Patterson, had won the title 25 years earlier.

Floyd Patterson was born into a large family in Waco, North Carolina on 4 January 1935 but grew up in one of New York City's black ghettos in Brooklyn. He got into trouble with the police early in his life and spent time in a reform school, where he learned how to box. A modest individual, Floyd ran up an impressive amateur record, culminating in a gold medal in the 1952 Helsinki Olympics as a middleweight before turning professional soon afterwards.

On Rocky Marciano's retirement in March 1956, Patterson won the vacant world heavyweight title by knocking out the light-heavyweight champion Archie Moore in five rounds, making him at 21 the youngest ever champion in the division. Patterson would hold that record for 30 years until Mike Tyson won the title at the age of 20. In an up-and-down and very controversial reign as champion, the Liston fight would be Floyd's tenth title bout.

As the details of the Patterson-Liston fight were being worked out in the winter of 1961 and spring of 1962, a major tragedy struck the boxing world. On 24 March 1962, Emile Griffith, a Virgin Islander based in New York, successfully defended his world welterweight title by stopping Cuba's Benny 'Kid' Paret at Madison Square Garden, New York. The two had fought twice before, with one win each, and there was bad blood between them. A major factor involved Paret deriding Griffith's manhood and alluding to his homosexuality, a taboo topic anywhere in 1962, let alone professional boxing. In the 12th round of the fight, Griffith cornered Paret and battered him mercilessly before veteran referee Ruby Goldstein, a respected official, intervened. Then, and since, many criticised Goldstein, a former boxer, for not stopping the fight sooner.

Regardless of any issue of blame, Paret was knocked unconscious and suffered two brain haemorrhages. Comatose, he was rushed straight to a hospital, where he was operated on to relieve pressure on his brain. The doctors' efforts would prove fruitless, however, as Paret's injuries were too extensive. Paret never regained consciousness and died ten days later. Paret's death was by no means the first fatality in professional boxing. Since 1900, an estimated 450 boxers had died prior to Paret. His death was not even the first ring fatality in the Garden, as a boxer had died there in 1933 and another in 1951.

Still, no fight ending in a fatality had been so high profile, and reactions were severe. In Washington, Senator Estes Kefauver called for more effective federal control, adding to his concerns about the mob's presence in the sport. There were calls across the US and other countries for the sport to be banned. The BBC halted all boxing broadcasts and several British newspapers carried editorials that something needed to be done about the dangers of the sport. Some even began calling for boxing simply to be treated like bullfighting or cockfighting and permanently abolished.

The furore soon died down when boxing legislators promised, and eventually delivered, more safety regulations, including the shortening of championship fights from 15 rounds to 12, although that change would take several years to be introduced. Meanwhile, negotiations and arrangements were being completed for Patterson v Liston and the bout was signed for the Chicago Stadium on 25 September 1962. Liston would initially work out at a training camp in South Fallsburg, in the New York Catskills, before switching to a camp on the site of an abandoned racetrack in Aurora, Illinois. Patterson used a training camp in Elgin, Illinois to prepare for what he considered the most important fight of his life.

At the weigh-in, Liston said, 'If I win, and I'm sure I can, I might fight Ingemar Johansson, although in truth, he should be locked up for impersonating a fighter. As for this young guy Cassius Clay I've been hearing about, he's been talking a lot but I'm prepared to take him on, but they would both have to fight Cleveland Williams first. Williams was the hardest puncher I ever fought and nobody wants to fight him. He can punch as hard as I can but he can't take it like I can, as I discovered when I twice fought him. Patterson? He will be the first fighter I've actually been mad at. I had a dream the other night about how the fight will end but I can't say anything about it. All I can say now is that the fight won't last long and I'll be the winner and new heavyweight champion of the world.'

Ticket sales were brisk, with a crowd of over 35,000 in attendance at the spacious ballpark. Closed-circuit television sold 600,000 seats at 247 locations, a record that would stand until Muhammad Ali and Joe Frazier fought in March 1971 at Madison Square Garden. Over 600 reporters from 49 states and 12 countries had successfully applied for press tickets and took up their places at ringside. By tradition, Liston was first into the ring as the challenger and was greeted by boos. When Patterson ducked between the ropes, he was cheered. If Floyd was the sentimental favourite, the smart money was on 'Old Stone Face,' a 7/5 favourite. Nevertheless, four former world heavyweight champions tipped Patterson to retain his title: James J Braddock, Jersey Joe Walcott, Ezzard Charles and Rocky Marciano.

The respective records of champion and challenger were not that dissimilar, with Patterson 38-2-0 and Liston 33-1-0. But there was a sharp contrast in their weights. Liston outweighed his shorter opponent by 25lbs, scaling 212lbs to Patterson's 187lbs. Patterson had said at his training camp that he would box out of a crouch but instead, once the fight started, he walked forward to face his challenger standing up.

With his ring boots planted firmly on the canvas, Liston landed a cracking left hook high on Patterson's head, causing the champion to quiver and appear to lose his balance. Floyd had not landed a single punch so far and a thin smile creased Liston's face. Keeping cool and remaining completely disciplined, Sonny flashed through a powerful right cross to the chin, followed by an equally fast right hook to the chin, and Patterson went down on all fours. 'Get up, get up,' yelled authors Norman Mailer and James Baldwin as they jumped to their feet. As the count reached three, the bewildered Patterson shook his head, his expression one of confusion rather than pain. As the seconds ticked away, he managed to get one glove off the canvas and struggled to prop himself up on one knee before falling over, his right leg doubled up under him, as referee Frank Sikora counted to ten. Patterson had lost his precious title in 2:06 of round one, making it the third-shortest world heavyweight title fight in history up to then.

Liston, a man of few words at the best of times, said in the dressing room, 'I always figured I would win and I now hope the public will give me some recognition. I beat the number one in the world, so what more can I do? I have a contract to meet Patterson in a return fight so we'll see what happens then.' Patterson said, 'I never had a chance to get to him. I started slowly. It was a 15-round fight and I wanted to feel him out. He started faster than I expected. I'm prepared to meet him again, hopefully in a few months.'

Boxing Illustrated reported, 'The whole thing was summed up in one caustic question fired at Patterson after the fight. When the beaten man said, "All I want to do is fight him again," a guy cracked, "Then why didn't you fight him tonight?"' Patterson said he was sorry he had let his fans down but promised he would do better next time. Fearful of being recognised, he left by a back door wearing a beard and dark glasses.

It would be nearly a year before the return bout took place. New York was still out of bounds because of Liston's association with mobsters and several other states went along with the ban, including Chicago. The rematch was finally set for Miami Beach on 10 April 1963 but Liston injured his left knee swinging a club on the local Normandy Shores golf course while playing with an 11-year-old boy he had befriended – 'Little Mike Zwerner, the best friend I ever had,' Sonny would say. The fight was postponed until later in the year, although the venue was changed after Miami withdrew following 'complications' which were never fully explained.

The new date set was 22 July 1963 at the Convention Center, Las Vegas, a city that would in a relatively short time become the self-styled entertainment capital of the world, not to mention a major fight location. Built in the Mojave Desert in Nevada, the crossfires and politics of the civil rights movement had little meaning there.

Vegas was a glitzy world unto itself and it was a world that very much wanted to boost itself in the name of its sole occupation – money. A big, lucrative world heavyweight fight would help to achieve that.

The last time the state of Nevada had held any such event was back in 1912, when Jack Johnson fought and beat Jim Flynn in a heavyweight championship fight. That one was held in Reno at a time when nobody had ever heard of Las Vegas. Prior to that, Reno put on James J Jeffries's brave losing fight with Johnson in 1910. Going further back, Cornwall's Bob Fitzsimmons knocked out James J Corbett in Carson City to win the heavyweight title in March 1897. Was it not high time for another heavyweight championship fight in Nevada, and this time one that would put Las Vegas itself on the celebrity map?

Viva Las Vegas. All roads and routes led to 'Sin City', where the high rollers and the gamblers and the hookers converged. By fight night, Patterson was the sentimental favourite but the big money was on Liston to repeat his earlier victory, though maybe not as quickly. A crowd of 7,816 packed the venue, with thousands of fight fans watching on closed-circuit television in cinemas across the nation. Celebrities introduced from the ring included former greats such as Sugar Ray Robinson, Rocky Marciano, Joe Louis and Billy Conn. Patterson was first to enter the ring to mild applause and waved to the crowd. Picked out by a spotlight, Liston was greeted with a mixture of cheers and boos.

At the opening bell, Sonny was the first to lead with a long left that Floyd adroitly ducked. But Liston kept moving in and in spite of Patterson's gloves-and-elbows defence, he was able to get through with two jabs, causing the challenger to fall into a clinch. Liston pulled himself free and landed three solid rights that sent Patterson down on one knee. The compulsory eight count was in force under Nevada rules but Floyd seemed too confused to take full advantage of it. Instead, he rose at four, a trifle wobbly, and when referee Harry Krause asked him if he was alright, he nodded.

Liston had retreated to a neutral corner before coming forward again and resuming his attack. Patterson made his one and only attempt to fight back by landing a swinging right on Liston's shoulder. Sonny took no notice and a burst of lefts and rights connected with Patterson's head, the final chopping right sending Floyd sprawling to the canvas. He got up at five, shaking his head to clear his senses but again failing to take advantage of the mandatory count. Liston moved in fast. Backing his man to the ropes, he landed three clubbing rights followed by a final right uppercut that sent the challenger down for the third time. On this occasion, there was no getting up. Patterson rolled over on to his side before getting to one knee, with both hands on the canvas, and tried desperately to get up as he was counted out. He was still dazed as he was helped to his corner. The time of the knockout was 2:10 of round one, four seconds longer than the first fight.

'I was beaten by a better man,' said Patterson in the dressing room. 'But I am not quitting. I love boxing. I want to try and fight my way up the ladder again. No, I wasn't afraid, just nervous and tense.' He then made the classic remark, 'I was doing fine until he hit me.' Liston was naturally in jocular mood. 'I predicted I would beat him in 84 seconds but it took a little longer. I would have done so had it not been for the mandatory counts,' he said.

The brash young heavyweight Cassius Marcellus Clay was firmly in the heavyweight picture now. Clay, who would change his name to Muhammad Ali inside two years, had climbed into the ring at the end of the fight, grabbed a commentator's microphone and shouted, 'It was a disgrace, a farce. I'm gonna whip this big ugly bear if he's brave enough to take me on. I'll be the greatest and the prettiest heavyweight to hold the title in history.' He tried to get near Liston but attendants hustled him away and he left the ring, still shouting what he was going to do with Sonny.

Clay grew up in a quiet black neighbourhood in Louisville, Kentucky. He had been focused on boxing since he was 12 years of age and trained with the single-mindedness of a future champion. Starting as an amateur in his hometown, Clay captured Golden Gloves and Amateur Athletic League titles on the way up and won gold as a light-heavyweight in the Rome Olympics in 1960. Turning professional the same year, he made rapid progress, showing almost unbelievable hand and foot speed. The brash young boxer's knack of self-promotion gained him a big following and he began to predict the round in which his opponents would fall. Clay was a one-man show, full of swagger and contempt, but the public and the media embraced him. In his third year of boxing, he had forced himself into the number one challenger's position and a championship fight seemed only a matter of time.

The scene was finally set for a showdown with Liston on 25 February 1964 at the Convention Center in Miami. As fight night approached, Clay promised to 'float like a butterfly and sting like a bee'. Liston was not impressed. He would let his massive fists do the talking. At the weigh-in, Clay appeared to go berserk, behaving so outrageously that the Miami Beach Boxing Commission fined him $2,500. His pulse was racing and Dr Alexander Robbins, who examined Clay, pronounced him 'scared to death' and had reservations about his fitness to fight. But by the time he entered the ring, Cassius was totally composed and his pulse was back to normal. It was Liston who looked tense and anxious. Still, Sonny was a 7/1 favourite and the only speculation surrounded how quickly he would dispose of his cocky challenger.

For the first four rounds, Liston was unable to land a solid punch on the fleet-footed Kentuckian. Clay swayed back from the champion's punches and moved swiftly around the ring, peppering Liston with stinging left jabs and jolting uppercuts from both gloves. At the end of the fourth round, Clay told his trainer Angelo Dundee that he had been blinded by something on Liston's gloves and wanted to surrender. 'Don't be crazy,' replied Dundee. 'You've got him. Get out there and keep dancing until your eyes clear.'

Clay would later tell this writer in an interview that all he could see was a 'foggy outline' of Liston, but the tired, frustrated champion was unable to land a telling punch. Liston plodded through the fifth and sixth rounds before spitting out his gumshield at the bell and refusing to go out for the seventh round. Referee Barney Felix indicated that the fight was over as a disconsolate Liston sat gloomily in his corner. Clay had predicted he would win inside eight rounds. Sonny's reign, which had promised to be an all-conquering one, had ended ingloriously. 'Cassius the Clown' had tamed the 'Big Ugly Bear'.

Liston told reporters later that he had damaged his left shoulder in the first round, making it impossible for him to jab properly. The next day, Liston's advisor Jack Nilon announced that his boxer had sustained the injury during training. A team of doctors pronounced the injury was genuine but the Miami Beach Boxing Commission withheld Liston's purse pending an investigation, particularly in view of the different versions of when, where and how the injury had actually occurred. The money was subsequently released but the suspicions about the whole affair would remain. When a return fight was planned for 16 November 1964 in Boston, the World Boxing Association banned it as a violation of its rules on rematches. It even went further by stripping Clay of its title, dropped both Cassius and Liston from its ratings and set up an elimination tournament.

With Liston already out of favour in Miami, New York and Chicago, Inter-Continental Promotions shifted operations 250 miles way to a century-old mill town in Lewiston, Maine, where a school ice rink was available on 25 May 1965, and probably on most other days. The location would be known as St Dominic's Arena. Though the fight was given wide publicity, fewer than 4,000 fans turned out, the smallest crowd at a heavyweight championship fight since the Ezzard Charles-Freddie Beshore bout in Buffalo, New York State in August 1953. However, the money came from closed-circuit TV, beaming it into 258 locations in the US and Canada, and all over Europe, including Britain, by the Early Bird satellite. Once again, Liston was favourite, this time at 8/5. 'I'll whip this loudmouth real good,' he had earlier told newspapermen while showing his clenched right fist at his training camp in nearby Poland Spring.

Clay came out fast and danced around. 'We sat back,' said George Whiting in London's *Evening Standard*, 'awaiting a waltz if not a tango.' Missing with a right, Ali followed up with another right to Liston's head. Liston was short with a left hook and also missed with a right to the body. Sonny was doing all the forcing when Clay suddenly landed a short, chopping right to the jaw and Liston went down on his back. What happened next was shrouded in utter confusion. Ali was shouting, 'Get up, you bum, get up', as Liston started to climb to his feet.

Referee Jersey Joe Walcott, the former world heavyweight champion, tried to usher Clay to a neutral corner and failed to pick up the count correctly from timekeeper Francis McDonough. *Ring* magazine editor Nat Fleischer called to Walcott to speak to the timekeeper, who had already counted up to 12 and ruled that the fight was officially over. Meanwhile, Clay was firing a salvo of wild punches at Liston. Walcott hurried over to the pair, separated them and raised Clay's right hand as the winner. The crowd called 'fix, fix'. Peter Wilson of the *Daily Mirror* called it 'a disgusting, revolting, utterly tasteless and nauseating travesty, and the worst apology for a world heavyweight title fight I ever saw'.

Once again, allegations of crookedness were never substantiated, even after some revealing facts came out. Inter-Continental Promotions, which staged the fight, had paid Clay $50,000 as an advance on his first title defence should he win the title, and the chief stockholder in that group was a gentleman called Charles Liston, known to one and all as Sonny. In the meantime, Clay had become a member of the Black Muslim sect and was now known as Muhammad Ali, abandoning Cassius Clay, which he claimed was a slave name.

Liston went on fighting for another five years, winning 14 bouts in succession, though mainly against inferior opposition. After reaching third spot in the world ratings, he was surprised on 6 December 1969 in Las Vegas when knocked out by the Philadelphian Leotis Martin in nine rounds after being ahead on all three judges' scorecards. Sonny had one more fight, the following June in Jersey City, where he stopped Chuck Wepner, said to be the role model for Sylvester Stallone's Rocky character, in ten rounds. On 5 January 1971, Liston was found dead in suspicious circumstances by his wife in their Las Vegas home. Another unsolved mystery was beginning to unravel.

Officially, the cause of death was listed as lung congestion and heart failure, as stated following the autopsy. Unofficially, it appeared to be a heroin overdose. Some police officials and Sonny's close associates believed he was murdered by loan sharks selected by mobsters after he had backed out on some big deals. On that theory, in a book published in 2016 entitled rather ambiguously as *The Murder of Sonny Liston,* the author Shaun Assael claims he *was* slain yet offers no conclusive evidence as to his findings, still leaving us in the dark. A man of mystery in life and death, Liston took the truth with him to his grave in an area known in Las Vegas as the Garden of Peace. Ironically, peace was something that eluded Sonny all his life.

Chapter 6

Flight of The Hawk

IN a career known as much for personal turmoil as brilliant performances, Aaron Pryor, billed as 'The Hawk', was one of the most talented and exciting boxers of the late 1970s and early 1980s. Standing in his corner, his eyes narrowing, and pointing his glove at his opponent, his battle cry was, 'What time is it? Hawk time! What time is it? Hawk time!' A bundle of fighting energy, the talented American was, at his best, a rampaging boxer who swarmed all over opponents with fiery aggression and ferocity. Champion of the world at light-welterweight, or junior welterweight as some organisations prefer to call it, the Associated Press news agency named him as the greatest 140-pounder of all time.

'With his great speed and the ferocity of his attacks,' said Bob Mee, the writer and historian, 'Pryor even rated comparison with the great Henry Armstrong, one of the few champions who could have matched his prodigious workrate.' Yet Pryor was also a wild card outside the ring and would become yet another sad victim of America's drug culture.

Pryor was already on the slide at 27 and drifted into a life of crack cocaine and despair. Not for the first time in boxing, and certainly not for the last, a talented fighter had hit the bottom. Sadly, to many, his name in boxing circles has become synonymous with self-destruction.

Pryor followed up a brilliant career as an amateur with an equally successful run in the professional ranks, where he won 39 of his 40 fights and went in against some of the best boxers in the world. But he got into bad company, ran with gangs, and spent time in jail and rehabilitation centres on charges of rape, kidnapping and an assault on a female guest at his home. His story is one of success, excess, failure and finally redemption.

Pryor's is also one of boxing's 'What if?' stories. 'Other fighters have come up short and had their troubles,' said Larry Merchant, the former Home Box Office commentator. 'But what is poignant about Pryor is that he was such a crowd pleaser. He was part of a great era. It took a special guy to stand out at the time because Sugar Ray Leonard blanketed everything. So Pryor was overshadowed. Certainly after his fight with another great, Alexis Arguello, he was more of a star, but through bad timing, or bad management, he missed his chances. How would he have fared against the big stars of the day? I don't know, but they would have been hellacious fights.'

Pryor was always proud of his hometown of Cincinnati, Ohio, where he was born on 20 October 1955. 'Some great fighters came out of Cincinnati,' he once told a magazine writer assigned to interview him. 'Freddie Miller, the great world featherweight champion of the 1930s, was one. A little later there was Ezzard Charles, the heavyweight champion who many say was also the best light-heavyweight of all time. Although Ezzard was born in Georgia, he was reared in Cincinnati and always regarded Cincinnati as his hometown. There were others, too, but Miller and Charles, I guess they would be the best known.'

One of seven children raised in a poor family, Pryor spent much of his time on the mean streets of his Over-the-Rhine neighbourhood, an area of crumbling buildings and rampant crime. Young Aaron was always in trouble with the law. 'All the cops knew me by name,' he often said. The Pryors had more than their share of trouble, sometimes involving guns and knives.

From this downtrodden environment came Aaron, a lonely kid craving attention.

Encouraged by a friend who used to frequent the local gym two or three times a week, Aaron joined up one evening and liked it so much that he vowed to become not only a boxer but a champion, too. At the very least, he hoped, the sport would bring him some love and make him less of an outsider. Pryor quickly built up an impressive record, winning two national Golden Gloves titles and a silver medal in the Pan American Games. In the lightweight finals of the 1976 national Golden Gloves tournament, he defeated future all-time great Thomas 'Hit Man' Hearns, who would become the first boxer to win world titles at five weights. Representing the US in international competition on 21 occasions, Pryor lost only once. His total amateur record was 204 wins in 220 bouts.

Pryor's one regret as an amateur was that he never competed at an Olympic Games. In the trials for a place on the US team for Montreal in 1976, Pryor was a hot favourite to win but was outpointed by Howard Davis, who would go on to win the gold medal at lightweight. There were suggestions that some Olympic officials did not want Pryor on the team because of what they termed his 'irrational and aggressive behaviour' outside the ring, but committee members strenuously denied this claim.

'Having the gold medal around my neck would have been the ultimate achievement as an amateur,' he recalled. 'You may remember that the Montreal Olympics turned out to be a great year for American boxers. They won five gold medals, including Sugar Ray Leonard at light-welter and the Spinks brothers, Michael at middleweight and Leon at light-heavyweight. It would have been nice had I been lucky enough to join them but that's the luck of the game, I guess.'

Consequently, Pryor was unable to use the Olympics as a springboard to a professional career as did Davis, Leonard and the Spinks brothers. Aaron vowed to do it the hard way, by proving himself in the ring. Turning to the paid ranks on 12

November 1976, he stopped Larry Smith, a former kick boxer, after 2:04 of the second round at the Convention Exposition Center, Cincinnati and earned $400. In contrast, Davis, his conqueror in the amateurs, was paid $185,000 for his first pro fight. Nor did Leonard come out of it badly, attracting endorsements and massive TV exposure.

While Pryor was gaining a reputation as a hard puncher with an exciting style, he was earning little money, being forced to stack shelves in a Cincinnati supermarket to supplement his income. When money started to increase, he was able to employ an agent but it was not until he met a local businessman named Buddy LaRosa that his life changed. LaRosa, who owned a chain of pizza parlours, bought out Pryor's contract and paid him $125 a week so he could focus primarily on boxing. LaRosa kept Pryor busy, with eight consecutive wins in 1977. Through 1978 and 1979, there were 11 more victories. Already with a high profile through regular TV appearances, it seemed only a matter of time before a title opportunity came Pryor's way.

It happened on 2 August 1980 at the Riverfront Coliseum, Cincinnati, where he had once sold concession tickets. In the opposite corner was Antonio Cervantes, the World Boxing Association light-welterweight champion and a power puncher. Pryor's purse was $50,000 and the fight would be nationally televised by the CBS network. The first Colombian to win a world title and the first from that country to be inducted into the International Hall of Fame in New York, Cervantes had first won the belt in 1972. He lost it briefly in 1976 but won it back a year later and put it on the line a further six times.

By 1980, Cervantes was past his best but still a formidable champion. Despite LaRosa securing home advantage for Pryor, Cervantes started favourite. Within 30 seconds of the opening round, Pryor was sent spinning to the canvas but he jumped up and waved his right arm to signal he was ready to resume battle as he took the mandatory eight count. Just before the bell, he shook the Columbian with a powerful left hook to show he still was very much in the fight. Following some fast action in the second and third rounds, Pryor caught the veteran champion in the fourth round with a left-right combination that sent him down for the full count.

With Pryor now the new holder of the WBA title and his winning streak at 25-0, LaRosa turned down an offer of $500,000 for Pryor to move up a weight and meet Sugar Ray Leonard for the World Boxing Council welterweight championship. He wanted more money. When the offer was raised to $750,000, LaRosa rejected that too and asked for $1m. The WBC then pulled out and Pryor instead accepted a $1m offer to meet WBC light-welterweight champion Saoul Mamby, a tough New Yorker of Jamaican origin, in a unification bout scheduled for 7 February 1981. However, the bout was postponed indefinitely after Pryor's girlfriend, who later became his wife, shot him during a domestic dispute.

While Pryor was recovering, a new date was planned by promoter Harold Smith. However, Smith disappeared amid allegations that he was involved in a $21.3m fraud against Wells Fargo National Bank. The fight was cancelled and Smith, whose real name was Ross Fields, was sentenced to ten years in prison after being convicted of 29 counts of fraud and embezzlement.

Pryor was then offered $750,000 to fight the Panamanian Roberto Duran but turned it down because his new attorney advised him not to sign anything until he had worked out a new agreement with LaRosa. By the time they had agreed a new contract, Duran had moved on and Pryor's chance was gone. Meanwhile, Aaron successfully defended his light-welterweight title eight times, all inside the distance and six times inside seven rounds. He was often knocked down but always got up to win.

Boxing periodicals were already lauding Pryor as one of the modern greats, but he took the fame and the acclaim in his stride. 'It's nice to be regarded so highly by your peers, sure it is, and I appreciate it,' he told one writer. 'But I'm in this game for money to take care of my family. They're the most important people.'

Pryor got on with the job of defending his title, retaining it twice in 1980 and twice more in 1981. In the spring of 1982, he signed to fight Sugar Ray Leonard in the autumn for the undisputed world welterweight championship, the exact date and venue to be decided later. His purse would be $750,000, the same figure he had turned down the year before. Leonard had won the title by coming from behind to stop Thomas Hearns in the 14th round of a thriller in Las Vegas the previous September. He was anxious to prove himself the best in the division and what better way to show it than to take on Pryor.

'I figured Pryor would be an ideal opponent,' said Leonard. 'He's tough, rough and a strong puncher. I've met those kind before but a match with Aaron intrigues me. 'I reckon I should be able to handle him.' When Pryor was asked to comment on Sugar Ray's remarks, he replied, 'This is the biggest and most important fight of my career but I'll do my talking in the ring as that's where it counts.'

Before meeting Leonard, Pryor was committed to defending his light-welterweight title against Roger Stafford in Buffalo, New York on 14 May 1982. Stafford was essentially a club fighter around the Philadelphia area but he was an experienced pro, with a smooth style and good hand speed. But he was not expected to provide too many problems for the world champion. A few days before the bout, Pryor was driving to Buffalo from his home in Cincinnati to taunt Leonard and hype their upcoming fight. On the car radio, he heard the shattering news that Sugar Ray had suffered a detached retina in his left eye in a sparring session and the fight was off. 'I just pulled over to the side of the road and cried,' said Pryor. 'I was completely shattered.' Leonard would announce his retirement in November. The Stafford fight was also called off as it was part of the contract Pryor had signed.

On 4 July, Pryor held on to his belt with an impressive stoppage in six rounds against Japan's Akio Kameda, who would later unsuccessfully challenge Terry Marsh, the International Boxing Federation champion, in London. In 1989, Marsh was charged and acquitted of the attempted murder of his former manager, the promoter Frank Warren.

Pryor was at ringside in Miami on the night of 12 November when world lightweight champion Alexis Arguello knocked out Kevin Rooney, the Irish-American who would later become Mike Tyson's trainer, in two rounds with a single shot, a perfect right hook to the chin. The Rooney bout would be at light-welter as Arguello was experiencing difficulties in making the lightweight limit. Pryor knew all about Arguello, a Nicaraguan exile living in Florida.

One of the greats with three world titles already to his name, he was a master offensive boxer and tactician who could adapt his style to take advantage of his opponents' weaknesses. He could hit, too. *Ring* magazine rated Arguello at number 20 in their 100 Greatest Punchers Of All Time list. But Pryor felt confident that a victory over the man from the heart of Central America would enhance his own reputation.

Arguello climbed into the ring before a crowd of 28,000 as a 12/5 favourite and was attempting to become the first boxer to win world titles in four weight divisions. He was also the sentimental favourite as Americans had clearly taken to this polite, almost embarrassingly sincere boxer. He had attracted sympathy after suffering personal misfortune. Arguello's home was demolished in the devastating earthquake in Nicaragua in the early hours of 23 December 1972, when the capital city of Managua was almost completely wiped out. The death toll was over 6,000, with 20,000 injured and over 250,000 homeless, including Arguello's family.

Later, his new house and possessions totalling almost $500,000 in value were confiscated by the left-wing Sandinista regime. A younger brother was killed fighting with the Sandinista guerrillas. But Arguello had overcome these tumultuous events with barely a trace of bitterness. He was supporting his mother and several brothers and sisters in Miami, as well as his wife and four children.

Arguello and Pryor represented total opposites. Arguello was the craftsman, able to box and punch, jab, slip and counter. Pryor was the all-action fighter, described by one writer as 'a whirling dervish who throws punches from crazy angles, a latter-day Henry Armstrong, who was a world champion at three weights and almost a third'. Arguello had a record of 72 wins in 77 bouts, 64 by stoppages or countouts, and had not lost in four years. Pryor, at 27 the younger man by three years, was on a 31-fight winning streak since turning professional, 29 by interventions or knockouts. Pryor's purse was $1.6m against Arguello's $1.5m.

This was quite clearly a contest between good and bad. The Miami-based Arguello had the bulk of the crowd on his side and Pryor was booed as he entered the ring, yet Aaron let nothing deter him. He had a job to do and nothing would prevent him from doing it – but it was not going to be easy. At the weigh-in, Arguello's veteran and revered trainer Eddie Futch, who had coached a number of world champions, including heavyweights Joe Frazier and Ken Norton, had told reporters, 'No matter what style an opponent employs, and Pryor will be no different, Alexis can come up with an effective strategy to counter and win.'

The fight was billed by promoter Bob Arum as 'The Ring of Fire,' a nod to the Johnny Cash song, after rejecting the suggestion by one of his assistants that it should be called 'The 'Battle of the Champions', an unimaginative tag that had been used many times before. It got off to a sensational start with Pryor belting away so fiercely to the body that it looked as if Arguello might be overwhelmed. The Nicaraguan fought back, slamming home a fine right to the jaw, but Pryor just grinned and was pumping away with both gloves when the bell ended what had been an exciting first round. It seemed to set the pattern of what was to follow as the pendulum swung one way and then the other.

Pryor received several warnings from South African referee Stanley Christodoulou for dangerous use of the head. Pryor's second, Panama Lewis, was also cautioned for shouting non-stop from the corner, with Christodoulou warning him twice to keep quiet or else he would have to be removed. Arguello's punches seemed hard enough to floor middleweights but Pryor, in the finest condition of his career at 140lbs, soaked them all up and kept stabbing left jabs into the challenger's face.

It was looking bad for Arguello in the sixth round when he was badly cut over the left eye. The referee examined the cut but waved the boxers on.

It was clear that Arguello was bothered by the injury and dabbed it with his glove as Pryor got through with effective short hooks and uppercuts. The ninth was the best round of the fight so far as Arguello rocked the Ohioan back on his heels with a big right and then Pryor rallied to land a barrage of solid blows to the head. Arguello often looked unsteady in the 12th as Pryor ripped in powerful shots, but the challenger gave as good as he got.

It was still anybody's fight going into the 13th, though Pryor was officially ahead on the scorecards of the two judges and the referee, who had a vote this time. Arguello won this round quite clearly and had Pryor badly shaken towards the end of it with a cracking right uppercut, causing him to walk unsteadily to his corner. Revived during the interval, 'The Hawk' left his corner quickly and swooped to rock Arguello with a tremendous right to the chin. The Nicaraguan tottered back to the ropes as Pryor blazed away with both gloves, landing at least six more crushing blows before the referee pulled him away and led Arguello to his corner at 1:06 of round 14.

Arguello sagged to the canvas and received oxygen as he lay on his back. He was later admitted to hospital for a check-up but was not detained. 'I waited to see Arguello's reaction for a few more punches but there was no reaction,' said Christodoulou. Danish judge Ove Ovesen and the referee had it 127-124 in

Pryor's favour while the other judge, Ken Morita of Japan, had Arguello in front by 127-125.

Arguello was too drained, physically and emotionally, to meet the media but Pryor paid tribute to him as a great fighter. 'I always felt in control of the fight but I could never relax,' he said. 'Arguello was always in the fight and always dangerous with that devastating right hand. I felt he was getting more tired as the fight went on but it was not until I tagged him in the 14th that I knew he was hurt. I hope the boxing world will now recognise me and my ability as a great champion.'

Unfortunately, Pryor's night of glory was tainted. Home Box Office television cameras caught cornerman Artie Curley holding up a plastic water bottle in the interval between the 13th and 14th rounds, and Lewis yelling, 'Not that bottle, the black one I mixed.' Lewis said it only contained tap water, in line with rules allowing boxers to consume only water in the ring, but doubts remained. Although Lewis was never formally sanctioned, the incident damaged his reputation and it was confirmed later in a documentary that he would often break apart pills used to treat asthma and pour the medicine into the water to give greater lung capacity in the later rounds.

The 'black bottle incident' raged on, and Arguello's adviser Bill Miller filed a protest to the WBA alleging that Pryor had been given an illegal substance between the 13th and 14th rounds. Miller also said he was disturbed that Pryor had not undergone a urine test and wanted the fight declared a no-contest. Pryor said he was given only a brand of mineral water in addition to ordinary tap water. 'The water was to help settle a stomach upset,' he explained. 'I have come too far to risk wrecking everything. Nor did I sniff anything between rounds. As for not having the urine test, no inspectors from the commission had required one from me.'

Showtime television analyst Steve Farhood remembered in 2017, 'The black bottle incident wasn't really much of a controversy and I think the reason was that nobody wanted to overshadow the fight, which was so fantastic. It was only in subsequent months and years that it became a big mystery.'

Lewis, the central figure in the controversy, was involved in an even more serious incident in New York on 16 June 1983, when he was accused of removing padding from Luis Resto's gloves during his fight against the undefeated prospect Billy Collins Jr. Resto won a 10-round unanimous decision over a bloody Collins, which was later changed to no-contest. Collins suffered a torn muscle in his eye, causing permanently blurred vision and ending his boxing career. Lewis's action amounted to illegal assault. There were also allegations of a big betting coup. Lewis had his licence withdrawn and was sentenced to six years in jail, serving three. Resto got three years. In 1984, Collins crashed his car in Tennessee and subsequently committed suicide. Many believed the tragedy was linked to what happened in the Resto fight.

Almost a year after the Pryor-Arguello thriller, which was the defining fight of Aaron's career and would be named *Ring* magazine's Fight of the Decade, the fighters met again, this time at Caesars Palace, Las Vegas. On the evening of 9 September 1983, before a crowd of over 11,000 in the 12,600-capacity arena, the man from Cincinnati put his world light-welterweight title on the line for the eighth time. He was going for his 34th consecutive victory. Considered the best boxer in the world along with middleweight champion Marvin Hagler, Pryor was expected to leave the ring as the winner and still champion. But Arguello had other ideas.

Pryor, with new trainer and chief second Emanuel Steward in his corner, made a good start, raking his opponent with heavy lefts and rights as Arguello did his best to slip and counter, but it looked as if the champion's blows were the stronger. Although Arguello took a count in the first round from a right cross and in the fourth from a left hook, he was still fighting effectively in the early stages. Pryor looked clumsy at times and seemed to overreach himself and fall off balance after missing with long right hands.

Towards the middle rounds, Pryor started to step up the pace and was scoring on the inside with powerful left hooks and uppercuts. Whenever the Nicaraguan scored with heavy shots, Pryor would often grin as if to say, 'If that's the best you can do, now it's my turn to show you what I can do.'

After nine rounds, Pryor seemed to have a commanding lead and certainly looked the stronger. Yet Arguello was still in there with a real chance. He hit his opponent with blows that would have dropped many other boxers for the count but the fierce exchanges were definitely draining him. At 31, the older man by three years, Arguello looked shaky as he went out for the tenth round. Pryor was ready to open up. Going after his man, he landed a barrage of hurtful punches as Arguello sank to the canvas to be counted out by referee Richard Streele after 1:48 of the round.

Pryor was leading on all three judges' scorecards. Chuck Minker of Las Vegas had him ahead by 85-83, James Jen Kin of Los Angeles marked it 86-83 and Seattle's Jimmy Rondeau saw it by the widest margin, 87-82. 'Arguello shook me a couple of times but I was never in any trouble,' said Pryor. The loser congratulated Pryor and said, 'My heart was there, my conditioning was there but you were just too strong.'

Pryor announced his retirement but his farewell did not last long – six months to be exact. 'I never really retired, I just rested,' he said in March 1984. 'I gave up the belt because the WBA insisted I defend it every six months. I now want to pick my own fights.' The newly created International Boxing Federation immediately recognised Pryor as its world light-welterweight champion. But the fight Pryor really wanted was a proposed multi-million dollar contest with WBA lightweight champion Ray 'Boom Boom' Mancini, insisting he would have no trouble moving down to the 135lb division to take on the exciting Italian-American in an all-Ohio showdown.

With talks going on for a planned fight, Mancini was sensationally beaten in 14 rounds by 4/1 underdog Livingstone Bramble, from the US Virgin Islands, in New York in June. 'Aaron Pryor actually cried,' said promoter Bob Arum. 'I saw the tears.' Pryor had by now a deep and destructive relationship with crack cocaine and the IBF stripped him of its title over his refusal to defend it.

He took on journeymen and club fighters, and suffered his only defeat when Bobby Joe Young stopped him in seven rounds in August 1987. It was Pryor's first fight in two years and taken while he was out on $50,000 bail on drugs charges. In September 1989, Pryor entered a no-contest plea to a charge of possessing an illegal pipe used for smoking cocaine, which was found in his car after he was stopped by police in Cincinnati. For periods, he lived on the streets and later estimated that he spent $500,000 on drugs.

An opponent named Darryl Jones, who had lost all his 13 fights, lost to Pryor in three rounds in Wisconsin in May 1990. Before the fight, Pryor had surgery to remove a cataract and repair a detached retina. He only got his licence back after agreeing to sign a waiver releasing the state from liability for any damage he might suffer in the fight.

Pryor was denied a licence by the Californian and Nevada commissions following medical reports declaring him to be legally blind in his left eye. His last fight was in a hotel in Oklahoma shortly before Christmas 1990, when he defeated unheralded Roger Choate after convincing the officials he was 'sound'. But his glory days were long gone and he hung up his gloves with a 39-1 record, 35 of his victories by either knockout or stoppage. Sylvester Stallone, star of the *Rocky* movies and who promoted Pryor in the last days of his career, remembered, 'Aaron could no longer keep throwing punches at the old alarming rate.' He was not forgotten and was inducted into the International Boxing Hall of Fame in New York in 1996 and the World Boxing Hall of Fame in California in 2001.

Pryor finally kicked his cocaine addiction in 1993 and would remain drug free for the rest of his life. He maintained his interest in boxing by training amateurs, and two of his sons, Aaron Jr and Stephen, became professionals. He lectured about the evils of drugs and started attending services at the New Friendship Baptist Church in Cincinnati, where he later became a minister. 'I serve the Lord. I gave my life to Christ. I'm living now and I've been having a great time,' he declared in 2012. 'I've been married to the same girl for 20 years. Things are just going really right for me.'

Pryor died from heart disease on 9 October 2016, just 11 days before his 60th birthday. The boxing world went into mourning at his passing. 'In the 1980s, Pryor blazed across the boxing landscape like a firestorm,' said Graham Houston in *Boxing Monthly*. 'The man from Cincinnati, Ohio was one of the most exciting fighters not only of his era but of any era.'

There is still talk in boxing circles of the career that might have been had Pryor not taken the wrong path. There was so much to do but it was a career that was always on the verge of unravelling. In a strange way, the fact that Pryor never fought a Leonard or a Duran or a Mancini adds to his mystique.

'As for the bad old days, Pryor talked about them sometimes,' recalled Don Stradley in *Ring* magazine in March 2017. 'But when he told his stories, he never went for laughs or shock value. It was more like disbelief. He talked of how much he'd lost and he'd tell you that going to church was what saved him. Mostly, he talked about his great rival Alexis Arguello and their friendship. Some fighters ignored Pryor but Arguello had the guts to fight him. Pryor never forgot. That the two couldn't have gone into old age together is a shame. Arguello died by his own hand in 2009. Like Pryor, he had a cocaine addiction. It appears the two were more alike than anyone knew, which may account for the strong bond.'

Chapter 7

Title fight ends on sidewalk

IT was said in the Roaring 20s that Harry Greb had 299 enemies – the men who refereed his fights. He complained regularly that referees interfered with his job in the ring and that they represented a kind of law and order between the ropes, and Greb did not believe in law and order. He admonished them for their constant warnings over extra-curricular activities, such as using his elbows and thumbs, rubbing the laces of his open gloves in his opponent's eyes and often planting a knee in the groin. Harry called the referees 'meddlesome cops'.

But he lost only eight fights and for all his foul tactics and rough-and-ready style, Greb was beaten only once on a disqualification – although whether nor not he should have lost more on disqualifications has never been fully explained. Greb was defeated inside the distance twice, both times in the second round. The first was in his seventh bout when he was knocked out by Joe Chip in 1913. Joe, the younger brother of the reigning world middleweight champion George Chip and with a 14lbs weight advantage, landed a powerful right to the chin that put Greb down and out.

The second loss by the short route happened two years later against Perry 'Kid' Graves when Greb broke his left arm after connecting with a hook to Graves's head. While Greb managed to finish the round, he was unable to continue and conceded victory to his opponent. In later years, both Chip and Graves were able to boast that they once beat the great Harry Greb inside the distance.

Known as the 'Pittsburgh Windmill' and the 'Human Windmill', Greb was not a great puncher as he did not give himself enough time to place his blows or put precise power behind them. His lack of a knockout punch would be his ultimate weakness and though he was able to hurt and bust up many opponents due to the constant onslaught of punches he landed on them, he rarely put them down and out.

Greb swarmed all over his rivals from first bell to last and many of his opponents admitted they never knew what hit them. Among his 299 fights, 183 were of the no-decision variety as Greb fought mainly in the days when it was illegal to render verdicts in most American states, and unofficial results would be given by the newspapermen at ringside. Perhaps the most remarkable fact about Greb was that for many years, and at his best, he had sight in only one eye.

Greb came up against most of the great boxers of his day and though he was officially a middleweight and a world champion in that division in an era of great 160-pounders, he regularly moved up to the light-heavyweight and heavyweight classes with considerable success. He challenged the heavyweight champion Jack Dempsey many times without success, even organising a campaign among many prominent newspapermen in New York.

The lame excuse put forward by the 'Manassa Mauler' and his canny manager Jack 'Doc' Kearns was that Greb was too small, but privately Kearns felt that Harry could be a rough and dangerous opponent for his boxer.

Greb was the only man to beat master boxer and defensive technician Gene Tunney, twice conqueror of Jack Dempsey in two world heavyweight championship fights. He once gave Tunney such a battering that Gene had to spend a week in bed afterwards.

Greb hated training and for many of his fights he did little preparation, depending on his ability to see him through. Few of his handlers ever tamed him. James 'Red' Mason, the most famous of Harry's managers, went on record as saying that Greb loved the high life and was a man who could not really be fully brought under control. On the day of his fight with heavyweight Tom Gibbons in March 1922 at Madison Square Garden, the unpredictable Greb went missing, providing Mason with a large-sized headache. 'I waited and waited at the Garden, and it's now only a couple of hours to go before fight time,' said Mason. 'I can't find him anywhere.

'I started making the rounds of all his favourite hangouts but Harry is nowhere to be seen. We are supposed to be at the Garden by 8pm and there is nothing for me to do but wait in the dressing room. Finally, around 9.30pm, in walks Harry with not a care in the world, and the fight is due for 10pm. He starts undressing and I say to him, "This is a fine time to show up. Where were you?" He laughs and punches me playfully in the ribs. "What ya worrying about, Red?" he wants to know. "We still got plenty of time yet." What was the use of arguing with him. He looked okay and what's more, he goes out and beats Gibbons over 15 rounds – the same Gibbons who made Jack Dempsey look like a bum a year later.'

Edward Henry Greb was born to a German immigrant father and a mother of German descent on 6 June 1894 in the steel town of Pittsburgh, Pennsylvania, which had a sizeable German community. Pius and Annie Greb raised Harry in what would now be called a blue-collar household. He worked as an electrician's apprentice for several years in a local plant before joining some friends who persuaded him to come to the gym with them. Greb went along and was so enamoured by the young boxers working out that he became a regular customer. Soon, he would take part in local tournaments, once boxing in Cleveland, Ohio. After five contests, all wins, he decided to try his luck as a professional.

After signing up with 'Red' Mason, Harry made his debut in a six-rounder against Frank Kirkwood a week short of his 19th birthday at the Exposition Hall in Pittsburgh on 29 May 1913. It was officially a no-decision bout but at the finish the newspapermen gave Greb the verdict. It would be the beginning of one of the most illustrious careers in boxing history. Averaging 22 bouts a year, he never really had time to train hard and depended on a few rounds in the gym and a short run around the local park to keep fit. Greb also spent his purses as soon as he got them. Fast cars, beautiful women and buying drinks for his pals would be the norm. He was also gaining a reputation for dirty fighting, with boos regularly heard at his fights. 'Listen,' he told one newspaperman, 'fighting ain't no fancy business, and I ain't fancy myself.'

In 1915 Greb had 22 fights, with 20 no-decisions, unofficially winning most of them. In 1917 he made it 37 fights, including a no-decision bout over six rounds with the talented Mike Gibbons, the 'St Paul Phantom'. Gibbons never won a world title but is considered by historians as one of the best 'near champions' in ring history. A master of footwork who could wear down an opponent with clever manoeuvres and defensive skill, he got the better of several champions in no-decision contests. Greb was so frustrated by Gibbons's shifty style, he shouted to his manager in one round, 'Next time, match me with one guy at a time.'

Greb was now mixing in the big league and keeping busy. Wins in 1917 over his old rival George Chip and former world light-heavyweight champion Jack Dillon added to his reputation. He outsmarted the reigning light-heavyweight champion Battling Levinski over ten rounds in September but Levinski's title was protected by the no-decision rule. Greb would have had to knock out Levinski to claim the title, and he had to be content with the newspaper decision.

Harry got the chance of a world middleweight title fight against the reigning champion Mike O'Dowd in St Paul,

Eight-times married
Kid McCoy was one
of boxing's most
notorious conmen

16 August 1924. Kid
McCoy (Norman
Selby) having his
fingerprints taken
by a police officer at
the City Jail after
his arrest, charged
with the murder of
Mrs Teresa Moers
and the wounding of
three others

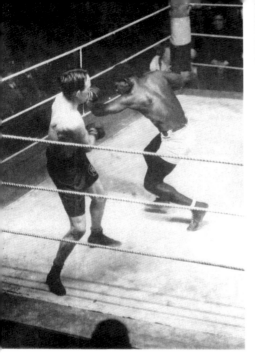

Mike McTigue, left and winner, backs off from an attack by Battling Siki in a title fight during the Irish Civil War

Battling Siki used to parade a fully-grown lioness on a lead down the boulevards of Paris

Chris Eubank, self-styled lord of the manor, enraged the establishment with his eccentric lifestyle

Steve Collins, his right eye cut, grazes Chris Eubank's jaw with a long left jab

Stanley Ketchel, the 'Michigan Assassin', left, squares off against world heavyweight champion and winner Jack Johnson

Muhammad Ali catches Sonny Liston with a left jab in their first encounter which ended when Liston retired after six rounds

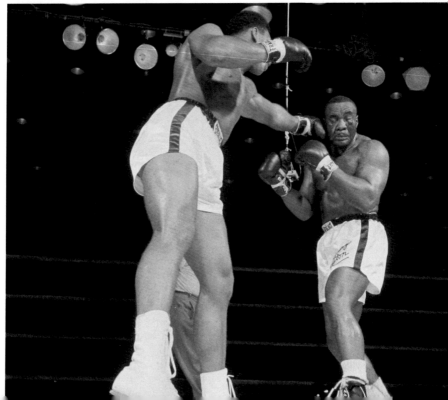

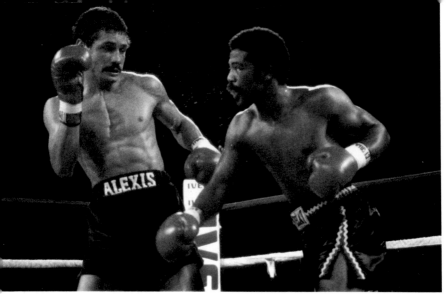

Aaron Pryor, here shaking Alexis Arguello with a right cross, was a victim of America's drug culture

Aaron Pryor is interviewed following his impressive win over Alexis Arguello after 14 thrilling rounds

Harry Greb, right, at the weigh-in for his return fight with Tiger Flowers, resulting in a second defeat for Greb

Harry Greb, left, and Mickey Walker in fighting pose before their classic world title fight

Roberto Duran, right, here on the attack against Sugar Ray Leonard, once knocked over a horse

Roberto Duran, right, awaits the next move from Sugar Ray Leonard in their third fight, won by Leonard.

Sugar Ray Robinson catches Rocky Graziano with a right to the head shortly before knocking him out in three rounds

Marvin Hagler, right, and Vito Antuofermo at the last bell in their drawn world title fight

Mike Tyson, one of the best of the modern champions

Joe Louis, right, gets under the guard of the roly poly Tony Galento at the start of their fight won by Louis in the fourth round

Beer-guzzling Tony Galento always threatened to 'moider da bum', even world champion Joe Louis

Minnesota in February 1918 in a no-decision match. The fight was extremely close and several newspapers could not agree who won. It was the clever O'Dowd and his sharp boxing against the aggressive, all-action style of Greb. Referee George Barton actually gave the fight to Greb, saying later that Harry's 'unique style of quickness and moving confused O'Dowd and the champion was unable to fathom his style'. Barton marked five rounds to Greb, two to O'Dowd with three even. The *New York Times* gave the fight to O'Dowd 'by a shade' but the *Pittsburgh Post*, undoubtedly showing a bit of favouritism towards the local boy, marked it for Greb. In the end, the general consensus of opinion was that O'Dowd won it narrowly. 'My chance will come again,' said Greb.

By now, Harry was in the navy and attached to the USS *Recruit* and later the USS *Sierra*, both berthed in New York. The *Sierra* used to transport new sailors from the US to Europe. The ship would drop them off at various European ports. While heading for France in November before sailing on to Britain, it was discovered that many American boxers were among the sailors and a boxing tournament was arranged for London. Greb was due to meet the European and French light-heavyweight champion Georges Carpentier, the 'Idol of France.'

On their way to the French port, the captain received news that the war was over. By the time Greb walked off the ship, Germany had signed the armistice. Soon the ship sailed for Britain, where they disembarked for London and the King's Tournament at the Royal Albert Hall. It would be an event between the navy and the army.

Greb had two fights and this time a verdict would be given, unlike in many US states that still adhered to the no-decision rule. The first match at middleweight, Greb's natural weight, was on 11 December, when he faced Corporal John Baker of South Africa and not Carpentier, as he had been expecting. Greb finished off the soldier in the opening round with a heavy right to the jaw that sent Baker down and very much out.

The following day was the final of the tournament and Greb found himself paired with a Britisher, Private George Ring – and it was trouble for Harry. His rough tactics did not go down very well with the crowd and Ring's supporters booed and made remarks like, 'Watch Greb's head, ref' and 'Throw Greb out, ref' as Harry butted, hit with the inside of the glove and used the occasional elbow in close. Hell, this was dear old England not America, where anything goes! Finally, after repeated fouls, the referee stepped between the two boxers in the fifth round and told Greb to go to his corner. He was being disqualified. Harry protested, as did his manager 'Red' Mason, but to no avail. The verdict stood and the Greb party left the ring to a crescendo of boos and catcalls.

Back in the US soon after Christmas, which the devil-may-care Greb celebrated in several nightspots surrounded by beautiful women until the early hours, he continued his rampaging form against the best fighters Mason and promoters could find in 1919. They were all the same as far as Harry was concerned, middleweights, light-heavyweights and heavyweights. With the 'Pittsburgh Windmill', size definitely did not matter. That year alone he had an amazing 45 bouts, more than many modern boxers would have in an entire career and a figure considered by boxing historians to be a record in a 12-month period.

Greb won newspaper decisions over the likes of Billy Miske, who would tackle Jack Dempsey for the heavyweight title the following year, and Bill Brennan, who would take Dempsey 12 rounds, again for the title, in 1920. Greb got the better of old rival Battling Levinski, the former world light-heavyweight champion, as well as future 175lb king Mike McTigue. A notable newspaper-decision win was over Willie Meehan, who had twice beaten and shared two draws with Dempsey in 1917.

Keeping up his busy career, Greb had 25 fights in 1920 and while he repeatedly challenged Dempsey for a heavyweight title shot, all he managed to get that year were six exhibitions with the 'Manassa Mauler'. One of them, in July at Dempsey's camp in New York, was particularly significant and was refereed by the Hollywood movie star Douglas Fairbanks. 'A big surprise was sprung on those present by the way Greb tore into the heavyweight champion,' reported the *Pittsburgh Post*. 'In the middle of the second round, time had to be called when Greb landed a hard right on Dempsey's left eye and split it open. Dempsey did not want to lose face, so he agreed to continue boxing but after a few more exchanges, he told his corner he would call it off for the day.'

Dempsey had been apprehensive about sparring with Greb in the first place and the general feeling at the time was that Harry would have given Jack a pretty uncomfortable night in a real fight. All Dempsey's canny manager Jack 'Doc' Kearns would say was, 'You'll get your shot, don't worry,' but it never happened, much to Greb's frustration and regret. In 1920, too, Greb won and lost to clever Tom Gibbons, with newspaper verdicts each time. Three years later, the same Gibbons would take Dempsey the full 15 rounds in a title fight.

But trouble loomed for Greb when he fought Kid Norfolk at Forbes Field, Pittsburgh over ten rounds on 29 August 1921. Norfolk was born William Ward but took his ring name from where he first saw the light of day, Norfolk Street in Virginia. He fought most of the leading light-heavyweights of his day, including a decisive points win over the former champion Battling Siki in the Senegal boxer's US debut. But like so many fine black fighters then, he was denied a title fight. Against Greb, Norfolk was heavier by 17lbs and had the better of the fight in four of the first five rounds, dropping the Pittsburger in the third. It was a rarity for Greb to be on the boards but Harry won all the last five rounds and was given the newspaper verdict when two of the three papers, plus the Associated Press, awarded him the win.

A few days after Greb died, the *New York Times* of 27 October 1927 carried a report by Harry's personal physician

Dr Carl S McGivern that Greb received a serious injury in the Norfolk fight when he was poked in the right eye by the thumb of Norfolk's left glove. It must be remembered that in those days, gloves were very light and allowed free movements with the thumbs. The gloves contained very little padding and were very flexible. Back then, too, boxing was not that far removed from bare-knuckle fighting and there were deaths in the ring periodically. Dr McGivern said the punch from Norfolk caused a retinal detachment that at first resulted in side vision only and gradually worsened until Greb was totally blind in the eye.

Incredibly, Greb was able to keep the injury a secret from all but his family and closest friends, fooling physicians during pre-fight physicals by memorising the order of the letters on the eye chart. His gradual loss of sight in the right eye led him to always go to bed with the light on. 'Greb was sensitive about the condition and did not want other boxers to know about it,' said his biographer Bill Paxton. 'If anyone who was boxing him knew he was blind in the right eye, they would use this to their advantage and throw more punches from that side as Greb wouldn't know they were coming. If the boxing commission knew he was blind in one eye, they would hardly have allowed him in the ring in the first place.' Fortunately, Greb's unconventional style of ring warfare, moving in and out and tossing punches from every conceivable angle, allowed him to continue boxing with his one good eye.

By now, boxing was legal in New York, although many other states continued to render no-decision verdicts. On 23 May 1922, Greb climbed into the ring at Madison Square Garden in Manhattan to face Gene Tunney in what would be the first of five bruising encounters. It would also be the defining fight of Greb's career. Tunney's American light-heavyweight title would be at stake and the match was set for 15 rounds. The winner hoped victory would lead to a world title fight with the reigning champion Georges Carpentier.

Tunney was a master boxer with a sharp left jab, excellent defence and good footwork. A native New Yorker and ex-marine, he would in his lifetime mix with literary giants such as George Bernard Shaw and Thornton Wilder, and could recite long passages from Shakespeare plays. He was an intelligent man outside the ring and inside it. Tunney was unbeaten in 49 fights over an eight-year period, in contrast to Greb, who had almost that many bouts in a single year, 1920. Tunney was the underdog. The odds were 3/1 on Greb to win on his attacking, all-action style, even though Tunney outweighed his man by 12lbs and was five inches taller, a considerable advantage to a skilful boxer such as Tunney. A crowd of 13,000 packed out the famous arena to watch the fight.

As always, Greb, on entering the ring, was a picture of confidence. With his dark hair slicked down and parted in the middle, and his face heavily powdered, he had the appearance of a 'street corner Don Juan', in the words of one writer. In contrast, Tunney was clean-cut and serious, square-jawed and handsome, with his light-brown hair in a modified crew-cut.

From the opening bell, it soon became evident that whatever confidence Tunney had was unfounded. Tunney never expected what was to befall him. Neither did the famous sportswriters at ringside, and they included Damon Runyon of the *New York Journal American*, Grantland Rice of the *New York Herald Tribune* and Westbrook Pegler of the *Chicago Tribune*. Greb was on the attack early on, bloodying the New Yorker's nose with a heavy right to the face. The punch was said to have broken Tunney's nose in two places. Tunney also finished the round with a deep cut over his left eye. This was going to be a war. In his report, which appeared the following day, Grantland Rice said, 'Tunney fell into a hornet's nest last night and came near to being stung to death.'

The second round followed the same pattern – Greb constantly on the attack and Tunney busily defending himself as best he could, using his left jab and moving all the time. There was just no way to keep off this aggressive battler as Greb was punching over and under Gene's defence, and using the laces of his gloves to rub into Tunney's face. Neither was Harry sparing with head butts, with no warning from referee Kid McPartland, an experienced official who had refereed many championship bouts. It seemed that McPartland was prepared for an 'anything goes' kind of fight and just let them get on with it, particularly with a dirty fighter like Greb involved. In complete contrast, Tunney was a clean boxer who abhorred illegal infringements and was always prepared to win fairly.

So it went, with Greb's non-stop style picking up the points round after round. 'All of Tunney's attempts to reach Greb's jaw were futile,' wrote Nat Fleischer, who had started *Ring* magazine a year earlier. 'The challenger had always flitted out of range by the time Tunney got a jab or hook started to the face. In the eighth, Greb was a marvel of speed.' Through the later rounds, it was the same story and it was to Tunney's credit that he stayed on his feet until the final bell.

Cut and bruised, Tunney had taken a heavy pounding. Not only was Greb unmarked but his plastered down hair had not been disturbed and he had not lost a round. Minutes before the official announcement was made, Tunney went over to the Pittsburger's corner, shook his hand and said, 'Congratulations Harry. You're the winner.' The new American light-heavyweight champion replied, 'Thanks Gene.' *Ring* magazine named it Fight of the Year for 1922. Tunney would go on to win the world heavyweight championship inside four years.

Grantland Rice said that it was 'perhaps the bloodiest fight I have covered'. The *New York Herald Tribune* columnist recalled, 'A great fighter, or brawler, Greb handled Tunney like a butcher hammering a Swiss steak. How the Greenwich Village Irishman with the crew haircut survived 15 rounds I'll never know, except that Tunney always enjoyed more and better physical conditioning than anybody he ever fought. By the third round, Tunney was literally wading in his own blood. I saw Gene a few days later. His face looked as though he'd taken the wrong end of a razor fight. To me, that fight was proof that Tunney meant to stick with prize fighting.'

Looking back in later years on the only fight he ever lost in an 83-bout career, Tunney remembered, 'Greb was never in one spot for more than a second. All my punches were aimed and timed properly but they all ended up hitting empty air. He'd jump in and out, slamming me with a left and whirling me around with his right or the other way round. My arms were plastered with leather, and though I jabbed, hooked and crossed, it was like fighting an octopus.'

Even though Greb was now a married man, this did not stop him visiting different speakeasies with friends to dance and drink until the early hours. Harry loved dancing outside the ring as much as he did inside it. Now that he was American light-heavyweight champion, winning his first title, there was every reason to celebrate.

The morning after the fight, Tunney and his manager, Frank 'Doc' Bagley, went to the offices of the New York State Athletic Commission to file a challenge to Greb for a return fight, accompanied by a $2,500 cheque that Gene had just received from his bank. There, commission chairman Frank Muldoon, looking at Tunney's stitched-up eyes, mouth and nose, said, 'Son, why don't you forget about Greb. He's not a normal fighter. There's no point in fighting him again.' But Tunney insisted, telling a very dubious Muldoon that he was convinced he would beat Greb this time. Years later, Gene would recall, 'I discovered through the early part of the fight that I could lick him next time. As each round went by, battered from pillar to post as I was, the discovery that Greb could be beaten became a positive certainty in my mind.'

They met in a return bout on 23 February 1923, again at Madison Square Garden. Tunney was a slight favourite in the days leading up to the fight, but several hours before the two men climbed into the ring a heavy influx of Greb money made

Harry an 8/5 favourite. As expected, at the opening bell Greb charged from his corner intent on destruction but was met by a series of hard left jabs followed by sharp body blows that prompted him to clinch for the first of what would be many times. Seated at ringside, Benny Leonard, the world lightweight champion, who had helped train Tunney for the fight, smiled. Gene was doing what he said he would do – going for the body.

Determined to let Greb know early on that he was prepared to respond in kind to the middleweight's roughhouse tactics, Tunney grabbed his man during a close-quarter exchange in the second round, which was marked by some head-butting by Greb. But Harry was not about to change his ways, nor be intimidated by anybody. Still, because of his effective body attacks, Tunney was gradually moving ahead.

'After doing well for the first six rounds, I suddenly became physically exhausted,' Tunney would remember years later. 'Greb relentlessly battered me about the ring from the sixth to the 11th round. They told me in my corner that I was losing, that if I wanted to win I would have to recapture the remaining rounds or knock him out. In sheer desperation, I came out at the start of the 12th and luckily hit Greb with a long right to the cheekbone that had everything I had in it. It knocked him to the ropes and he slowed up considerably. Fight, fight, hit, hit, I kept repeating to myself, and I did.'

Greb reverted to his rough and tough aggressive style in the final three rounds, with several low blows and elbows thrown in for good measure. But Gene stuck to his sharp boxing and solid body punching. His corner told him before going out for the 15th round that he had the fight under control and was a certain winner and new champion. Tunney himself wasn't sure. There were still three vital minutes to go, when anything could happen. Gene did take the last round on his better ring generalship, as tired as he was.

The arrangement was that if the two judges, Charles Miles and Charles Meegan, disagreed, the verdict of the referee, Patsy

Haley, would decide the outcome. As it happened, Miles had Greb the winner while Meegan voted for Tunney. Haley also went for Tunney, a result that gave Gene the split decision – and his old title, the American light-heavyweight championship.

The verdict was met with a chorus of boos and catcalls, with the majority of the crowd feeling that Greb's overall work entitled him to the decision. Asked the next day why he voted for Tunney, referee Haley said that Greb's foul tactics, including holding and butting, lost him the fight, despite the Pittsburgher's apparent winning margin on points. Most sportswriters at ringside thought Greb had won, or at least should have been given a draw. Grantland Rice of the *New York Herald Tribune* said the result 'was probably the most outrageous ever rendered in the state'. Harry Newman of the *Chicago Tribune* wrote, 'Most of the fans seemed to be of the opinion that a draw would have been more equitable.' The *United News* reporter Westbrook Pegler said, 'Many on hand seemed to think that Greb was entitled to no worse than a draw.'

In a snap poll of other writers, five said it should have been a draw, four gave the decision to Greb and four felt Tunney won. William Muldoon, chairman of the New York State Athletic Commission, said, 'The decision in Tunney's favour was unjustifiable. I thought Greb should have received the decision after his determined fight.'

Greb reckoned there would be a third fight with Tunney as the score was now one win each. Fight number three would decide who was the better man once and for all. Three weeks after the second fight, however, Greb's wife Mildred died after a prolonged battle with tubercolosis. Despite Harry's reputation as a wild character, a hellraiser who partied until the early hours and was constantly surrounded by beautiful women, he was devoted to Mildred, a former chorus girl, and spent much of his time at their Pittsburgh home. When she was ill, he took her to a sanatorium and rearranged his fight schedule. But shortly after contracting pneumonia, she passed away on 18 March 1923, leaving Greb to look after their three-year-old daughter, Dorothy. Fortunately, his sister Ida and her husband would help raise her, allowing Harry to continue his busy ring career.

As well as a third fight with Tunney, Greb had been casting his sights on the world middleweight title for some time now and issued several challenges to the reigning champion, Johnny Wilson, a southpaw. A New Yorker of Italian extraction, Wilson was alleged to have associations with the underworld who 'arranged' many of his fights. He had won the title in May 1920 but his connections steadfastly ignored calls from Greb's people for a title fight.

Finally, Greb's manager had a bright idea. He would make sure Harry was seen in nightspots and speakeasies having a good time. Waiters would bring him glasses of coloured water all night and Greb would act the drunk as he rolled home in the early rounds. Wilson and his manager Marty Killelea fell for the trick and asked promoter Tex Rickard to put on a Greb-Wilson fight. 'This will be an easy one,' Killelea told Wilson. Rickard, who never missed an opportunity of promoting a big fight in New York, especially an attractive one as this, signed the combatants to clash at the Polo Grounds on 31 August 1923.

On the day of the fight, there were persistent rumours that the match was fixed for Wilson to lose, and that he could pick up a bigger purse than if he won. Frank Marlowe, one of the men on Wilson's team, who had part of the champion's contract, allegedly had connections with underworld figures all the way up to public enemy number one, 'Scarface' Al Capone. The rumours reached the offices of the New York State Athletic Commission and officials warned both boxers that close scrutiny would be maintained before, during and after the match. There would be no room for any skulduggery.

In any event, even if Wilson were to lose his title, it would hardly be deliberate. It would be because Greb was simply the better man. Wilson had been regarded as something of a 'cheese champion', a derogatory term that implies a boxer was not worthy of his title, which in Wilson's case was true as long as Greb was around. The rumours that the fight was fixed and that Greb would take it easy had reached Harry's ears. He strongly denied such gossip. 'First I've heard of them,' he said.

Greb started fast in his usual manner, both hands firing as Wilson went on the retreat. Harry wanted to make a good impression from the outset. This was his big chance and he wasn't going to mess it up. Nevertheless, Wilson's better boxing and ring technique won him the first round. Referee Jack O'Sullivan warned Greb several times about butting and punching low. It looked like being a typical Greb fight, or rather a Greb war – and that's what it was. In the fifth round, Harry was probing the thumb of his left glove into Wilson's eye socket. 'All right Greb, what do you think you're doing?' barked O'Sullivan. Greb replied, 'Gouging Johnny in the eye, ref. Can't you see?'

At no time did Wilson look like hanging on to his title. There were calls from Wilson's supporters for their man to 'box, box, box' but the challenger would not be denied. How could you hold off the 'Windmill?' This was Greb's golden opportunity to win the middleweight championship of the world and he was not going to let it slip away.

After 15 hard rounds, Greb was proclaimed the winner and new champion by announcer Joe Humphries, a familiar figure at big fights and known for his booming voice and commanding presence in the centre of the ring. Greb, as promised, had brought the title back to Pennsylvania, which had been home to two other 160lb champions, Frank Klaus and George Chip.

This is how the *New York Times* saw the fight, 'Greb won every round except the first and last. He completely baffled Wilson with a swirling attack which did not end until the bout finished. When the final bell ended the hostilities, Wilson was a sorry sight. The bridge of his nose was cut from a blow in the second round, his mouth was bleeding, his lips were puffed and raw, he had a slight growth under his right eye and his left was also closed.'

The *Chicago Tribune* said, 'There is no doubt whatsoever that Harry Greb is a worthy middleweight champion. Wilson, too, was probably the most unpopular fighter that ever won the title. Greb simply was fighting rings around him.'

Greb told reporters in a packed dressing room, 'I felt all along that my speed would be too much for Wilson. I think I showed everyone out there that I am Wilson's master. Now, any middleweight in the world can have a crack at the title. I don't intend to remain idle. If Wilson wants a return bout and a promoter will arrange the match, I am agreeable. I am sorry that there were reports that I had agreed to any arrangements before the fight, but they were proven wrong. My record anyway speaks for itself.'

Fifty years later, Wilson, then 80, came up with a completely different version of the fight, or at least the way he saw and remembered it. Interviewed by Peter Heller for his book *In This Corner*, Wilson said, 'For about three rounds, I really hurt Greb in the stomach. Around the third, I think I started to tire until about the tenth. I came on around the 11th, 12th, 13th, 14th and 15th and started plastering him around the ring. The referee called it a draw. The commission had put two stooges in there as judges, Frankie Madden, who was a lightweight in the old days, and Bat Masterson, a former gunslinger from Dodge City. Then they changed the judges. That title should never have been lost. If they had two neutral judges in there, I probably would have saved my title. They might have given me the decision.'

Greb would give Wilson a return bout five months later, this time at Madison Square Garden. It was another rough brawl, with both fighters repeatedly warned for illegal tactics. Harry stayed on the outside mainly while shaking up the challenger with smashing uppercuts to head and body. Wilson put up a better, smarter fight than last time, using his superior skill in several rounds to sidestep many of Greb's strong attacks. In the last two rounds, however, Harry came on strong and dominated the sessions to wrap up the decision.

'The fight lacked any spectacular skills,' said Regis Welsh in the *Pittsburgh Post*. 'The only real fireworks came in the ninth and 11th rounds, which Greb took by such a wide margin that it looked like a bad match. Harry had too much nerve, too much heart and too much ability for Wilson to come within reaching distance of him. The pasting that the contender took was just as complete as any ever administered to a novice mixing with the titleholder.'

Now for the rubber match with Tunney. Greb wanted it, Tunney wanted it and the public wanted it. Promoter Rickard wasted no time in setting it up. The venue would again be Madison Square Garden and the date set was 10 December 1923, with Tunney's American light-heavyweight title on the line over 15 rounds. The judges were different this time, as was the referee, Lou Magnolia being in charge. Greb decided to do a lot of hard training for a change by running in Central Park and doing some sparring, rope skipping and bag punching in a local gym. He wanted to be fully fit and ready for his previous conqueror. Just seven days earlier, Greb had successfully defended his middleweight title in his hometown of Pittsburgh by easily beating Bryan Downey over 10 rounds. Two championship fights inside a week. Only Harry Greb could do it.

It started fast, Greb going on the attack in his customary style, but Tunney knew he would have to keep his man at a safe distance so as to get his rhythmic boxing going, snappy left jabs, solid rights to head and body, uppercuts in close. Greb's speed was proving a problem and his all-action style, not forgetting his usual butting and hitting on the break, meant that this was no picnic for Tunney. Harry was constantly going forward, smothering the New Yorker's more scientific style, notably in the middle rounds. In the closing session, Greb had one of his best rounds when he drove his opponent back across the ring, but it was all a little late. The bell clanged and it was all over. Tunney was the winner on points and still American light-heavyweight champion.

Most of the newspapermen thought it was a fair decision and agreed that Tunney had won nine rounds, with four going to Greb and two even. Jack Lawrence of the *New York Herald Tribune*, who had pushed Jack Dempsey back into the ring three months earlier after he had been pushed out of it by big Luis Firpo, gave Greb only three rounds. One of the reporters who thought Harry won was Regis M Walsh of the *Pittsburgh Post*, perhaps understandably as he was a close friend of Greb. 'Tunney, his eye cut, his mouth and nose bleeding, windblown and tired, climbed out of the ring amidst loud hooting while Greb, who won praise for his earnest and ever-aggressive fighting, stood silently for a few seconds after greeting Tunney and listened to the jeering which boomed against the rafters as the prejudice of the local judges and referee became an established fact, instead of a myth or a dream or even a mistake.'

After three hard battles between the two boxers, with not that much between them a fourth fight was called for. Because there were no knockdowns in any of the fights, people were still not convinced which fighter was the better at light-heavyweight. Tunney, on his way to the heavyweight championship of the world, needed a more decisive victory over Greb to settle any unanswered questions. So fight number four was scheduled nine months later. This time, the match would be at the Olympic Arena in Cleveland, Ohio. Unlike the previous three fights, this would be a no-decision bout under the rules in operation in Ohio at the time. The verdict would not be in the hands of two judges and a referee but would be decided by the newspapermen around the ringside. Whichever boxer received the majority of their opinions in the newspapers the next day would be declared the winner. The date: 17 September 1924.

With the long passage of time, some sources had Tunney outweighing Greb by as much as 17lb while others had Gene with a nine-pound advantage. Either way, Tunney was much heavier and was able to use the extra poundage in the clinches by bearing down on the smaller man. Once again, the referee had the most trouble. This time, the third man was Matt Hinkel, who was busy pulling the fighters apart, with Greb repeatedly drawing Tunney in close as Gene tried to get his skilful boxing and cleaner punching going. As the rounds went by, Greb was punching away relentlessly with both gloves as Tunney moved around the ring, jabbing, hooking and uppercutting. At the last bell, some newspapers made Greb the winner but the majority felt a draw was the fairer result. Referee Hinkel said he would have ruled it a draw, too.

With each of the four bouts providing excitement for the fans, there was a demand in the newspapers for a fifth match. The public wanted it. Greb wanted it. Tunney wanted it. The final fight between these two great protagonists was set for 27 March 1925 and the selected venue was the St Paul Auditorium in Minnesota. As in the last fight, it would be a no-decision decider.

A few weeks before the fight, Greb was driving in Pittsburgh with two glamorous women in his car when he was held up at gunpoint by five men after stopping outside a local park. Greb jumped out of the car, knocked the gun out of one of the robbers' hands and sent him spinning to the pavement with a left hook, bloodying his face. At this juncture, another of the robbers came forward but Harry got there first and sent him down with a right hand, again a bloody mess. With that, the other three ran away.

Tunney was by this time just a year away from winning the heavyweight championship of the world from Jack Dempsey in a stunning upset. Greb stepped on the scales at 167lbs while Tunney was 181lbs, 14lbs heavier – and this time it was official. The odds were at even money and the 8,000 crowd expected another thriller. Alas, the fifth bout did not match up to their previous encounters. Greb started in his customary fast fashion, rushing Tunney to the ropes but generally Harry seemed slower as the rounds passed while his opponent appeared revitalised. Greb's manager 'Red' Mason told his man in the seventh round he was losing his grip on the fight. The final bell rang as the two boxers were in a clinch.

The newspapers next day agreed that Tunney won in what was 'an uneventful fight'. The *Chicago Tribune* summed it up with the headline: 'Tunney Shades Greb in Sleepy Bout at St Paul'. Harry now finally agreed that Tunney was his master. He went into Tunney's dressing room and told the victor, 'Gene, you're ready for anyone now, including Dempsey, and you'll lick him. I know. You can't miss, kid, and when you're the big champ, remember it was Harry Greb who told you so.'

One year and a day later, Tunney would go into the ring in Philadelphia to face Dempsey, and win. Interviewed a few weeks before the fight by Ed Van Every, sports editor of the *New York Evening World,* Greb said, 'I told Dempsey there was no way he could beat Tunney and I'm going to place my first bet on Gene. Dempsey is favourite but I have a chance to risk $1,000 against $2,500 on Gene's chances and I will have plenty more riding on Tunney before I'm through. I've sparred with Dempsey and fought Tunney five times. You never know how good Tunney is until you box him.'

Tunney would write in his autobiography *A Man Must Fight,* 'Few human beings have fought each other more savagely or more often than Harry Greb and I. The first of our five fights is for me an enduring memory, a memory still terrifying. All five of our fights were of that order of savagery.' In another interview, Tunney talked of Greb in this way, 'The moment we signed for any of our fights, he was my enemy and he detested me. But after each fight it was a different matter and it remained that way until we were matched again. If ever an athlete deserved a monument to his greatness, to his endurance, to his sportsmanship, it was Harry Greb. Anything he did to you – and he did everything he could to dismember you – you could do back to him and he wouldn't complain.'

With three successful defences of his world middleweight title behind him in May 1925, Greb had been reading of challenges being thrown out by Mickey Walker, the world welterweight champion who was anxious to capture a second world title. New York newspapers took up the chant. At first, Harry ignored them but at the same time he was mindful that he would have to put his title on the line against somebody soon – and Walker was now the number one contender. Eventually the match was signed between the two champions and their respective managers for the Polo Grounds, New York. The date: 2 July 1925. It promised to be a good fight between two of the world's best fighting men. The big question was: Could Mickey concede weight to the middleweight king? Many experts felt he could.

Mickey was one of the greats. Named 29th in the current *Boxing News* list of its 100 greatest boxers, the trade paper noted, 'Walker would march into his rivals before unloading bombs with his squat, muscled pistons. He mastered the art of bobbing and weaving away from his opponent's punches, which was vitally important for a fighter with such a come-forward style.' In his eighth fight, in 1919, Walker was knocked out by a fast right to the jaw in the first round by the more experienced KO Phil Delmont. 'It was the best lesson I ever had,' Mickey would recall. 'Never take your eyes off an opponent, whether he was experienced or a novice.'

Similar to his fighting style, Walker also went through managers like a knife through butter. The most famous one would be Jack 'Doc' Kearns, best known for guiding Jack Dempsey to the heavyweight championship of the world. Few could handle Mickey, who was most definitely his own man. The ladies in his life found that, too. He was married seven times to four different women and cavorted with movie stars, high society and mobsters. Kearns would insist on Walker training hard, despite his wild lifestyle, and Mickey would agree, albeit reluctantly. Not that Kearns was averse to indulging in the lavish lifestyle created by his boxer. The 'Doc', too, was something of a playboy.

Born in Elizabeth, New Jersey on 13 July 1901 of Irish extraction, Edward Patrick Walker was the champion scrapper in Keighry Head, the tough Irish section of the town. Popular because of his good nature and cheery smile, he loved nothing better than a good fight and when he became a professional boxer at the age of 18, Walker quickly established a reputation as one to watch. Compact and heavily muscled, he soon became known as the 'Toy Bulldog', a nickname that stuck with him throughout his 16-year career. Walker packed power into his 5ft 7ins frame. Outside the ring, he lived life to the fullest, spending money as soon as he got it. He would run through millions, like sand through a sieve, living the life of a playboy, but his off-hours carousing did little to affect his prowess in the ring.

Between 1919 and 1921 Walker had nearly 50 fights, mainly in the New Jersey area. In November 1922 at Madison Square Garden, he battered an ageing Jack Britton over 15 rounds to win the world welterweight title and would defend it successfully four times. As 1924 became 1925, Walker and Kearns reckoned that they were ready for Greb and his middleweight title. Negotiations went ahead for the fight , to be held on 19 June 1925 at the Polo Grounds, home of the New York Giants and the New York Yankees baseball teams.

For the Walker fight, Greb trained at his Atlantic City camp for ten days, mainly doing roadwork, before leaving for New York and finishing off his preparations at Philadelphia Jack O'Brien's gym, where his workouts consisted of mainly handball and shadow boxing. Walker worked out at Johnny Collin's camp at Summit, New Jersey, where he did roadwork and went through his paces with four different sparring partners. The fight was postponed to 2 July, when Walker had to have treatment for an ingrown toenail.

As expected, both had expressed supreme confidence in their chances. Greb started as an 8/5 favourite and as people saw how fit he was, the odds on Harry increased to 2/1. Greb wanted to bet on himself so he did something the night before to change the odds.

Stanley Weston wrote in *Boxing and Wrestling* magazine some 30 years later, 'A group of well-known gamblers were shooting the breeze in front of Lindy's restaurant. It was about 2 o'clock in the morning. Suddenly, a yellow cab rolled up to the kerb and out fell Harry Greb in a seemingly drunken stupor. One of the gamblers, Arnold Rothstein, who had bet a bundle on Greb, looked down at the guy who was going to carry his marbles and broke into a cold sweat. Two heavily painted showgirls hopped out of the cab and helped Greb back inside. Then the cab shot away. The gamblers looked at each other and then, as if a tornado had struck, they disappeared in different directions, heading for the nearest telephones. They called all over the country and hedged their bets off Greb and on to the well-conditioned Walker.'

The public fell for the ruse and the odds soon swung in Walker's favour. It was said that Greb bet thousands of dollars on himself to win as he reckoned he was in the finest condition of his life. He looked it, too, as he climbed into the ring after Walker had entered it. Greb weighed 159lbs and Walker 152lbs. With a crowd of over 65,000 in the ballpark, the receipts would reach $339,040, bringing wide smiles to the face of promoter Humbert Jack Fugazy, a one-time barge fighter from New York and now a serious rival to regular promoter Tex Rickard and the powerful Madison Square Garden organisation.

As Walker waited for the bell, he was remembering the words of Gene Tunney when interviewed by Henry L Farrell, sports editor of United Press. 'There was only one way to beat Greb, and that was to take the steam out of his punches with body blows,' said Gene. 'If you don't, he'll throw so many thumbs, wrists, elbows, shoulders and fists at you that you'll never get started. He's too quick to get caught with a smack in the jaw.'

As James A Fair recalled in his biography of Greb, 'Clang went the bell for two of the greatest champions who ever shuffled shoes in resin dust. For five rounds Greb, old, slow and sick, took one of the most frightful beatings any man has ever had to take. He was fighting back but his attempts were feeble, and Walker was strong and contemptuous. You winced as you contemplated what Walker would do to him in the next round.

'The bell rang for the sixth round and what you saw you couldn't believe. Comparatively fresh, Greb jumped out of his corner, moved into Walker and tied him up. Walker stepped back, then came in with a two-handed barrage, aimed at Greb's middle. It didn't land. He tried again and missed. Then Greb ran in on him, spun him and stepped back and hit him while he spun. You were seeing a miracle. The "Pittsburgh Windmill" was sweeping now, sweeping everything before it.'

By the 11th round, Greb had the fight won and it was only a matter of time before he would be declared 'winner and still middleweight champion of the world'. Harry was taking the rounds by wide margins on his constant punching to head and body, as well as some fine jabbing. While Walker was always in there with a real chance with his sharp hooking and uppercutting, it was Greb who was landing the harder punches.

Walker remembered in his retirement years, 'In the 14th round, I saw his right hand coming. I can see it now. It looked as big as a balloon shooting toward me. I raised my left shoulder to protect my chin, confident I could block the blow. But somehow it slipped past and landed high on my jaw. I was knocked ragtime, not off my feet but I was silly. You know, like a man walking in a dream. It nearly tore off my roof.'

At the final bell, both boxers threw their arms around each other. Greb knew he had won. Walker knew he had lost. It was a unanimous decision, with most of the newspapers giving Walker only a handful or rounds. Regis M Walsh of the *Pittsburgh Post* had it 12-3 for Greb. Damon Runyon of the *New York Journal* said, 'Greb remains the wonder of the pugilistic age. But Walker had to have plenty of stamina and courage to survive that pounding in the 14th round. Walker gave a demonstration of fighting heart at that moment such as is rarely seen in the ring.'

The fight was not over yet – at least not the unofficial one. A few hours later, Greb went into Billy Lahiff's tavern on West 48th Street for 'a few quiet drinks', in his own words, when who should he see sitting at a table but Walker and his manager Jack 'Doc' Kearns, accompanied by several ladies. The story goes that they drank and danced until the early hours before relations seemingly turned sour.

'After stumbling out into the morning air,' recalled Walker later, 'all of a sudden Harry grabs me by the back of the neck and says, "Just to show you, Walker, I can lick you anytime, any place, anywhere and now I'm going to give you a walloping right now." He made a rush for me so I stepped back and let him have a swift left hook to the chin. In a few seconds we were grappling on the floor and rolled out into the street. When we regained our feet, and Greb was pulling on his coat, which was hanging off, I took the opportunity of whacking him with a stiff left hook. We were still slugging each other when an Irish cop I knew, officer Pat Casey, who was on the beat, bundled us into separate taxis.' A few hours later, Greb rang Walker and said 'Mickey, I'm really sorry for what I did, but don't forget – I can still lick you any day of the week.'

As for the official encounter, *Ring* magazine deservedly named it Fight of the Year for 1925. Meanwhile, Greb was determined to maintain his busy schedule. Only two weeks after the Walker bout, he climbed into the ring at the Taylor Bowl in Cleveland, Ohio and won a newspaper decision over 'Slapsie' Maxie Rosenbloom, a future world light-heavyweight champion and movie actor. Harry would have 25 fights that year. Not even a serious car crash interfered too much with his ring activity.

On the way to the town of Erie, Pennsylvania for a charity boxing tournament on the night of 19 August 1925, his car skidded to avoid two other cars and overturned. Rushed to hospital with two fractured ribs, cuts and bruises on his back and chest, doctors said he was lucky to be alive. But survive he did, and he was back in action two months later with a win over

Tony 'Young' Marullo over ten rounds, repeating his victory over the same opponent in a world middleweight title defence in his next fight.

The coming of 1926 marked Greb's 13th year as a professional and the New York authorities were anxious for him to defend his title again. What they did not know was that he was completely blind in one eye. Meanwhile, Harry was going to do something completely different. He had always held great sympathy for African-American boxers being denied title fights because of the colour of their skin and he had never drawn the colour line. Now he would meet the formidable Tiger Flowers in a championship fight. It was a noteworthy gesture as Greb was allowing an African-American to fight for a world boxing title for the first time in nearly 20 years. After this fight, it would be 11 years before the colour line was finally broken when Joe Louis won the world heavyweight championship.

Flowers was a deeply religious man known as the 'Georgia Deacon' and recited a passage from Psalm 144 before every bout. A talented southpaw, he began boxing in 1918 after quitting his job in a shipbuilding plant in Philadelphia and racked up an impressive record with few losses, fighting his way to the number one middleweight contender's spot. The match was set for 26 February 1926 at Madison Square Garden.

On fight night, Greb entered the ring as a 5/1 odds-on favourite but it was Flowers who looked the likely winner in the early rounds, backing Greb up and nullifying the champion's attacks. Harry came back in the middle rounds but was often guilty of wrestling his man and pushing him back to the ropes, getting several warnings from referee 'Gunboat' Smith, a former White Hope in the Jack Johnson era. Though Greb was 31, he was a year younger than Flowers but his busy career and hectic lifestyle seemed to be catching up with him. Opinions varied as to which fighter won the closing rounds but at the finish referee Smith held up Flowers's right hand as 'winner and new champion'. The verdict was disputed in the newspapers the next day, with several agreeing that a draw might have been a fairer verdict. A disconsolate Greb said, 'I thought I'd done enough to protect my title but there will be a next time.'

There was – six months later at the same venue. Sadly for Greb, it was another split decision and a second victory for the 'Georgia Deacon'. This time Flowers concentrated on body attacks but Greb's sharper boxing in the middle rounds gave his many supporters hope. Harry was resorting to his foul tactics such as butting, elbowing, holding and slapping, only for Flowers, normally a clean boxer, to give as much as he got in illegal tactics. At the bell, the two judges gave the fight to Flowers but referee Jim Crowley awarded it to Greb. The page one headline in the *Pittsburgh Post* read, 'Greb Wins Most Rounds but Flowers Retains Crown.'

Greb never fought again and related to a friend that he was planning to open a gym in downtown Pittsburgh. In September 1926, a month after the second defeat by Flowers, he went into hospital and had his right eye removed and replaced with a glass prosthesis. In October, while driving in Atlantic City, he was involved another car crash. Trying to avoid two farmers whose vehicles were blocking the road, he swerved and went down an embankment, resulting in severe head injuries, damage to his nose, several cuts on his face and a loosening of the glass eye.

Rushed to hospital, Greb underwent an emergency operation from which he never recovered. The *New York Times* reported, 'Following the operation Greb fell into a state of coma from which he failed to rally, and death was due to heart failure induced by the shock of the operation combined to injuries received in the accident.'

Gene Tunney was one of the pallbearers at Greb's funeral in Pittsburgh. Exactly one month and a day earlier, Gene had beaten Dempsey for the heavyweight title, just as Greb said he would. Turning to a friend on the way out of the graveyard, Tunney said, 'To me, Harry Greb was a great fighter, the greatest fighter I ever saw.'

Chapter 8

Fifth Horseman of the Apocalypse

I T was the early spring of 1972 and the telephone was ringing in Ray Arcel's apartment on Manhattan's Lexington Avenue. When Arcel, one of America's legendary boxing trainers, picked up the receiver, the call was from a prominent promoter/manager in Panama City named Carlos Eleta. 'I'd like you to train my kid Roberto Duran,' said Eleta. 'He's from Panama City and he's a great prospect.' Arcel, who was 72 and semi-retired, asked what Duran had done. Eleta replied, 'He's been a pro for three years now and has had all his fights in Panama except one, when he knocked out a former world champion from Japan in one round in New York.'

When Eleta and Duran arrived in New York, they were met by Arcel and Freddie Brown, who would be Ray's assistant. Brown, from New York's tough East Side, was another great trainer and probably best known as Rocky Marciano's cut man. 'When we started with Duran, it was sheer murder,' remembered Arcel, who would train 20 world champions in his long career. 'Training him was like riding a young colt. There was the language barrier, too.

'Neither Freddie nor I spoke Spanish and Duran knew no English. We had to use an interpreter. Most difficult of all was trying to discipline a young street fighter and instil the thought in his mind that you were capable of doing him some good. In the end, we didn't tell him what to do. Our job was to condition him, not tell him how to fight. He already knew how to do that. He was always his own man.'

Bobby Goodman, the fight publicist, recalled, 'Arcel was the calm guy but Duran and Brown fought like cats and dogs. It was sheer war. You must remember that Freddie was a hard taskmaster and demanded everything be done right or not done at all. Duran would scream and holler and curse in Spanish, then he'd come right back and apologise and do exactly what Freddie wanted him to do.' What Arcel and Brown taught him was technique – how to cut down the space between him and his opponent, and to manoeuvre his rival into corners. They also showed him how to punch in fast combinations and to move his head and body so it was difficult for the opponent to retaliate.

Nicknamed 'Manos de Piedra,' or 'Hands of Stone', Duran was a natural fighter first and foremost, a brawler and an in-fighter from the back streets of Panama. His one purpose was to destroy his opponent in the shortest possible time, and he was not too bothered about the methods he used. With 119 professional fights spanning 33 years – one of the longest careers in history – Roberto won world titles at four different weights. But it was at lightweight where he reigned supreme.

Duran's victory over Scotland's Ken Buchanan in 1972 summed up his whole career – savage and merciless, with not an ounce of compassion. With his jet-black hair and cold, grey, shark-like eyes, his ring appearances took no account of basic sportsmanship or even of the rules. His attitude was that his fights were only going to end one way, in triumph for Duran. He was a modern version of Harry Greb, the legendary world middleweight champion.

Most experts and historians rate Duran in their top ten. In a recent *Boxing News* poll among eight leading writers, five had him at number seven and one placed him at number eight. Bert Sugar, the author and broadcaster, placed Duran eighth in his book *Boxing's Greatest Fighters*, behind Sugar Ray Robinson, Henry Armstrong, Willie Pep, Joe Louis, Harry Greb, Benny Leonard and Muhammad Ali. The Associated Press rates Duran the best lightweight of the 20th century. It was *The Guardian* that probably described him best, 'Duran was a beast, an animal, a rampaging monster whose only thought was to hunt down and destroy his opponent. He was death on legs, the Fifth Horseman of the Apocalypse, terror given form.' He is also only the second boxer in ring history to have competed over a span of five decades, the first being the former world heavyweight champion Jack Johnson.

Like many Panamanians, Roberto Carlos Duran was of native American and Spanish descent. He was born on 16 June 1951 in the Spanish-speaking area of El Chorro, a slum suburb of Panama City, at a time when it was reputed to be the drug-trafficking and money-laundering capital of the world. This was the same overcrowded and totally underprivileged area that would be razed to the ground in 1989, when US armed forces invaded the city to topple the corrupt President Noriega.

The second of nine children, Duran lived in a one-room house with his mother, Clara Esther Samaniego. His father, Margarito Duran Sanchez, an American of Mexican descent, left the family home when Roberto was 18 months old. Twenty-one years later, after Roberto became famous, his father reappeared, claiming to have been in the US army in Panama before being posted back to the US before Duran was born. He said Roberto's mother had taken up with another man. Roberto would say in his autobiography, 'I didn't see him again. All those years he was gone from my life, I didn't spend a lot of time thinking about him. Why should I? He was nothing to me.'

Duran had a tough childhood. Always poor, he had no schooling from the age of 13 after being expelled for punching another boy in the lower regions of his body. He often slept on the streets, raiding dustbins for any scraps of discarded food. 'I would do anything to try and get money for my family, even though I was only a child,' he recalled. 'I was a shoeshine boy, chopped wood, sold newspapers, worked as a house-painter, raided the mango plantations and sold them and then used the money to buy milk and rice, and that's what we had to eat and drink all day. I would do anything to get money for my family. My family, though, was only one of many who had this kind of life. There were lots of families in the same situation. But you survived. You had to.'

One day, he was caught stealing coconuts from a local plantation and was caught by the owner, a wealthy businessman named Carlos Eleta, who was a keen sportsman and racehorse owner. By a strange twist of fate, as recounted earlier in this chapter, Eleta would come back into Duran's life years later, first as his promoter and later, and more prominently, as his manager.

Down on the local beachfront, Duran got into free-for-all fights organised by a local and only the last man standing got paid. It was tough work for the adolescent and it provided the hallmark of a street fighter, and a good one. He recalled that he would not have got into boxing at all had it not been for his elder brother Domingo, or Toti as he was called.

'Toti was a boxer before me and he used to train at the old Neco de La Guardia gym,' Duran said. 'Toti would have this little gym bag with him. It wouldn't hold much, just wraps, gloves and the mouthguard. Not even his boxing shoes would fit into it. It was more like a lunch box. As I watched the trainer put the headguard on Tito, then the protective cup, for a sparring session with a professional boxer named Adolfo Osses, a bantamweight, I was fascinated. Then he put on his shorts and got into his robe. When I asked Tito how I could get all that stuff, he said, "Become a boxer." That's how it all started.'

Duran went down to the gym with Tito several times a week and registered as an amateur boxer. He was 14. Inside two years, he had run up a record of 13 wins in 16 bouts and become something of a local hero. While it was Tito who introduced him to the sport and he was always very grateful to his brother, Duran's own idol would be Ismael Laguna, one of Panama's all-time greats. Known as El Tigre, Laguna was a classy boxer with a solid punch and good defence. When Duran heard Laguna was challenging for the world lightweight championship against Carlos Ortiz in Panama City on 10 April 1965, he made up his mind to be there.

With no money in his pockets, he got to the national stadium by jumping on to a cattle truck and made it into the area when they opened the gates during the last three rounds of the 15-rounder. 'I managed to get up to the ringside and was mesmerised by the whole spectacle,' he remembered. 'Laguna won the decision to become champion and watching him, I knew that this was what I wanted to be.'

Duran turned professional as a bantamweight on 23 February 1968, when he won a unanimous decision over four rounds against Carlos Mendoza in Colon. Mendoza was another newcomer, with only one fight to his credit, but Duran was much quicker to the punch and the victory gave him great confidence. In eight more fights that year, he knocked out or stopped seven opponents in the first round and one in the second. Five took place in Panama City and the remainder in Colon. Boxing writers in both cities were beginning to take notice of this exciting young 118-pounder, who had an aggressive style and a solid punch in both gloves.

Duran's first manager was a jockey, Alfredo Castillo, but when Carlos Eleta watched him in some of those early fights in 1968, he approached Castillo about buying Duran's contract. As well as making his money in business, Eleta was involved with boxing and had also been a tennis champion. 'I've promoted boxing and managed boxers but Roberto is something special,' he said to Castillo. 'How much will you sell me his contract for?' Castillo said he had spent around $150 on the boxer and suggested he would sell the contract for $300, a figure Eleta agreed on. Eleta had big plans for Roberto.

Duran went through 1969 unbeaten and it was the same in 1970, when his record reached 20-0, with only three fights lasting the scheduled distance. In 1971, Duran added four more wins before making his US debut at Madison Square Garden on 13 September. His fight against Benny Huertas was on the undercard of the world lightweight championship fight between defending champion Ken Buchanan of Scotland and Panama's Ismael Laguna, who had twice been champion himself. Laguna was the great boxer Duran had long admired and he often said it was a great thrill to be sharing a bill with him that day. With two legendary trainers, Ray Arcel and Freddie Brown, in his corner, Duran stopped Huetas in 66 seconds.

Back in Panama City for Christmas 1971, Duran was soon in the ring again with two more local wins before news came through that he had been matched with Buchanan, with the Edinburgh boxer's world lightweight title on the line. A classy boxer and hard hitter with both hands, and arguably the best lightweight Britain had ever produced, Buchanan got an early start in the fight game when, at the age of eight, he was taken to the local cinema by his father Tommy to see *The Joe Louis Story*. He was enthralled.

As a Christmas present, Buchanan got a pair of boxing gloves from an aunt, so a future in the ring seemed his destiny. He followed a successful amateur career by turning professional at 20, winning the British lightweight title at 22 and the world title two years later. Now here he was defending his championship at the fabled Madison Square Garden. What's more, Buchanan was fully confident he could handle the rugged Panamanian and keep the title on his side of the Atlantic. Buchanan was 2/1 favourite the moment the fight was signed and remained that way.

'Buchanan disrespected me but what really made me mad was that he said I was a lucky boy because I never had to fight my way, step by step, the way he had,' Duran would write in his autobiography. 'But he didn't know Roberto Duran. I was raised in the streets, had to hustle for food every day. I told reporters, "I've been fighting every single day of my life since I was a little kid and I always felt nobody could beat me. I have no respect for him. I'm undefeated – he should respect that." I trained hard for the fight. I didn't care if I was the underdog. I trained as if I was going to fight 25 rounds. Ray Arcel, my co-trainer, said to me, "I suppose you won't go back to Panama if you lose." "If I lose, I'll kill myself," I told him.'

The fight drew a capacity crowd of 18,901, who paid $223,901, a new indoor record for a lightweight championship fight. Buchahan, at 133lbs, was the heavier by one pound. A quick glance at the fight statistics on the programme showed that Duran, at 21, was six years younger than the Scot and had won all his 28 bouts, as against Buchanan's 43-1-0 record. The Scot was played into the ring by bagpipes while Duran favoured a group of flamenco dancers and a band featuring a drum solo.

No sooner had the bell sounded after referee Johnny LoBianco issued final instructions than Duran practically ran across the ring to get at Buchanan. A flash overhand right sent the Briton down in the first 20 seconds but he jumped up straight away and indicated that he had merely slipped, although LoBianco gave him the mandatory eight count. It was not a good start for Buchanan and things did not improve as the fight wore on. Ken used his fast, strong left jab in an attempt to hold off his rampaging challenger, but Duran would not be denied. This was his big night and nothing was going to stop him.

The Panamanian often missed badly with wild swings and hooks as Buchanan used his superior technique to move around the ring and spear Duran at long range. At the same time, he hoped that Roberto would tire and slow the pace down. It never happened. Duran kept up the pressure with strength-sapping hooks and uppercuts to head and body. A left and right to the head shook Buchanan in the fifth round but the Scot rallied and a hard left hook sent Duran's mouthpiece flying into the crowd. Buchanan had sustained a cut under the left eye by the end of round eight, a few seconds after Duran had clearly given him a knee in the groin, though LoBianco did not issue a warning.

Buchanan's attempts in the ninth and tenth rounds to stay on top of Duran were cancelled out by the challenger's potent body shots, not to mention his repeated illegal use of the head. Several ringside reporters would note that the Panamanian was only just short of kicking the Scot as he poured in jabs, hooks, swings and uppercuts. It was to Buchanan's eternal credit that he was able to stand up to Duran's relentless barrages round after round. At the end of the 12th, Roberto had a commanding lead on all three judges' scorecards. In the 13th, Duran was finally warned for butting as he continued to charge forward, hurling a blizzard of leather at the beleaguered Buchanan. But Ken was made of stern stuff and that was an unmistakeable fact.

As the bell sounded to end the 13th round, both men were still exchanging blows. As LoBianco moved in to separate them, Duran fired a low, almost casual right hand that landed squarely in Buchanan's protective cup. The Scot grabbed his groin, his face contorted in pain, before keeling over and rolling on the canvas. Buchanan would claim the punch was destined to land below his testicles in an upward course, where the cup offers less protection. His handlers helped him to his corner, where he slumped on his stool, followed by LoBianco and the ringside doctor. After looking at Buchanan, who was still in agony, LoBianco turned away and waved his hands in the air to indicate the fight was over, just as the warning buzzer went for the start of the 14th round.

LoBianco then went over to Duran's corner and raised the Panamanian's right arm in victory by a technical knockout, although many sources, including *Ring* magazine, have always regarded such a result as a knockout. At the time of the finish, both judges had Duran ahead 9-2-1 and 9-3 while LoBianco's card had him in front by 9-3. Columnist Red Smith reported in the *New York Times* the next day that LoBianco had to award the victory to Duran, even if the punch was a low blow, 'as anything short of pulling a knife is regarded indulgently in American boxing'.

Buchanan, his face cut and bruised, protested, 'I'm okay, I'm okay,' though he was still clearly in great pain. His American trainer Gil Clancy claimed that Duran had even kneed the Scot before the low blow, and without a warning. In an immediate post-fight interview, LoBianco said, 'Buchanan was hit after the bell but Duran could not stop the punch and I let it go. Remember, Buchanan was wearing a protective cup, as was Duran, as a protection. I stopped the fight when I saw the condition Buchanan was in. It was very obvious he was in no shape to carry on. It was a culmination of punches that he had taken that caused him to collapse, not just one single punch.'

Buchanan would recall to this writer in his retirement years that Duran 'got away with murder in that fight'. He also admitted that he had underestimated the Panamanian and wanted a return match, which Duran refused. Buchanan never forgave Duran for that and while he admitted that Roberto was the best boxer he had ever fought, the Scot nevertheless refused to appear on any subsequent American TV show to pay tribute to Duran.

Following his controversial victory over Buchanan, Duran had two wins in the first round in non-title bouts. But his wild side was beginning to surface. He was drinking and started to carry a gun 'just in case anybody started trouble', as he put it. He was driving his Volkswagen in the hills one evening when a rainstorm came up. Braking sharply to avoid an oncoming car, the Volkswagen skidded down an embankment and overturned. Roberto split his lip in two parts when his face came into sharp contact with the steering wheel. Rushed to hospital, he was treated for facial injuries and a cut on his right elbow. He had already been committed to a non-title fight in New York a few weeks later against Esteban DeJesus, the Puerto Rican lightweight champion. Rather than disappoint the Madison

Square Garden promoter, Duran decided to go through with the fight, even though his injuries had not fully healed.

On the night of 17 November 1972, after several celebrities were introduced, including featherweight legends Willie Pep and Sandy Saddler, it was time for Duran and DeJesus to climb through the ropes for their scheduled 10-rounder. While DeJesus had fought in good company up to then and won seven fights in a row, he was still relatively unknown outside Puerto Rico. But that would now change. There was a sensational start when DeJesus put Duran, the 2/1 favourite, on the canvas with a hard left hook, the first time the Panamanian had been on the boards. Stunned more than hurt, he was up at six, shaking his head as if he could not believe what had happened.

Duran kept out of trouble for the rest of the round but the Puerto Rican was always coming forward with snappy left jabs and hooks, often following through with strong uppercuts and combinations. His confidence gradually draining, Duran found it hard to get through his opponent's defence and while he showed bursts of aggression, particularly in the eighth and ninth rounds, it seemed a lost cause. DeJesus was generally landing the most effective punches. The three judges marked their cards 6-3-1, 6-2-2 and 5-4-1 all for the Puerto Rican. In his dressing room, an angry Duran began to cry then screamed before punching the walls until his knuckles bled.

DeJesus offered Duran a return fight but the terms were not right. Meanwhile, Roberto got down to defending his world lightweight title. He put it on the line three times in 1973, starting in January with a fifth-round knockout over California's Jimmy Robertson, a stoppage in eight rounds against the Australian aborigine Hector Thompson in June and a win in the tenth over Ishimatsu 'Guts' Suzuki of Japan in September, all in Panama City. With demand from the controlling bodies now growing for Duran to face his lone conqueror Esteban DeJesus, a title fight was set for the new 18,000-seater Gimnasio Nuevo Panama in Panama City for 16 March 1974.

Despite his previous loss, Duran was installed an early favourite at 2/1. Roberto knew he had to win this one but the Puerto Rican would have none of it. 'What I did before, I can do again,' he told local sportswriters after finishing a workout at a local gym. Nevertheless, nobody else but DeJesus would have accepted the conditions of the championship fight. Not only was the fight in Panama but the referee was a Panamanian, and all three officials were Panamanian. As one visiting boxing writer remarked, 'That's called eliminating the variables.'

DeJesus told reporters that the officials would not be needed in any event as he planned to knock out the champion. Yet there was one real problem – his weight. DeJesus knew from the start that he would have trouble getting inside the 135lb limit and had actually requested a postponement, but the promoter had turned him down. As it was, he made the weight with ounces to spare. Duran, too, weighed in right on the limit. One of the judges at ringside would be Emma De Urrunaga, the world's only female ringside official at the time. As it turned out, her scoring would not be needed.

The fight started in dramatic fashion and once again Duran found himself looking up at his opponent. DeJesus started strongly. A straight right followed by a fast left hook sent Duran staggering backwards and down as he tried to keep his balance. The Puerto Rican, tasting victory like a police dog on the scent, went after his man on rising and landed another left hook that sent Duran to the floor for the second time, with the fight only 60 seconds old. The Panamanian jumped up without a count and indicated to his corner that he was alright. DeJesus never got another chance. Nor would he ever recapture that early momentum.

In a second round packed with action, Duran stayed on top, guarding his chin, and kept after the challenger with barrages of punches. From the third round onwards, Duran turned boxer-fighter, snapping back his rival's head with left jabs, uppercutting and hooking in close. DeJesus did manage to win the sixth round by scoring well at long range and Duran returned to his corner with a cut over his right eye. Roberto went out for round seven in confident mood and shook up DeJesus with smashes to head and body. It would have been over in the eighth if the challenger had had his way. After taking an eight count on his knees, he was ready to call it a day, a bad day, when he returned to his corner. 'It's all over,' he said to his manager/handler Gregorio Benitez. But Benitez, an uncompromising character who always believed he knew best and was the father of the boxing great Wilfred Benitez, barked, 'Get out there. You can't quit now.'

He was wrong. As Duran would recall in later years, 'Up and down, all over, I kept pounding him. It was as hot as hell in that stadium, which was better for me as I trained in that kind of heat all my life. It wasn't so good for him and I sensed his strength ebbing as the rounds passed and I just needed to finish him off. After taking him down with a five-punch combination in the seventh round, I finished him off in the 11th with a left hook to the head, a shot to the body and another right cross to the head, when he took the full count.'

DeJesus said in the dressing room afterwards that he wanted another fight with Duran. 'The heat in Panama sapped my strength,' he said. 'I lacked the punching power to put him away. I lost six pounds during the fight. Next time, I would want the fight in Puerto Rico. I only arrived here five days before the fight. I should have been here at least three weeks to become comfortable in the searing heat, but there was a delay caused by a row with my manager and the promoter over plane tickets.' The third fight would not happen for a few years yet. In any event, it was extremely unlikely he would ever recapture the glory of their first fight, even in his own territory.

'Picture Duran and you picture a wild-swinging, heavy-hitting youngster with stamina to burn,' reported *Boxing Illustrated* from ringside. 'He's still a heavy hitter who can swarm all over you. Nobody accused him of being an accomplished boxing strategist. His three title defences after he stopped Ken Buchanan did nothing to change anyone's opinion. But against DeJesus, he became a complete fighter. He showed more style and boxing knowledge than he had ever done previously.'

DeJesus would go on to win the world lightweight title in 1976 but his career went into decline and he developed a drug habit. Driving to a family celebration on 27 November 1980, DeJesus was involved in a traffic dispute with another driver, a teenager. Leaping from his car and brandishing a .25 pistol, he shot the teenager in the head. In court, DeJesus was convicted of first degree murder and sent to jail for life. A model prisoner, he took up baseball and excelled at it, playing for the Puerto Rican All-Star prison team three times. Soon after, he learned he was HIV positive, like his brother Enrique, who had often shared needles with him and subsequently died of AIDS. Sent to a facility for the re-education of addicts, DeJesus became a born-again Christian in 1984.

When it became public knowledge that DeJesus had become an AIDS sufferer, the Puerto Rican governor Rafael Hernandez Colon pardoned him. After returning to spend his last days with his family, DeJesus was visited by many celebrities, including his old nemisis Roberto Duran. The compassionate Duran lifted his former opponent out of his bed and hugged him at a time when so little was known and so much feared about AIDS. DeJesus died on 12 May 1989 at the age of 37, a month after being released from prison.

Meanwhile, following his title defence against DeJesus, Duran successfully put his lightweight title on the line eight times. Seven ended inside the distance, including a third fight with DeJesus in Las Vegas when he stopped the Puerto Rican after 2:32 of the 12th round on 21 January 1978. Duran's manager Carlos Eleta would recall that he changed Roberto's corner after entering the ring because his boxer claimed he heard a voice from a witch advising it.

Never mind the witch's warning, the boxing fraternity was impressed with Duran's form. 'Roberto Duran could be the man American boxing needs to revive interest in the divisions other than heavyweight,' said *Boxing International*. The former champion Ken Buchanan repeatedly challenged him to a return but Duran refused, 'There's no point. What I did before I can do again.'

At ringside for the third Duran-DeJesus fight was Sugar Ray Leonard, a very promising welterweight from North Carolina, who had turned professional 11 months earlier and was on a six-fight winning streak. He would soon play a key role in Duran's career. Fast, stylish and powerful, as well as being handsome with no 'bad boy' image, Leonard would become one of the greatest boxers of the modern era, winning world titles at five different weights.

Born Ray Charles Leonard, the fifth of seven children, he was named after his mother's favourite singer. His childhood was uneventful. He stayed at home a lot, reading comic books and playing with his dog. Ray's mother Getha would say, 'He was a quiet boy and didn't talk too much. We never knew what he was thinking but I never had any problems with him. He always went to school.'

When Leonard was four years of age, his family moved to Washington DC and later to Maryland, settling in Palmer Park, a middle-class, predominantly black neighbourhood. It was at a recreational centre in Palmer Park where Ray was introduced to boxing under the guidance of Janks Morton and Dave Jacobs, who ran operations. He picked up the sport almost naturally. Going from novice class to open competition inside two years, Leonard ran up an amateur career embracing 150 bouts, of which he won 145. At the 1976 Olympics in Montreal, he topped it all by winning gold in the light-welterweight division.

Turning professional in February 1977 with a then-record signing-on fee of $40,000 and borrowing Sugar Ray Robinson's nickname with permission, he was now proudly billed as Sugar

Ray Leonard. After two years, he was in the world welterweight ratings. On 30 November 1979 in Las Vegas, now firmly established as the hub of world boxing, Leonard won the WBC title by stopping Wilfred Benitez of Puerto Rico with just six seconds remaining in the 15th round. Benitez was put on the canvas by a powerful left uppercut followed by a blitz of combination punches that convinced referee Carlos Padilla to intervene.

Meanwhile, Duran was experiencing much difficulty getting inside the lightweight limit, even though he was still winning. The prospect of moving up to the welterweight division with its 147lb limit, where he would be more comfortable, seemed an irresistible one. Not only that, it would give Duran the chance to fight his way to a second world title.

Leonard made the first defence of his welterweight title on 31 March 1980 in Landover, Maryland, where he knocked out Britain's Dave 'Boy' Green from Chatteris, Cambridgeshire in the fourth round with a brutal four-punch combination. Leonard would later describe the finishing punch as 'the most perfect left hook I ever threw'. The Englishman was unconscious before he hit the floor and referee Arthur Mercante went through the formality of counting him out. Green slowly came to and was assisted to his corner, much to the relief of Leonard, who had fears of a ring fatality.

By now, Duran was a fully fledged welterweight, having earlier relinquished his lightweight belt under the one-title-only rule. With Leonard keen to establish himself as a champion who feared no challengers, a showdown was in demand. The championship fight was set for the Stade Olympique in Montreal on 20 June 1980 and it would be a joint promotion by boxing's two greatest rivals, Don King and Bob Arum, between whom there could hardly have been a greater contrast. King was a hustler and former jailbird while Arum was an academic who had studied law at New York University and Harvard Law School. Then again, opposites can often make the best partners, even in boxing.

As the fight approached, the American sportswriter and author Sam Toperoff wrote, 'Duran was a punishing hitter to be sure, but he was much more, more even than his remarkable ring record of 71 victories in 72 bouts, later reversing his one loss, would show. Ring records can deceive gaudily. They can be pumped up as easily as silicone breasts. Not the case with Duran. He'd fought everybody willing to step into a ring with him on the way to the lightweight championship he held for almost ten years, through 12 title defences. But Duran was considered a phenomenon not merely on the basis of statistics. Duran was Duran because of how he fought. There were no other fighters around quite like him. He was a throwback in more ways than one, a mysterious, dark figure from some tropical and mythic past.'

Leonard Gardner, whose novel *Fat City* had been turned into a boxing movie by John Huston eight years earlier, also saw Duran as the winner. Roberto's good record and his work in the gym made an indelible impression on Gardner. 'I saw him land a right hand that left me spellbound,' he said. 'It reminded me of some of the great fighters I had watched on television as a kid. It was a picture-perfect punch. But what impressed me even more was his exuberance. He was so full of energy and seemed to really enjoy what he was doing. I was at the gym one day and when he finished he was ready to leap right out of the ring. The ring was a good four or five feet off the floor, so this absolutely terrified his trainers Ray Arcel and Freddie Brown, who seemed to be watching him every second. Later that night, when I got back to my hotel, I phoned a friend in California and advised him to bet on Duran.'

Duran had his supporters, to be sure, but it was Leonard, with the help of saturation TV coverage, allied to his brilliant skills, who had replaced Muhammad Ali as the new glamour boy of boxing. Sugar Ray climbed into the ring as a 9/5 favourite. *Inside Sports* carried pictures of the two boxers on its cover and a poll inside that included former champions Ali and Sugar Ray Robinson, as well as writers like Red Smith and Bert Sugar, showed the majority shared the view that Leonard should retain his title for the second time. Arthur Mercante, hoping that he might be named as the referee, declined to pick a winner, although there had been earlier suggestions that he also favoured Leonard.

On fight night, which was wet and chilly, a crowd of 46,317, the largest ever for a fight in Canada up to then, passed through the turnstiles. Receipts from a combined closed-circuit television audience at over 300 locations totalled around 1.5 million in the US and Canada, with delayed TV broadcasting rights adding to the coffers of promoters Arum and King. Duran would earn $1.6m and Leonard nearly $8.5m, eclipsing the record $6.5m that Muhammad Ali collected in 1976 for his third fight with Ken Norton.

Billed as 'The Brawl in Montreal,' Duran planned that the fight would live up to its name. He would turn it into a brawl from round one and never allow the smoother, slicker Leonard to get into his normal rhythmic style. Surprised that Duran had started so fast and not conserved his energy for a few rounds, Leonard played the Panamanian at his own game, standing his ground and fighting it out. 'They were not smart tactics,' his trainer Angelo Dundee recalled. 'We kept telling him to box, in and out, but he wanted to knock Duran out. He was a guy who always liked to do things his way.'

Leonard's usual grace and movement were being taken away from him by Duran's incessant rushing and swarming style. Dundee was screaming, 'Box him, box him', but he stayed in front of the challenger, using his jabbing and hooking to pick up points. It seemed a dangerous route to take as the tactics saw him hit with some terrific blows from both hands. A heavy right staggered Leonard in the second round as he tried to punch his way out of trouble and Duran was not averse to hitting low if he got the chance, with no warnings from referee Carlos Padilla.

'When I hit Leonard with the left hook, he felt it,' Duran would write in his autobiography. 'I had to demonstrate that I was smarter, faster and that I could put up with a lot more than him. He committed an error by putting too much Vaseline on his body, so that my punches would slide off him. He would hug me and that's the mistake he committed because I could take my hands off him much faster and uppercut and hook him.'

The pattern had been set early on, with Duran boring in and forcing Leonard back on to the ropes. The rounds flashed by, with both men punching and wrestling, but it was the stockier, shorter Duran who came surging forward like a great wave, threatening to sweep over Leonard. Sugar Ray seemed to be coming back from the fifth through to the eighth, firing punches with both gloves and jerking back Duran's head with right uppercuts and left hooks. But the Panamanian was always ready for toe-to-toe combat. Leonard would recall, 'Every time I gained an advantage, he would surge back. I felt I was losing control of the fight.' Leonard's wife, Juanita, passed out after the eighth round, unused to seeing her husband being hit so often.

Duran regularly resorted to butting but there were no warnings from the referee. Leonard had a bad 11th and 12th rounds as Duran's superior strength told. He shrugged off Leonard's counters and thumped in his own shots to head and body. Sugar Ray called on all his reserves of stamina and courage to hit back viciously in the 14th round, but Duran always surged back. In a thrilling 15th round Leonard gave as good as he got, letting loose with left and right smashes as though his life was at stake. It was a magnificent last stand. He won the round but it was not enough to save his title.

Harry Gibbs from London had it 145-144 for Duran and Raymond Baldeyrou of France scored it 146-144, also for Duran. Italy's Angelo Poletti had it even at 147-147, so rendering it a majority decision. An hour later, Bob Lee of the World Boxing Council announced there had been a mistake in the tabulation of the scorecards and that Poletti had actually scored it 148-147 for Duran, making the decision unanimous. It was Leonard's first loss after 27 consecutive wins.

At ringside was Budd Schulberg, author of *On the Waterfront* and other classics. Recalling the fight in his book *Sparring with Hemingway,* he wrote, 'Duran was a classic example of the importance of thinking in boxing. Leonard was a great fighter who was in there fighting Duran's fight, punching with him. He was doing everything wrong. At the final bell, Duran had thrown his arms in the air in an instinctive sign of victory and Leonard was looking down on the canvas as if he knew he had lost. It was close, only a point or two on official cards and most of our unofficial ones. Leonard was making sounds about retiring but the next day he was seen on [ABC TV's] *Wide World of Sports* telling Howard Cossell that was ready to pursue Duran to any ring in the world to win back his crown.'

True to form, a date and venue was set for the return – 25 November 1980 at the Superdome in New Orleans. This time, Leonard vowed to regain the title, *his* title as he put it. Duran told reporters, 'Deep down, Ray *knows* I'm the best welterweight in the world and he'll find out when the bell rings.' Sugar Ray, however, was determined to correct his failings in the first fight – and did so in quite spectacular fashion. From the opening bell, he danced around and picked off Duran with spearing left jabs and hard hooks and uppercuts. The Panamanian was frustrated at not being able to catch his will-o'-the-wisp challenger, who never seemed to be in one place for long.

Sugar Ray was employing the tactics Angelo Dundee had told him to use in the first fight, when he had ignored his trainer. This time he kept to the plan, hit and move, hit and move. Roberto's lead fell short in the second round and Leonard got inside and scored with a cracking right to the jaw. By the third, Duran was beginning to connect with his punches and won the round as he trapped the challenger on the ropes for long spells, pounding away mainly to the body. Leonard came back in the fourth and landed solidly. Shortly before the bell,

Duran missed with a charge near Sugar Ray's corner and ended up halfway through the ropes on his knees. Leonard's workrate dropped in the fifth, although he was still on his toes, moving around the ring.

Duran had a good fifth, driving the challenger back with a two-handed attack, but Leonard took over in the sixth, boxing well behind a stinging left jab. He caught the Panamanian with a good right hook and it was noticeable that Duran was now slowing down and landing few meaningful punches. Duran seemed bemused in the seventh as Leonard wound up a right hand above his head, as though he was about to deliver a bolo punch, before suddenly snapping a left jab into Duran's face. Later in the round, Leonard dropped his hands and pointed to his chin. An angry Duran fired with his right but Sugar Ray pulled his head back and allowed the punch to sail harmlessly past.

'Round after round, you could see the frustration building in Duran,' said Bobby Goodman, public relations officer for the Don King promotion. 'This was a fight that neither he nor his brains trust had ever imagined. Leonard's strategy was brilliant but it was like he was making fun of Duran, and Duran felt disrespected by his tactics.'

Midway through the eighth round of the fight, which was still officially close, Duran suddenly straightened up. Throwing up his arms in a dismissive gesture, he muttered to referee Octavio Meyran, 'No mas, no mas box', which Meyran took to mean, 'No more, no more boxing.' Leonard did not seem to fully grasp what was going on and after doing an Ali shuffle he raced over to Duran and landed two punches to the midsection, with no response. Duran then suddenly turned his back on Leonard and, scowling and gesticulating, walked to his corner, had a few quick words with the handlers and left the ring.

It took a little while for the ringside reporters to realise exactly what had happened, but when Leonard went cartwheeling across the ring and began to climb on to the ropes in celebration, it was clear that the fight was over. The time of the sensational finish was 2:44 of round eight. The unthinkable had happened. The great Roberto Duran, 'Hands of Stone, *Manos de Piedra*', the indestructible macho man, had given in, quitting in the middle of a world title fight, unable to stand the ridicule.

Duran declined to meet the media afterwards to offer an explanation, preferring to let his team supply information, which was often contradictory. World Boxing Council president José Sulaimán told Red Smith of the *New York Times* he understood that when Duran threw a right hand in the eighth round, something happened to his shoulder. Duran claimed he had cramps. In his autobiography in 2016, he said (a) Leonard was humiliating him by sticking out his tongue (b) the crowd had started laughing and (c) he hadn't been 100 per cent physically or mentally prepared.

It was reported the following day, inaccurately as it turned out, that Duran's purse had been withheld. In truth, he was paid before the fight in agreement with the organisers Don King Promotions. The Louisiana Boxing Commission, however, announced they were fining him $7,500 for his 'unsatisfactory performance'. Duran paid the money, drawn on the account of King's company.

Duran's two trainers, Ray Arcel and Freddie Brown, walked out and he took up with a new set of handlers nowhere near the same standard or calibre. He had only two fights in 1981 but he seemed to be getting back to form in both. New Jersey's Mike 'Nino' Gonzales went into the ring with a 24-1 record but left it a clear loser. Italy's Luigi Minchillo, who held the European light-middleweight championship at the time, was also outscored. Duran felt more comfortable at the new weight and said he would be campaigning at 154lbs in future. But then he suffered another setback against New York's triple-world-title holder Wilfred Benitez.

The fight was for Benitez's world light-middleweight championship, which the World Boxing Council called the junior middleweight title. Held in Las Vegas on 30 January 1982, the bout went the full 15 rounds, with the decision going to Benitez, a 9/5 favourite. Discouraged, Duran stayed out of the ring for eight months before going in against the somewhat eccentric British-based Jamaican journeyman Kirkland Laing in Detroit, getting well beaten on points over ten rounds. *Ring* magazine would designate it as the 1982 Upset of the Year. Don King stormed into the dressing room after the fight and declared he would never promote Duran again. 'You're through,' he exclaimed. The next day, Duran signed with King's great rival Bob Arum of Top Rank Promotions. Arum felt the Panamanian could still deliver the goods, providing he got down to hard training and curbed his wild side.

Arum succeeded in getting Duran another shot at the world light-middleweight title by pairing him with Davey Moore at Madison Square Garden on 16 June 1983. A talented New Yorker from the Bronx and undefeated, Moore held the rival World Boxing Association version of the title and entered the ring before a turnaway crowd of 20,061, the largest attendance at the iconic venue since the second Muhammad Ali-Joe Frazier fight in 1974.

Moore ducked between the ropes a 2/1 favourite but Duran knew this was a make-or-break fight. He was on the attack from the opening round, ripping in punches with both gloves. A left jab had Moore flinching and covering his right eye. The New Yorker would later claim that Duran had thumbed him. Duran finished the round by slamming in a hard right to the body as the crowd roared encouragement and the Panamanian walked back to his corner with the air of a delighted student who had just received top marks in his exams.

Moore's nose bled in the second round and his right eye was looking puffy. He fought well but was having trouble coping with Duran, who was slipping and rolling under his blows. In the second round, the Panamanian was still dictating the fight and while Moore caught him with a solid left hook to the chin towards the end of the round, Duran came back with a right uppercut-left hook combination. Both men were battling away after the bell before Mexican referee Ernesto Magana pulled them apart.

By round four, Moore had come back and landed several shots to the head that sent spray flying from Roberto's matted black hair, but Duran punished him with left hooks and right uppercuts. By the sixth, Duran seemed to be hurting his man with every punch and in the closing 40 seconds of round seven, a big right dropped Moore for a count of eight. The New Yorker managed to hang on to the bell.

Duran went all out in the eighth and while Moore tried his best to hold on, the challenger would not be denied. He landed thumping right-handers and jarring left hooks as the crowd yelled for the fight to be stopped. A white towel fluttered into the ring, thrown by Moore's corner, but at first the referee did not see it. Only when Duran's handlers rushed into the ring did Magana finally spot the towel and indicate that it was all over. The time was 2:02 of round eight. Besides knocking the life out of Moore, Duran had become the seventh boxer in history to win world titles at three weights, joining the elite class of Bob Fitzsimmons, Tony Canzoneri, Henry Armstrong, Barney Ross, Alexis Arguello and Wilfred Benitez. He cracked open a bottle of champagne in his hotel room to celebrate.

'I've returned to be the real Roberto Duran, and it's been a long time,' he said. 'When everybody was saying I was finished, here I am world champion again.' The headline in *Boxing News* was 'Duran top of the Hit Parade again.' The British trade paper described the fight as 'a stunning, upset triumph which made up for his surrender against Sugar Ray Leonard two years ago and his subsequent poor form. It was like a master against a novice as he gave Moore a terrible hammering to head and body. At the finish, Duran shed tears of emotion while all around the packed arena the fans rose and chanted his name. He is once again a hero to the Latin American fans and also back home in Panama. The legend lives on.'

Eyebrows were raised when Duran talked of moving up another division and taking on the formidable world middleweight champion Marvin Hagler, later issuing a challenge to the shaven-skulled Hagler. Boxing people shook their heads. Three world titles, fine. Four? Never. Besides, Hagler, a southpaw, was one of the most formidable 160lb champions of all time, with seven successful defences of his title behind him. In the end, with a promised $10m purse split down the middle, the match was arranged for 10 November 1983 at Caesars Palace, Las Vegas, where the 14,600-seater arena was quickly sold out. *KO* magazine asked 25 sportswriters for their opinions and all tipped Hagler. At the weigh-in, Duran forecast that Hagler 'would go down for sure'. The menacing Marvin was unmoved. 'Destruct and destroy,' he glowered. Hagler entered the ring a 4/1 favourite.

With around 2,000 flag-waving Panamanians roaring their man on, the lighter Duran was unable to get through Hagler's guard early on, with the middleweight champion, coming off 11 straight victories, keeping him at bay with a stabbing left jab that he often turned into a hook. Duran was warned several times for low blows. Hagler started to switch from southpaw to orthodox in the middle rounds to confuse Duran but the Panamanian was always coming in, never afraid to mix it with the stronger Brockton fighter. It was fairly even for 11 rounds, with Hagler doing the boxing and Duran the fighting. Sensationally, all three judges had Duran ahead going into the 14th round. Hagler knew he had to do something to save his title and in storming 14th and 15th rounds, he opened up with blistering attacks to wrap up a close but unanimous decision.

Most of the newspapermen around ringside thought that Hagler had won more rounds than the judges credited him with. George Kimble of the *Boston Herald* wrote, 'Hagler didn't need a mirror to know he'd been in a fight. Duran landed more punches and inflicted more damage than Hagler had absorbed in his seven previous defences put together. It was the first time he had to go the distance in defence of his title and the cut below his eye reminded him that the old lion named Duran still had some teeth.'

Duran took the defeat in his stride. 'The better man won but Hagler didn't do anything special. He's just a strong fighter,' he said. Moving back to his more comfortable division, light-middleweight, an offer was made to meet the talented Thomas Hearns, known as the 'Hitman', though Hearns, from Detroit via Memphis, Tennessee, would later bill himself as the 'Motor City Cobra'. Either way, the nickname suited him. Hearns became the most famous product of Emanuel Steward's Kronk gym in Detroit. He had represented the USA in international tournaments as an amateur but had few knockout victories. Yet under Steward's coaching, Hearns developed into the most feared hitter of his era, an era of heavy punchers.

In time, Hearns would become the first boxer to win world championships at five weights. He was light-middleweight champion when a defence against Duran was first mooted. The Bahamas was picked as the location but when local backing failed to materialise, the fight was moved to Caesars Palace, Las Vegas, where it was hastily christened by promoter Bob Arum as 'Malice at the Palace'. The date was 15 June 1984. In a boxing era already swimming in big money, Hearns was guaranteed $1.8m and Duran $1.6m for the fight, which Hearns viewed as a necessary step to force the bout he truly coveted – a clash with Hagler. 'I don't need to just win, I need to be devastating,' said Hearns, confidently predicting a knockout in two rounds.

This was one fight in which Hearns said size would matter. At 6ft 1in, he was six inches taller than Duran and had a reach advantage of 11ins. Under a darkening sky in the outdoor arena, Hearns scored early in the first round, flicking out left hands as Duran sought an opening. Lunging in with his head down, and throwing a long right, Duran was suddenly met with a crashing right and took a mandatory eight count. It was not going to last long. Going out for round two, Duran wrestled

Hearns into a clinch and after some heated exchanges, the Detroit boxer landed a thunderous roundhouse right to the chin that sent Duran spinning to the canvas, face down. With Duran virtually out cold, referee Carlos Padilla declared it all over on a technical knockout at 1:07 of round two, the round that Hearns had predicted.

Duran had no excuses. 'Damn, I tried to get under those long arms and he knocked me crazy with that right hand,' he said. He talked about retirement after the fight. In his autobiography 32 years later, he wrote, 'When I got back to Panama, it was a relief to tell the world I was done with boxing. I had money in the bank and I could look after my family, which is why I got into boxing in the first place.'

Like most great boxers, the lure of the ring was still strong and while he stayed away from boxing for the rest of 1984 and throughout 1985, he put on the gloves again at the start of 1986 and won seven out of eight fights without causing any great excitement. With the world middleweight title coming into dispute, the World Boxing Council agreed to a match between their champion, Iran Barkley, and boxing's forgotten man, 37-year-old Roberto Duran. It would be the Panamanian's last great hurrah. The big-hitting Barkley, from New York's Bronx and a former world championship bronze medallist as an amateur, was fully expected to send Duran back into retirement. Barkley was no pushover, having beaten Duran's conqueror Thomas 'Hitman' Hearns in his previous fight. But the totally unexpected happened at the Convention Center in Atlantic City on the night of February 24 1989.

As Jack Obermeyer reported in *Boxing News*, 'Father Time had his clock turned back as the now most assuredly legendary ring craftsman Roberto Duran took the 12-round split decision against Iran Barkley. It was a time-capsule performance before 7,090 hearty souls, who had braved a freak and massive coastal blizzard to what most felt was the final chapter to an always and forever three-weight champion. Duran, the former Panamanian tough street fighter, employed all the guile and even more the will to outlick a champion hell-bent on teaching him a lesson for the frightful beating he had bestowed upon his buddy, the late Davey Moore, in 1983.'

Barkley fought hard and stunned Duran several times, noticeably in the eighth round, but the man from Panama always fought back stubbornly. He dropped Barkley for six in the 11th round with a hard left-right combination and while the New Yorker won the final session with a final burst of activity, it was not enough to save his title. The split decision went to Duran, who took a world title at a fourth weight, once more unleashing his inner gladiator.

It was the once-great Duran's last stand. In his next fight ten months later, he lost a decision to his old rival Sugar Ray Leonard in a dull encounter. Inactive throughout 1990, with his weight ballooning and mired in debt and tax problems, Duran returned in March 1991 for one meaningless fight, which he lost in six rounds. He carried on defiantly seeking another title fight but was pounded to defeat in three rounds by WBA middleweight champion William Joppy in August 1998. A month after his 50th birthday, Duran had his last fight when he was hammered to a unanimous points defeat by Hector Camacho, a three-weight world champion from Puerto Rico. The fight, on 14 July 2001, took place at the Pepsi Center in Denver, Colorado, where only 6,597 turned out at the 19,000-capacity arena. Duran got a cold reception. The once-golden days had turned to rust.

With a record of 103-16, including 70 inside-the-distance wins, Duran finally retired. He subsequently survived a serious car crash after undergoing life-saving surgery, opened a restaurant in Panama City, did a few movies and had his life story turned into a documentary starring Robert DeNiro. Duran often plays in a salsa band and travels extensively. 'The first time I went to London, I thought they would hate me for beating their idol Ken Buchanan,' Duran admitted. 'But they adored me. It's too bad I never boxed in Britain. I'd have loved to.'

Chapter 9

Rocky road from a Brooklyn slum

I T was 8 May 1945, VE Day, with six dark years of war finally at an end. Officially, it would be another two months before Japan surrendered to end hostilities in the Pacific following the atom bombing of Hiroshima and Nagasaki. But that did not stop New Yorkers celebrating as never before. The streets around Times Square, Wall Street and Rockefeller Center were whitened by snowstorms of paper cascading from office buildings. Ships on the Hudson and the East River sounded their sirens. Workers in the garment centre in Midtown Manhattan threw bales of rayon, silks and woollens into the streets to drape passing cars with brightly coloured cloth. Then the workers swarmed out of their shops, singing and dancing, drinking whisky out of bottles, wading in their own confetti.

Among the revellers was a 26-year-old New York middleweight named Rocky Graziano, who was making steady progress towards his goal, the middleweight championship of the world.

Overcoming an impoverished and delinquent childhood, he would soon achieve his aim. In doing so, he became involved in a trio of ring battles with Tony Zale, the 'Man of Steel' from Gary, Indiana, that remain to this day among the most thrilling ring battles of all time.

While he lacked skill and finesse, never bothering too much with defence, Graziano had a true taste for action that turned him into a tremendous drawing card at the box office. Promoters loved him, especially Mike Jacobs, who promoted most of his big fights in the 1940s. 'When you had Rocky, you had action,' Jacobs said. 'He was that kind of fighter, a true warrior who came to fight. He packed out small fight clubs and big arenas because fans knew what to expect when he ducked between the ropes.' The tousle-haired kid had the X factor in abundance. It was W C Heinz, one of America's most prolific chroniclers of the sweet science, who probably put it best when he said, 'When Rocky Graziano fought, you could almost walk on the tension.' *Ring* magazine rates him as 23rd in their list of the greatest punchers of all time.

If Rocky created the headlines inside the ring, he also made them outside it. He fought the way he lived – on the edge. Continually embroiled in controversy, he went AWOL in the army and had a prison record. He was friendly with mobsters and would temporarily lose his licence for failing to report a bribe offer. Nothing came easy for Graziano. His turbulent and violent life story was the subject of the Oscar-winning movie *Somebody Up There Likes Me*, with Paul Newman as Rocky.

But when Graziano got into his ring shorts, boots, socks and robe and had his gumshield placed in his mouth, it was action all the way. A powerful slugger, he would absorb a tremendous amount of punishment while awaiting the opening he sought for a knockout. The *Boxing Register*, the official record book of the International Boxing Hall of Fame in New York, notes that Rocky's tally of 52 knockouts or stoppages in 83 fights is proof of his punching ability. In his penultimate fight, when years past his best, Graziano was still good enough to put Sugar Ray Robinson on the canvas, albeit briefly, in a world middleweight title fight.

'Rocky hated every opponent he ever fought,' recalled Rex Lardner in *Sport* magazine in January 1956. 'He hated them with an all-consuming, fiery hatred. Chewing his nails, throwing quick, practice rights and reading comics didn't take the edge off his anger. Essentially, when troubled, a generous and gentle if profane young man, Rocky admits he didn't care how he won so long as he won. He rabbit-punched. He hit out of clinches. He held fighters on the way down as they tried to get to their feet. He clambered over the referee to get at groggy opponents and he hit after the bell.

'In all his years of boxing, he stuck to a single pattern – he charged across the ring, threw his arm back, lunged forward and swung. Unless he was paralysed by a body blow, he never paused and he never moved back. He was constitutionally unable to block punches, just as he was unable to learn to jab or feint or throw a short punch. His trainers found that instructing him in technique was the most difficult and most frustrating thing they could do. Fists, it had been impressed upon him from the age of about five, were for punching. It was as though his hair-trigger temper and sustained rages were beneficial instincts for survival.'

Graziano was born Thomas Rocco Barbella in a cold-water flat in Brooklyn on 1 January 1919 to Italian parents. His father, Nicola Barbella, was a moderate boxer known as Fighting Nick Bob but gave up the sport when discovering he was not getting anywhere. In any event, he was constantly drunk with his cronies and worked occasionally on the docks. He could never hold down a job. Consequently, the family were extremely poor. They later moved to the Lower East Side, where the young Rocky was forever in street fights. He learned to look after himself before he could read or write. His father kept boxing gloves around the house and he would encourage junior and his brother Joe, who was three years older, to fight one another. But in the streets, it was a different story. They had to fight to survive.

'Like everyone else in our neighbourhood, I had a real tough time of it from the beginning,' Graziano would recall in later years. 'We were on drugs or whatever but I would find out later that the drug scene was not for me and I got out of it. But without the drugs, I was still always getting into trouble with the authorities. You get branded as a troublemaker and it kinda sticks to you all your life. You never really shake it off and that's how it was for me.'

Rocky seemingly thought that school was not really a good idea and he was forever in trouble with the teachers and regularly stole other kids' lunches. Outside the classroom, he got into even more trouble and spent years in reform schools, jails and Catholic institutions, continually clashing with the authorities. Running with a gang, they regarded stealing as a way of life, easy money. They stole cars, bicycles, radios and jewellery from houses, anything they could lay their hands on. Breaking open slot machines was a regular occurrence. Later on, Rocky would say he only stole things that began with an 'a' – a car, a radio, a bicycle and so on. 'Running from roof to roof, I fell once but I fortunately caught a couple of clotheslines, broke one, broke two but the third one stopped my fall to the pavement,' he remembered. 'If it wasn't for those clotheslines, I would have been hurt badly or killed.'

Graziano would quickly admit that boxing saved him, as it did many other wayward kids. After spending several months in the New York Reformatory for robbery, he heard about a boxing tournament being run locally by the Metropolitan Amateur Athletic Union. Anxious to give boxing a try, and encouraged by his father, he handed in his name to the trainer Tony Zaccaria and he was in the competition. He had three bouts, all wins, before qualifying for the final, which he won on a third-round knockout. Accepting the gold medal with pride, he sold it the next day for $15 and decided this was a good way to earn cash without being chased by the police.

It was now 1939, with war clouds already looming over Europe. At 20 years of age, Rocky realised he would have to pull himself together if he wanted to make any real progress in life. Other bouts came his way, all victories but without any medals on offer. Alas, his past life was never far away and his old habits caught up with him when he was caught stealing at his old school and found himself interred at Coxsackie Correctional Facility before being shifted to the New York Reformatory, serving five months in total.

On probation, Graziano went back to his local gym, determined to go straight once and for all, though he knew it was not going to be easy. In the gym, he chatted to the resident trainer Eddie Coco about taking part in several more amateur bouts before eventually turning professional. 'I won a batch of competitions all over New York,' Graziano recalled. 'I beat everybody and wound up being a good fighter. I felt I could get into the ring with anybody and beat them. That's how confident I felt.'

Rocky made his professional debut in a scheduled four-rounder at the Broadway Arena, a popular fight club in Brooklyn, on 31 March 1942 and beat Curtis Hightower on a stoppage in the second round. A powerful right to the chin did the trick. A couple of weeks later, he was brought before the court and charged with violating the conditions of his probation and sent back to reform school, this time to Rikers Island, a correctional institution on the East River. It was said he later instigated a riot at a local club.

On being released after two months, Rocky got his call-up papers from the military and found himself stationed at Fort Dix in New Jersey. Trouble soon loomed, however, and after causing a disturbance in the mess hall following a heated argument with several other recruits and striking an officer, he was called before two military personnel to explain his actions. Expecting to be prosecuted and sent back to military jail, he ran away from the rigours of boot camp. Returning voluntarily to Rikers Island over a week later, he was pardoned and given the opportunity to box under the army's aegis.

Deciding that the war could be won without his services, Rocky went back to his budding boxing career. In his first year, 1942, his record read 5-1-2, all his wins either coming by knockout or stoppage in small clubs in New York, such as the St Nicholas Arena and the Broadway Arena. By 1943, Graziano had stretched his tally to 20-3-3 and graduated to boxing's most prestigious arena, Madison Square Garden, three times, twice in main events. Boxing people were beginning to take notice of this Italian-American kid with the mop of dark hair who was wiping up rivals. Rocky had several managers, each one going their separate ways, before he met up one afternoon with Irving Cohen at Stillman's Gym.

Cohen would manage over 500 boxers in a career spanning more than 30 years but he would always be associated with Graziano, his only world champion. Noted for his integrity in a sport well known for its shady connections, particularly in the 1940s and 1950s, Cohen was born in Russia but left for America in his teen years. A former amateur boxer, he worked as a lingerie salesman before becoming a fight manager. A calm, quiet man who rarely raised his voice, the 5ft 6ins Cohen did not fit the stereotype of the loud, insensitive manager with a large cigar clenched between his teeth. Cohen and Graziano got on well. Irving was always aware of Rocky's often fiery temper and, in the words of one trainer, 'gave his boxer a long leash'. It was Cohen who changed Rocky's name from Barbella to Graziano, his grandfather's surname, and turned Rocco into Rocky.

Happy with Graziano's progress, Cohen reckoned that by the time world champion Tony Zale came out of the navy at the end of the war, Rocky could get himself into the leading contender's spot with his brawling, all-action style. World titles were technically frozen at the outset of the war and even though champions in the lower weight divisions continued to defend their titles, those in the four heaviest classes, from welterweight to heavyweight, Freddie 'Red' Cochrane, Zale, Gus Lesnevich and Joe Louis respectively, were exempt from championship defences.

Graziano came unstuck in his final two fights of 1944, when he topped the cards at Madison Square Garden against the shifty Harold Green, a 20-year-old from Brooklyn. In both fights, and on the advice of his corner, Green kept moving away from Rocky's punches, mainly long-range swings, preventing Graziano getting close enough to unleash his bombs. In the ninth round of the first fight, on 3 November, Rocky did catch his man with a looping right to the chin but Green recovered quickly and reverted to his style of slipping out of danger quickly and keeping up his fast left jab. In the return a month later, it was the same story – Graziano advancing, seeking the big finishing blow but failing to land it, and Green moving, moving, moving, frustrating all Rocky's efforts.

'Green kept me away with left jabs and hooks from both hands and whenever I charged him, he was on his bicycle and getting out of danger,' Graziano would recall in his autobiography *Somebody Up There Likes Me*. 'If he couldn't get on his bicycle on the times I trapped him, he grabbed hold and clinched. I never got one good shot at the guy and I felt terrible. When the decision went against me, as I imagined, I told my manager Irving Cohen, "Get me that bum again, and I'll kill him."

'In that second fight, he jabbed and hooked and ran all the time. Then, in the tenth and last round, I finally landed a solid roundhouse right on his chin and he went down. I wasn't to know that there were only ten seconds of time left, and the referee only got to six when the bell went. I was deprived of a knockout. They had to score it by rounds and it was Green's fight. Everybody but Green knew he won that fight. It took the referee and both Green's handlers to pick him up off the canvas and hold up his hand. Then they carried him out of the Garden. The next day, some of the papers said I got him with a lucky street-fight punch. This didn't bother me. I knew now that if I could knock the bum out too late in the tenth, next time I could knock him out anytime I wanted.'

Graziano would get a chance of revenge in a third fight. He was now at the crossroads of his career. The New Year was looking bright. Cohen was offered a headliner at Madison Square Garden on 9 March 1945 against a sensational youngster from Philadelphia named Billy Arnold. Rocky jumped at the chance. It would be an opportunity to get among the winners again after the Green losses. Arnold was a fast, slick boxer with a good punch in both hands and was considered a real prospect along with another youngster who was also showing high promise. His name was Sugar Ray Robinson.

Arnold, a 19-year-old, had an impressive record, with 26 knockouts or stoppages in 28 winning fights, 11 of them in the first round. He was an 8/1 favourite, with some sources listing him at 10/1 and 12/1. Graziano's record was 35-6-5. In any event, Rocky paid no attention to the odds, reckoning that what happens in the ring was what counted. Nevertheless, Arnold received a tremendous reception when he climbed into the ring before an excited crowd of 14,037, whereas Graziano got only a mild welcome.

Arnold acknowledged the fans' appreciation and jigged around in his corner. Rocky chatted to his seconds, hitting one glove into the other, anxious to get started. He had worked out at his training camp in New Jersey with big Joe Baksi and felt in top shape. Baksi, one of the leading contenders for Joe Louis's world heavyweight title, would come to London a few years later and hammer Britain's best, Bruce Woodcock and Freddie Mills, into heavy defeats.

Round one and Graziano was on the attack straight away, hooking, swinging and uppercutting his slick rival, who countered with accurate punches straight out of the textbook. Arnold caught Rocky with a glancing right to the chin but missed with a follow-up left hook. Graziano was now putting the pressure on his fancied rival and won the round narrowly. In the second round, Arnold opened up and connected with a strong left hook over Rocky's lowered right hand, which shook the New Yorker to his heels. Billy quickly followed through and subjected Graziano to a heavy pounding from both hands as the crowd roared. Ringside writers agreed they did not think the fight would go on much longer as Rocky held on, praying for time to get his rhythm going. Referee Frank Fullam was casting anxious glances at Graziano but the bell ended any thoughts he might have had of stopping the fight.

The bell for round three rang and Rocky left his corner like a greyhound out of the traps. Arnold moved in fast, too, punching away with both hands on his advancing and always-dangerous opponent. Then it happened. Billy pulled back to throw a left hook but Rocky got there first with a looping right that caught Arnold on the point of the chin. Billy was badly hurt but stayed on his feet.

This is how writer Jimmy Breslin remembered it for *True* magazine over 20 years later, 'Rocky had the killer instinct and it was working overtime as he rained punches on Arnold and then got in one good right which dumped Billy on the ring apron. Somehow, Arnold got up, just beating the count. Graziano raced after him again and once more Arnold slipped onto the ring apron from a right hand. This time he pulled himself upright and staggered along the ropes to his feet at six. He was dazed but his eyes were clear. Referee Fullam looked at him, then stepped out of the way and Graziano tore in. He grabbed Arnold by the throat with his left hand and began to hammer rights into the helpless fighter's face. Arnold sagged into a neutral corner for a seven count, got up again and was caught by one wicked Graziano right before Fullam decided it was all over at 1:54.'

In the dressing room, Graziano was delirious with excitement, 'I told you I'd do it and I did. Sure, Arnold was a massive favourite but they all underestimated Rocky. He never hurt me. I just wanted him to open up and when he did, I got him. I beat the devil out of him. I've erased the handwriting on the wall. I now belong to this new world I've come into and I'm never going back to the old one. I hear the vice-president of the United States, Harry Truman, was at ringside. Good for him and I hope he enjoyed the fight and my performance.'

Over in Arnold's dressing room, the atmosphere was sombre, like a wake, which it effectively was. 'What hit me?' Billy kept saying. He was unmarked except for some psychological scars. In less than seven and a half minutes of action, a great prospect was killed off and a future champion was born. Arnold never recovered and eventually quit the sport, always lamenting what might have been had he beaten Rocky.

Graziano's manager admitted to the newspapermen that he was against the Arnold fight when it was first offered to him, even though Rocky really wanted it. 'I didn't think he was really ready for the fight,' said Cohen, 'even if he himself couldn't wait to get into the ring. This guy was a real comer and Rocky wasn't always in the best of condition. What if Arnold knocked all that super-confidence out of him and beat him? It would have been a good thing. It would have brought him back to earth, if you know what I mean. He'd have trained harder next time, and probably beaten Arnold. Rocky would have taken on Joe Louis if I'd have allowed it. Personally, I thought Arnold would beat him so Whitey Bimstein and I figured that as long as he was losing fights for $4,000, he might as well lose a fight for $10,000.'

Graziano was now on a roll, with the newspapers calling him a future world middleweight champion. Two months later, following a fourth-round stoppage of Solomon Stewart, he went in against Al 'Bummy' Davis in a ten-rounder at Madison Square Garden. Davis, a New Yorker from the Brownsville district, was a roughhouse fighter, a villain, but he was at the end of his career by then. Yet he felt he had the beating of Graziano even though, being a welterweight, he would be giving away considerable poundage. The fight turned into a real war. Davis went down in the first round and Graziano hit the deck in the second. Davis visited the boards again in the third as bedlam reigned in the famous arena.

When the bell rang to end the third round, 'Bummy' dropped his hands and turned to his corner just as Rocky fired a right to the jaw and Davis sank to the boards. Al Buck of the *New York*

Post wrote, 'The blow that did the damage came at a time when the ring was full of handlers for both fighters. It was clearly an illegal punch but Young Otto, the referee, ignored the protests of Lew Burston, Davis's manager. "I asked Otto to stop the fight and disqualify Graziano but he refused," said Burston. "Instead, he ordered the fight to continue." Davis, hurt and bleeding, was knocked off his feet and took a count of nine. When he got up, Rocky smashed right after right to Davis's chin. Al was still on his feet when Otto stopped it.'

That was Davis's last official fight. An unscheduled one in Brooklyn would follow later in the year, with tragic consequences. Around that time, the borough was plagued by a rash of robberies perpetrated by a gang of thugs who operated out of a large limousine. The newspapers reported they had already robbed six taverns the previous week and shot a 16-year-old girl to death.

On the night of 21 November, 'Bummy' was drinking a beer with some friends at Dudy's Bar, which he had once owned, when four of the gang alighted from their limousine and entered the premises. Waving their pistols, they ordered the few customers to stand at the end of the bar with their hands up and took the night's takings, around $150. As they started to leave, Davis jumped forward and smashed a left hook into one of the guys' faces, which sent him reeling backwards. Another gunman opened fire and shot 'Bummy' in the neck, spine and right arm before the robbers escaped in their getaway car. But not before 'Bummy,' dazed and bleeding, stumbled after them and intended to give chase in his own car before falling face down on the pavement. He was dead before the ambulance reached the scene. A villain in the ring, a hero outside it.

With the middleweights keeping clear of Graziano, Rocky took on the world welterweight champion Freddie 'Red' Cochrane, again at Madison Square Garden, on 29 June 1945. Cochrane, from New Jersey, had won the title in 1941 but had not been called on to defend it because of the war. In an overweight bout with his title not on the line, he faced Graziano before a crowd of 18,071. For eight of the scheduled ten rounds Cochrane outboxed his heavier opponent, easily avoiding Rocky's swings and long-range hooks. In the ninth, Graziano caught him with a powerful right hand to the chin and Cochrane went down, but the bell rang at the count of six. In the tenth round, with victory in his sights, Rocky again landed his vaunted right to the temple and Cochrane went down for the full count. *Ring* magazine named it Fight of the Year.

In a return bout before an even bigger crowd at Madison Square Garden, Graziano was again the victor when he put Cochrane down for no fewer than seven counts before a left and right to the jaw in the tenth and last round laid him out flat on the canvas. Cochrane would never defend his welterweight title successfully. In his first defence in February 1946, he was knocked out in four rounds by Marty Servo.

Before the end of a successful 1945, Graziano had a rubber match with Harold Green, stopping his two-time conqueror in three rounds at the Garden. Green would later claim that he was approached by mobsters a few days before the fight to deliberately lose for a 'substantial fee' and while the sport was being infiltrated by the underworld, a trend that had started in the 1930s, Green's allegations were never proven.

Ruby Goldstein, who refereed the fight, remembered, 'The feeling between them was bitter and this time Rocky took charge from the outset. Soon after the finish, I was about to start for the dressing room when Green suddenly blew his top. He stormed about the ring, resisting the attempts of his handlers to control him and stirring up a pocket-sized riot that the city police and special cops quelled only after an anxious few minutes.'

Graziano was now the most exciting middleweight around and in the big money, picking up $50,000 a fight on average. But the real cash would come as champion. A world middleweight title fight with Tony Zale was already being mooted by promoter Mike Jacobs for late summer 1946 at the Yankee Stadium. First, though, Rocky had to answer a challenge from Sonny Horne. A very promising middleweight from Ohio, Horne had an impressive winning record and his people also had a fight with Zale in mind. Slick and a hard hitter, with an impressive record in the amateur ranks, where he won several Golden Gloves titles, Horne paired off with Graziano at the Garden on 18 January 1946. He managed to avoid Rocky's bombs for ten rounds but his opponent landed enough hard shots to take a unanimous decision.

It was back to the Garden for Graziano's next fight against world welterweight champion Marty Servo on 29 March. It would be a ten-rounder without Servo's title on the line. A native New Yorker, Servo's promising career had been interrupted by service in the US Coast Guard but he resumed activities in peace time and won the title in 1946. When his manager Al Weill, who would later take Rocky Marciano to the world heavyweight title, got a big offer to fight Graziano, he accepted. It would turn out to be a very bad career move for Weill and Servo.

Outweighed by 14lbs, Servo was down three times in the second round from Rocky's powerful smashes before the one-sided bout was stopped at 1:52 of the session. Servo's nose was badly injured and he was forced to relinquish his welterweight title and retire. He would make an ill-advised comeback, including a knockout loss in the first round, before quitting for keeps. The way was now clear for Graziano to face Tony Zale for the middleweight championship of the world. Rocky would be up against one of the great 160-pounders, a chilling puncher who was also a good boxer with a sharp left jab that he could quickly turn into a deadly hook. The champion was one man who knew how to take care of himself when the bell rang. 'When Zale hits you, it's like someone stuck a hot poker in your belly and left it there,' was how one of his opponents, Billy Soose, described a Zale punch to the body.

Born of Polish ancestry on 29 May 1913 in Gary, Indiana, Anthony Florian Zaleski was as tough as the steel city in which he grew up. Every man and boy seemed to work in the mills and young Tony was no exception. As a result of the death of his father when he was two, Tony developed a deep sense of guilt and an impenetrable shyness. When he was suffering from a temporarily worrying infant illness, his father had cycled to a drug store to buy medicine, only to be knocked over by a car and killed on the way home. For months, whenever he saw a man on a bicycle, Tony would tell his anguished mother, 'Daddy's coming ...'

Child labour laws and trade union ideals meant nothing in those grim cathedrals of industry. 'It seemed like I worked in the steel mills since I was weaned,' he once said. 'Breathing the burnt air, catching with a bucket the hot rivets that could burn a hole right through you if you missed.' He remembered complaining to his brother as they walked through the factory gates, 'I feel like I was born here.' The response was, 'Stop bitchin'. Be thankful you got a job.'

When Zale was working out at a boxing gym one night, a coach looked at him and said, 'You look like you're made out of steel.' The nickname 'Man of Steel' stuck with him for the rest of his life. It seemed to suit Tony perfectly and as he made progress in boxing, his strong psyche enabled him to hit hard and take a good punch in return. But his introduction to the sport in the first place was modest enough. As a growing boy and on the advice of his brothers, who were active in amateur boxing, he went down to the local boxing club 'to see what it was all about'. Zale would recall in later years, 'Going down to the club that first night changed my life. I knew at that stage that I wanted to be a boxer. I loved the atmosphere of the club, the boxers doing their paces, the whole thing. I joined up soon after. The hardest thing I found was trying to hit the speed ball but I eventually got the hang of it and it soon became part of my routine.'

Zale had 95 amateur bouts, winning 85, with 50 ending inside the distance, and had a cupboard full of cups and medals. He was still in high school and while several boxing managers wanted him to sign up as a professional, Tony was reluctant. He had his steady job in the steel mills and although the work was hard and draining, the money was good. He would wait until graduation before making any firm decision about testing the waters on the paid side of the sport. After graduation, he decided to quit the mills. 'I figured I had nothing to lose,' he remembered. 'I felt the prospects were good in the fight game and made up my mind to take the plunge.'

With little boxing activity in Gary, Zale moved to Chicago, a good fight town, and started his career by joining up with a local manager Harry Shall. He had his first fight in the Windy City on 11 June 1934 and outpointed Eddie Allen over four rounds. After nine straight wins, he came unstuck, losing a decision to Billy Hood. Tony quickly realised that he needed more than a punch and average boxing ability to succeed. There would be more losses along the way, in Zale's case another five defeats before the end of the year. Even though he won six fights, the setbacks dampened his enthusiasm.

Somewhat discouraged, Tony returned home to work in the steel mills before two boxing managers in Chicago began making enquiries as to his whereabouts. On discovering the promising middleweight was back in his old hometown, Sam Pian and Art Winch sent Zale a telegram asking him to return to Chicago, where they would look after his affairs and put him on the right track. Pian and Winch would be his managers until he retired in 1948. They had a strong team of boxers under their experienced guidance and had taken the great Barney Ross to the world lightweight and welterweight championships.

Zale returned to the ring on 25 February 1935 with a points win over Young Jack Blackburn and while there would be the occasional setback, he made enough progress to be ranked the tenth best middleweight in the world in *Ring* magazine's annual ratings of 1939. Pian and Winch secured a non-title bout early in January 1940 for Zale against Al Hostak, a tough Czech from Indianapolis, who was recognised as world middleweight champion by America's National Boxing Association (NBA), a forerunner of the current World Boxing Association. A heavy underdog, Zale won the decision over ten rounds. Tony's managers demanded a title shot. Six months later, they got it when Zale stopped the champion in 13 rounds at Seattle's Civic Stadium. Hostak was down three times before referee Benny Leonard, the former world lightweight champion, intervened as the towel came fluttering in from the defeated champion's corner.

Zale twice defended his NBA title before defeating Georgie Abrams over 15 rounds for the universally recognised middleweight title at Madison Square Garden on 28 November 1941. Abrams, from Virginia, entered the ring an 8/5 favourite. Contemporary newspaper reports show that Abrams had little defence against Zale's solid body blows and admitted he was lucky to escape a knockout. Three months later, despite a gutsy performance, Zale was outsmarted by the 15lbs heavier Billy Conn, the former world light-heavyweight champion, losing on points over 12 rounds. In May 1942, Zale received his call-up papers and enlisted in the US Navy, after which the title was frozen until the end of the war.

On his return to civvies in 1946, Zale found that a young New Yorker named Rocky Graziano, six years his junior, had been making headlines in newspapers and magazines with displays of vicious punching that had earned him a series of sensational knockouts. Soon, the demand for a title defence against Graziano was gaining momentum – Rocky, the kid with bombs in his gloves, against the experienced 'Man of Steel'. It had all the ingredients of an explosive match.

Promoter Mike Jacobs set up the eagerly awaited fight for 8 July at the Yankee Stadium ball park, with Graziano getting 25 per cent of the gate and Zale 35 per cent. Rocky was immediately installed favourite at 12/5. When the fight was announced in early January, Zale, who had not fought since losing to Billy Conn in February 1942 before enlisting in the US Navy, engaged in six warm-up bouts, winning each by knockout. Graziano, in any event, had been busy all along and regarded the Zale match as 'just another fight, though this time with a world title at stake', as he told newspapermen. It would be the first undisputed world middleweight title fight in almost 17 years, since Mickey Walker decisioned Ace Hudkins in 1929. As it happened, Zale picked up a virus at the end of June and the fight was rescheduled for 27 September at the same venue.

As fight night approached, the odds on Graziano dropped to 7/5 and even 6/5 because of Zale's impressive workouts at Stillman's Gym in New York. Joe Louis, the reigning world heavyweight champion, who had been undecided when the bout was first announced, now went over to Tony's side. 'Zale is too much of a tremendous body puncher for Graziano, who is inclined to leave himself open too much for comfort,' said Louis. Newspapermen slightly favoured the more youthful Graziano but Gene Kessler of the *Chicago Daily News* tipped Zale to win and gave three reasons: One, Zale had regained most of his old form in his workouts; two, Graziano looked overconfident in his workouts and, three, Zale was stronger and had the heavier punch.

A crowd of 39,872 turned out, producing at the time the largest gate in history for a world middleweight championship fight, a total of $342,497. It was also the second largest amount for a non-heavyweight fight up to then, exceeded only by the Benny Leonard-Lew Tendler bout for the world lightweight title at New York's Polo Grounds in 1923, which took in $450,000. Zale entered the ring at the middleweight limit, 160lbs, outweighing the challenger by six pounds. After referee Ruby Goldstein called the two men together for their final instructions, they returned to their corners to await the first bell.

From the very outset, it was action all the way, with the big crowd constantly on their feet. This was no Boston tea party, or New York tea party for that matter. Each fought as though their very lives depended on it. It would be a battle for survival. Zale had the better of the opening round, hooking to body and head, and driving Graziano back to the ropes. Inside a minute, Zale connected with a short left hook that caught the New Yorker on the point of the chin and sent him to the canvas. Rocky, momentarily dazed, reached out for the ropes, desperately trying to pull himself upright. He managed to climb to his feet at four and went right in against Zale, firing lefts and rights, and the round ended with both fighters swapping punches. But it was Zale's round.

In the second, Graziano seemed to have fully recovered from the early knockdown and was connecting with long rights to the face. He followed up with three more rights and Zale responded with a sharp uppercut that made the challenger blink. Suddenly, a left hook to the head and a right under the heart sent Zale skidding under the bottom rope. He looked in real trouble but the bell came to his rescue at the count of three. The fight was certainly living up to its publicity and expectations, and indications were that it was very unlikely to last the full 15 rounds, or even reach the halfway stage. But there was a big worry for Zale. He complained to his cornermen of a throbbing pain in his right hand and it was feared he had injured his fist.

Winch put pressure on certain points of the hand and when he dug his finger into the base of Zale's right thumb, Tony winced in pain. Winch said nothing in case it would undermine his boxer's confidence but when Zale went out for the third round, Winch told his partner Pian that the hand was broken. It was noticeable that Zale was using his left more than his right, but he was still able to keep Rocky at bay with stabbing left jabs and left hooks. Graziano was full of fight and rocked the champion with two powerful left hooks to the mid-section. Zale risked his damaged right hand with a shot to the head and suddenly it was Graziano who looked in real trouble as the bell clanged.

The fourth was another slugfest, as was the fifth, and while Zale managed to land with his weak right hand, he was doing most damage with his left jabs and hooks. Still, it was Graziano who was doing the most effective punching, both at long range and in close, and Zale, his face a bloody mess, was tottering around the ring. It was only Rocky's wildness that allowed Tony to stay on his feet.

At the bell, Zale was so hurt that he started to head for the wrong corner before realising his mistake. Damon Runyon, covering the fight for the International News Service, scribbled on his notebook, 'I'll take 10/1 on Zale', tore out the page and passed it to a colleague. Nat Fleischer of *Ring* magazine, who served as timekeeper for the fight, would recall that he doubted if anybody in the ballpark gave Zale a chance of coming out for the sixth round. 'I remember saying to somebody next to me at ringside, "Too bad, it'll be all over in the next round. Zale can't possibly stand up to any more of that kind of punishment."'

In Zale's corner before he went out for the sixth round, his two seconds and trainer Ray Arcel worked him over frantically. They doused him with cold water, applied ice to his neck, massaged his legs and slapped his face to bring him back to life. 'That fifth round was just a murderous one and we don't know how Tony survived it, with his broken hand and all that,' Arcel would say later. 'Graziano was winning hands down. I said: "Listen Tony. Don't let this guy take away your title. Go out there and hit him with all you've got. Just load up and take a chance."' Over in Graziano's corner, the scene was little short of jubilation. 'You've got him, Rocky,' said Whitey Bimstein. 'He's all yours.'

The warning buzzer sounded seconds before the bell rang and Graziano sprang into action, landing a solid right to the body and missing with a follow-through left hook. Zale suddenly stepped inside and connected with his suspect right hand to the body. It was enough to shake Graziano and Zale followed through with a whiplash left hook to the head and the challenger was on the canvas in a squatting position with one hand on the bottom rope. As Goldstein counted off the vital seconds, Rocky struggled to grab a higher rope with his left hand and managed to haul himself to his feet, but it was a second too late. Goldstein had ready counted to ten. The time was 1:43 of round six and boxing had a new world middleweight champion.

In the dressing room, Graziano said, 'I don't remember the left hook that finished me but the right to the body was the most damaging punch. It knocked all the wind out of me. I heard the count at eight, nine and ten but it all came fast. It kinda crept up on me.'

Zale said, 'I always figured Rocky was going to be tough and I was under no illusions about his ability. I knew too that he punched hard and you felt it every time he landed. But I was always confident I could beat him. When my right hand went in the second round, I had only one alternative. Save it as much as I could and use my left. It worked. My co-manager Art Winch told me after the fifth round that Graziano was more tired than I was and that I had to give it all I'd got in the sixth. It worked. Rocky's a good guy and we'll always be pals, no matter what happens in the ring.'

Referee Goldstein remembered, 'For five rounds it was desperate in there. Graziano was what is known in the ring as a head-hunter and he was bombing Tony's jaw and skull with punches it didn't seem anyone could take and survive. Zale was hurting Rocky, too, for he was a torturing body-puncher, but by the end of the fifth round there were cries from the ringside to call a halt. I went to Tony's corner and Tony said, "I'm all right, Ruby." Now there's never a fighter who says "I feel lousy. Get me out of here." They all say they feel great. Courage and pride keep them from admitting it.

'In the sixth round, Zale hit Rocky with a dreadful punch to the solar plexus. It was as if Rocky's legs had been cut from him. He sprawled on the canvas and was still struggling to get up at the count of ten. As he got up within a split second after the count, there was apparently some bewilderment on the part of the spectators well back from the ring who thought he might have beaten the count. But there were no complaints from Rocky or his team.'

James P Dawson said in the *New York Times*, 'Zale had to be a great champion to win. He had to pace himself expertly and had to weather a storm of blows that would have crushed a man with less courage, less stamina. His foe was a crude, primitive fighting type, a younger man with only a little boxing skill but a Stone Age man when stung – throwing punches furiously, recklessly, viciously from all angles, with crushing, paralysing power. It was a blazing battle for the middleweight title, a glorious chapter in ring history.'

A return bout was inevitable and while both boxers had agreed to meet again, there were protests that other contenders deserved to be considered. The three most prominent challengers were Charlie Burley of Pittsburgh, New York's Jake LaMotta and Marcel Cerdan, the European champion from Morocco, which was then under French control. While LaMotta had his legion of supporters and was the only man to have beaten Sugar Ray Robinson at the time, there was strong support for Cerdan, who had already made an impressive US debut with a good win over Georgie Abrams. But most boxing people seemed to point to Burley as the number one man. A Graziano-Burley fight never happened.

Sadly, many fighters refused to box him. It seemed Burley was too good for his own good and too much of a risk. World champions would have nothing to do with him and Burley would go through his entire career without ever getting a title shot, even though he won 83 of his 97 fights. It was a sad reflection on boxing in the 1930s, 1940s and 1950s, his campaigning years.

While tentative plans were being made for a Zale-Graziano return, Rocky and his team found themselves in deep trouble with the authorities for failing to go through with a bout against Rueben 'Cowboy' Shank of Colorado on 27 December 1946. Rocky withdrew from the fight three days earlier after complaining of a back ailment, but it had been reported that a syndicate of New York gamblers had bet as much as $135,000 on Shank, who was a 4/1 underdog and given little chance against Graziano.

It meant that a win by Shank would have resulted in a payout of over half a million dollars for the bettors. Graziano would tell a grand jury that he was approached by 'a man in a dark suit' at Stillman's Gym and made the offer. Under the rules of the New York State Athletic Commission, a boxer is obliged to report a bribe offer. Commissioner Eddie Eagan, a former gold medallist at the 1920 Olympics in Atwerp, suspended Graziano in the state.

While New York was now out of bounds for a return Zale-Graziano fight, Abe Greene, president of the rival National Boxing Association, announced that his officials could make any matches involving Graziano as they saw fit. The return fight was now set for the Chicago Stadium. The date: 16 July 1947. In the lead-up to the fight, a poll of 25 United Press writers believed Zale would emerge victorious while eight thought the hard-hitting Graziano would pull off an upset. Only one of the 25 scribes thought the fight would go the full 15 rounds. Mike Jacobs had promoted the first fight but he was now unwell, meaning that Irving Schoenwald would stage the rematch.

It had been a sweltering day in the Windy City. The temperature outside the stadium measured 90 degrees and according to Jack Cuddy, a United Press editor who had brought along a thermometer, it was 105 degrees at ringside. It was felt that if the heat was going to have an effect on the outcome of the fight, then Zale, the older of the two, would suffer the most. According to a Zale biography co-written by his nephew Thad Zale and historian Clay Moyle, 'The stifling heat that night must have reminded him of his days in the steel mills back home in Gary, Indiana'.

An attendance of 18,547 braved the heat and produced a new record of $422,918 in paid receipts for an indoor boxing tournament. It would remain a record for an indoor event until 1961, when the third world heavyweight championship fight between Floyd Patterson and Ingemar Johansson produced a figure of $485,000 at the Miami Beach Convention Hall. Among the attendance for Zale v Graziano II were stars of stage, screen and radio, including Al Jolson, Frank Sinatra and Harry James, as well as prominent financiers, industrialists, lawyers, doctors, political leaders, managers and matchmakers. Boxers included two former world heavyweight champions in Jack Dempsey and Gene Tunney, as well as reigning welterweight champion Sugar Ray Robinson.

No sooner had referee Johnny Behr called the two fighters together and the bell rung than they went for each other. This one looked like matching the first fight for sheer thrills. Rocky connected with some cracking rights to the jaw and Tony replied with stabbing left jabs and a combination of hooks and uppercuts. Midway in the round, Graziano hurt Zale with three heavy rights that caused his knees to buckle but the 'Man of Steel' refused to go down. At the bell, Graziano went back to his corner with blood streaming from his left eye while his right eye was swollen. The first round was clearly Zale's.

Looking back on the fight in his autobiography eight years later, Rocky said, 'This was no boxing match. It was a war and if there wasn't a referee, one of us would have wound up dead. I still can't look at the pictures of that fight without it hurting me and I get nightmares that I am back in the ring on that hot July night and I am looking through a red film of blood. The cut that opened my left eye felt like he crashed a butt of a gun over my eye. I couldn't see out of it. The corner closed it between rounds but in the second, Tony hit it a number of times and the blood started running again.'

Graziano moved out fast in the second round and tried a left hook to the jaw, but Zale countered with a succession of short rights and left hooks that reopened the cut over Rocky's left eye. He was clearly hampered by the injury, having to defend himself at every opportunity. It was same at the start of the third round, which was a bad one for Graziano. Zale caught him with a whipping right to the chin that sent him down but he jumped up, more surprised than hurt. Nevertheless, Graziano was falling well behind against a champion at his best.

Describing that third round later, Rocky said, 'The third was the worst round I ever lived through in the ring. Before I could put a glove on Zale, he belts me a right to my jaw and the arena is spinning and when it stops I'm sitting on the canvas looking up with one good eye blinking through the blood. I jump to my feet before there is even a count. But before I square off he is all over me again, whamming me in the middle, trying to cut off my wind like he did in Yankee Stadium. He caught me an awful whack like a policeman's stick had socked me across the belly and it doubled me over. My head is knocked to the left, to the right, like it is going to come off my neck. My arms and legs feel like they are made out of lead and I almost topple over. When the bell rang, I ached from head to foot.'

Round four was more of the same, Zale pitching and Graziano catching. Referee Behr had gone over to Rocky's corner to have a close look at the left eye and did not like what he saw. 'If it hadn't been a championship fight, I would not have let him last out the round,' said Behr later. 'His corner pleaded for one more round and I reluctantly agreed. But it was looking bad.'

Knowing the fight could be stopped and his dream of the big title all over, Graziano fought with renewed passion in the fourth round. The blood had been stemmed and he was still in there with a chance. By now, Zale seemed to be tiring and the New Yorker kept up a constant attack, often driving the champion before him. Graziano seemed to have found a second wind and he won both the round and the following session on sheer punching power and non-stop aggression.

Thirty seconds into the sixth round, Rocky landed a solid right to the head that caused Tony's knees to buckle. He recovered fast and shook the Brooklyn battler with a heavy right but Graziano would not be denied. With the crowd on their feet, Rocky sent his opponent reeling into the ropes with lefts and rights. Three more rights to the head sent the champion down for a count of three and when he arose, the hungry challenger was all over him, draping him over the middle strand and pounding him at will. Jimmy Cannon of the *New York Post* counted a total of 36 unanswered punches that landed on Zale before referee Behr moved in and stopped the massacre at 2:10 of the sixth round. Rocky Graziano, the kid from the Brooklyn slums, was the new middleweight champion of the world.

Zale and his team felt that the fight should not have been stopped and when somebody put the question to the referee, Behr asked if everybody was forgetting that three weeks earlier, Jimmy Doyle had died after being beaten by Sugar Ray Robinson in eight rounds in a world welterweight title fight. 'What do you want in the ring, murder?', he said. 'I should have stopped the fight at the end of the fifth because Zale's eyes had ceased to focus. But because he was the champion, I let him go out for the sixth and by then he was a completely helpless target – with absolutely no hope of recuperating.'

Graziano returned to Brooklyn as a conquering hero but soon there were calls from Zale's people that Tony deserved a chance to regain the title, preferably in Chicago, his adopted hometown. Problems arose, however, when news came through that Rocky, already under suspension in New York, would not be allowed to box in Illinois. The state's athletic commission had issued a ruling barring dishonourably discharged servicemen from boxing in Illinois. Atlantic City was then suggested before New Jersey was selected because it was closer to New York fight followers. The venue was the Ruppert Stadium in Newark on 10 June 1948.

Graziano entered the ring as a 12/5 favourite and it showed in his confidence as he made his way towards the ring for what would be the final act of their torrid trilogy. Rocky felt what he did in their last fight he could do again. Promoted by the Tournament of Champions, it would be the first of their three bouts to be captured on film. A crowd of 21,497 turned out, with receipts, including broadcast and motion picture rights, generating a gross gate of $405,646. There was speculation that the winner, expected to be Graziano, would defend his title in

September against the French-Moroccan Marcel Cerdan or Sugar Ray Robinson, who was anxious to move up from welterweight and challenge for the middleweight championship. Both challengers would be big drawing cards.

Both men started cautiously, unlike in their previous encounters, but with a minute to go in the first round Zale stepped in fast and caught Rocky with a solid left hook to the jaw that dropped him to the boards. He was up without a count and waded into Zale, but it was the challenger who came off best in the fierce exchanges. It was clearly Zale's round. The second started just like the opening session, with both men feeling each other out. Graziano fired a left hook that missed but managed to shake his man with a looping right that forced the challenger into a clinch. This was Rocky's round.

The third opened fast before Zale got through with a damaging left hook to the chin that sent Graziano to the deck. He rose on shaky legs before missing with a long left hook that exposed him to another two-handed Zale attack. A big right followed by an equally hard left hook to the jaw sent Graziano down again. Grasping the lower rope, he hauled himself to his feet at the count of seven. Zale was on to his prey again, determined to end it. He caught Rocky with a crunching right to the ribs and followed with a powerful left hook to the jaw. Graziano went down, poleaxed, and lay there, flat as an ironing board, as referee Paul Cavalier counted him out at 1:08 of round three. Rocky had been world middleweight champion for just 11 months.

Nat Fleischer of *Ring* magazine said it was the most thrilling finish since Joe Louis had beaten Max Schmeling in the first round ten years earlier. Zale had now become the first middleweight to regain the title since Stanley Ketchel beat Billy Papke in 11 rounds in 1908. 'On several occasions prior to the finish, Graziano was on the verge of collapse,' wrote Fleischer. 'The cockiness he displayed as he entered the ring, and during the time the introductions were made, was soon battered out of him. Zale has now gained a place among the immortals in the middleweight division.'

Graziano continued his career but would never be far from trouble. Matched with the former world middleweight champion Fred Apostoli on 1 December 1948 in California, Rocky was suspended by the state's athletic commission for running out on the fight. The suspension covered not only California but all the US states, as well as Britain, the European continent, Cuba, Mexico and Canada. He was subsequently pardoned following several appeals and re-instated. Resuming his career, Rocky remained a serious contender with an impressive streak of 20 wins and one draw before getting another chance at the world middleweight title, which was now in the capable hands of Sugar Ray Robinson. The match was scheduled for 16 April 1952 at the Chicago Stadium.

A capacity crowd of 22,264 saw Graziano come out fast, his right hand cocked, ready to land on the elusive champion. He got few chances as Robinson moved swiftly around the ring, keeping out of danger while at the time picking up points. Rocky did connect in a dramatic third round, when a right swing landed on the champion and sent him down on one knee. He was up without a count as Graziano sought the follow-through punch. It never came. Sugar Ray countered one of Rocky's rushes with a perfectly timed right-hand punch that landed on the point of the former champion's chin and sent him down and out at 1:53 of the third round.

'I was sure I could beat Robinson,' Rocky told author Peter Heller in 1973. 'I had him down in the third round. I put everything into that right hand and I let it fly. It seemed that the whole world was screaming, "Come on, Rocky, come on Rocky." All my life, those three words were the sweetest to me. But he got up and won. I think personally that Robinson was the greatest fighter I ever fought. Pound for pound, a fantastic fighter.'

Graziano intended to hang up his gloves permanently after the Robinson fight, even though promoter James D Norris of the

International Boxing Club was anxious for him to continue as he was still a major drawing card. When Norris offered him a ten-rounder against Michigan's Chuck Davey, who was unbeaten in 36 fights, for a $50,000 purse, Rocky felt it was an offer he couldn't refuse. It would be his final ring appearance and took place at the Chicago Stadium on 17 September 1952.

A graduate of Michigan State University and one of television's early stars when the medium was in its infancy over 60 years ago, Davey was a slick southpaw and was expected to give the veteran ex-champion problems with his speed and versatility. That's how it worked out. Graziano's plan was to advance and maintain pressure on his opponent, driving Davey into corners and going for the big punches. It didn't work out like that. Davey refused to stay still, punching and slipping away, catching Rocky with that unerring right jab. Graziano chased his man as the rounds progressed but it was Davey who did the effective scoring. Referee Frank Sikora and all three judges marked their cards in Davey's favour. Newspapermen were almost unanimous in their 8-2 judgement.

With a 67-10-6 record and a place in the history books assured, Rocky announced his retirement at a press conference the following day. He soon became established as a regular TV personality and in the 1960s opened a restaurant in Manhattan called Rocky Graziano's Pizza Ring. He died from heart failure on 22 May 1990 aged 71.

Chapter 10

Blue collar warrior who wouldn't be denied

THE shaven-skulled southpaw from Brockton, Massachusetts was mean, moody, menacing and magnificent. With his cold, grey eyes and fists of destruction at the ready once the bell sounded, Marvin Hagler was one of the greatest boxers of all time. His 12 successful defences of the world middleweight title place him fourth on the all-time list behind Carlos Monzon, Bernard Hopkins and Gennady Golovkin.

It was said that Hagler fought a disbelieving world as well as the best middleweights of his generation. Unlike other 160-pounders before him, he never moved up a division as a contender in a bid to capture a title in a heavier class. Instead, he was content to bide his time for a middleweight title shot. Sidetracked for many years, he trusted nobody and nothing, and battled on year after year, inspired by the grim faith that one day he would make it to the top.

It was Marvin's stubbornness, determination and narrow-mindedness that got him there. 'If they cut my head open, they will find one boxing glove,' he once said. 'That's all I am. I live it.' He boxed in an era of outstanding 147lb and 160lb boxers such as Sugar Ray Leonard, Thomas Hearns and Roberto Duran. A switch-hitter, Hagler could change his style from puncher to boxer and back again to suit the occasion. In 1982, Marvin was so dominant that he was persuaded to add the 'Marvelous' moniker to his name by deed poll and nobody disagreed with the sentiment. 'Nothing can intimidate me,' he once said. 'I just go out to destruct and destroy.'

A diligent conditioner all his life, for six weeks before a big fight, Hagler would take himself off to a place he called his jail. It was a beach hotel among the dunes called the Provincetown Inn, near Cape Cod in Massachusetts. Parts of the building dated back to the early 1900s. The owner was an eccentric entrepreneur named Brook Evans, who liked to accompany Marvin on his early-morning runs on the sand. Hagler would toil there day after day, relentlessly driving himself into shape and harnessing the bitterness that made him the fighter he was. When he was not training, he would sit in his room, staring out across the Atlantic Ocean. In the evening, after his meal, he would watch videos of his opponent or of his own workouts.

George Kimble, esteemed sports columnist with the *Boston Herald*, always credited Hagler, along with Leonard, Hearns and Duran, as the four boxers who saved the sport in the early 1980s. 'By the late 1970s, boxing had lapsed into a moribund state and interest in it was on the wane,' he wrote in *Four Kings*. 'In 1980, however, the sport was resuscitated by a riveting series of bouts involving an improbably dissimilar quartet, Hagler, Leonard, Hearns and Duran. The "Four Kings" of the ring would fight one another nine times throughout the decade and win 16 world titles between them.'

Hagler was considered the best middleweight in the world for several years before he got a shot at the title. One-time world heavyweight champion Joe Frazier once told him, 'You know Marvin, you have three strikes against you – you're black, you're a southpaw and you're damn good.' It was regrettable that on the night Marvin did win the world title in September 1980, a riot followed at Wembley Arena in London, where thugs turned the venue into what one writer called 'a viper's pit of hatred'.

Hagler was born in Newark, New Jersey on 23 May 1954. His father Robert walked out on the family when Marvin was a child, leaving his mother Ida Mae to raise two boys and four girls on social welfare. He grew up in the playgrounds and the streets, 'cruising sidewalks, hanging out, playing sports, boxing shadows, dreaming big,' he once said. 'I always wanted to be somebody. Baseball, I'd play like Mickey Mantle or Willie Mayes. Basketball, I'd be Walt Frazier. Boxing, I'd pretend to be Floyd Patterson or Emile Griffith.'

On 12 July 1967, when Marvin was 13, a riot lasting nearly a week broke out in Newark in which 26 people were killed and $11m in property damage was caused. Young Marvin had initially watched with fascination as looters scurried about on the street below, but when a bullet came through the window his mother ordered her six children to crawl on the floor. They had to go from room to room in that position to avoid exposing themselves to the gunfire. For days, the family were prisoners in their little tenement flat. At the end, the whole ghetto neighbourhoods of the once vibrant city lay in ruins. Buildings were abandoned, garbage and mattresses were strewn in the streets and cars were stripped.

Within two years there was another riot when up to 1,000 blacks roamed the streets, smashing store windows, looting and throwing bottles at police cars. This one lasted only two nights and nobody was killed but several of the tenements, including the Haglers', sustained further damage. There was only one alternative. Within a year, and with the help of a social worker, the family relocated to Brockton, Massachusetts, where Ida Mae had relatives. 'The authorities finally tore down those buildings and until they did, you could see the bullet holes in the walls,' she would remember.

Brockton itself was a city in some decline but people were not shooting themselves on the streets – at least not on a regular basis. The city was put on the map as the birthplace and home of Rocky Marciano, heavyweight champion of the world in the

1950s. Rocky had worked in a shoe factory in Brockton before becoming a professional boxer.

Marvin was always a boxing fan, watching the greats on TV and reading about them in magazines. So it was no surprise when one evening he walked into the gym set up by Marciano and the Petronelli brothers, Goody and Pat, and said he wanted to be a boxer more than anything else.

'I gave him the pros and cons as I would any lad coming in,' remembered Goody. 'I explained that if he did well, it will teach him self-respect and make him a better person, but that there was nothing easy about it. He would have to work hard and get up in the morning and do roadwork. It would cut down on his social life and no matter how good he might be, he was going to get hit and he was going to like it. When I asked Marvin if he still wanted to go ahead, he said, "Yeah – and one day I'm going to be champion of the world." I said, "That's great, kid, and when you're the champion, I'll be your trainer."'

Hagler came back to the gym the next night, and the next, and soon he was progressing faster than many of the other kids there. Goody and Pat put his name down for a bout in a local tournament and he won. Naturally right handed, Hagler fancied a southpaw stance and seemed more comfortable that way. Goody left him alone on the basis that he was happier boxing with his right hand extended. It worked because Marvin had a successful amateur career, losing only two of his 52 contests, including victory in the US Amateur Athletic Union Championships in 1973.

When Hagler and Goody agreed to enter the professional ranks, Marvin's first promoter, Sam Silverman, had initially reasoned that since many managers were reluctant to pit their boxers against southpaws, it might he easier to book fights for a left-handed Hagler. But after three fights, Silverman advised Petronelli to turn him back into a southpaw. 'He's more devastating that way,' said Silverman. Although Marvin would be listed as a southpaw for the rest of his career, he had become virtually ambidextrous. He could and often did befuddle opponents by switching from one hand to another in the middle of a round.

Hagler began to shave his head while still an amateur. The original idea was that it might cause an opponent's gloves to slide off his head, but the combination of the shiny head and a goatee beard vaguely gave him the appearance of Mephistopheles, a character featured in German folklore who originally appeared in literature as the demon in the Faust legend. It was felt that Hagler rather liked the reaction this produced when an opponent sized him up for the first time.

The look, though, would later become fashionable among sporting figures and perhaps most notably in the Kojak television series, which was still somewhat novel in the mid-1970s. As he was making his way towards the ring for one of his early fights, Hagler overheard a couple of fans making a friendly wager on the outcome. 'OK,' one them said, 'I'll take the black Kojak.'

Although Marvin was dominating local opposition, he might as well have been fighting in a vacuum for all the attention he was getting. It was not until he was matched with the rated contender Sugar Ray Seales, another southpaw, that he came to the attention of the general boxing public and the fight media. Seales, born in St Croix in the US Virgin Islands, had been an outstanding amateur with a 338-2 record. Representing America as a light-welterweight in the Munich Olympics of 1972, he had four wins before defeating Bulgaria's Angel Angelov in the final – the only US boxer to win gold in the Games that were marred by the murder of 11 Israeli athletes by Palestinian terrorists.

When he climbed into the ring set up in a television studio in Boston on 30 August 1974, Seales had run up 21 straight wins as a professional, while Hagler's record was 14-0. Before an audience of invited guests, Hagler won the decision over ten rounds to hand Seales his first loss. A rematch was soon arranged, this time in Seales's adopted hometown of Seattle, Washington on 26 November.

While one judge voted 98-96 for Seales, 4-2-4 in rounds, the other two returned identical 99-99 scorecards, leaving the result a draw. Ringside writers felt it was improbable enough for one of the judges to mark eight rounds even, but for two of them to do it in the same fight was considered absolutely flabbergasting. Hagler and Seales would meet for a third time, five years later in Boston, and this time Marvin did not leave the result in the hands of any judges by stopping Seales in the first round.

Hagler suffered his first defeat on 13 January 1976 when losing a disputed decision to the cagey South Carolina middleweight Bobby 'Boogaloo' Watts at Philadelphia's Spectrum Arena, which would shortly become familiar to moviegoers as the scene of Rocky Balboa's battle with Apollo Creed. Marvin appeared to dominate the ten-rounder but referee Hank Cisco called it even and, worse still, both judges scored it for Watts. The decision was so shocking that J Russell Peltz, director of boxing at the Spectrum, was embarrassed.

On his way to the dressing room to console Hagler, Peltz ran into the promoter Sam Silverman sitting forlornly outside. 'Sam, I'm sorry,' said Peltz. 'Ah, I've been around forever,' Silverman replied with a dismissed wave of his hand. 'I'm used to it.' Allen Flexer, the president of the Spectrum, called around to Peltz's office later that night and said, 'How can they do things like this?' The following morning's headline in the *Philadelphia Inquirer* read, 'Welcome to Philadelphia, Marvin Hagler!' *Ring* magazine called it 'a blatant bad decision and as disgraceful a verdict that was an insult to the intelligence of the disgruntled paying public and the sport of boxing itself.' In recalling the fight in his retirement years, Hagler said, 'I won every round and Watts knew it.'

Marvin was back at the Spectrum two months later against the New York-based Willie 'The Worm' Monroe on a night a blizzard hit the gate badly, with only 3,200 turning up. Hagler took the fight at two weeks' notice. The decision again went against him and while it was reported in the Boston newspapers that it was another hometown larceny, most agreed that Monroe, who was trained by the former world heavyweight champion Joe Frazier, did enough to win. Hagler himself thought so, too. 'I've a few things to learn,' he said. 'But I have a feeling Willie already knows them.'

Spectrum owner Peltz would recall, 'In my mind, that remains the only fight Marvin Hagler ever truly lost. Monroe had the best fight of his career. Willie just had one of those nights every fighter dreams about.' Hagler would not lose another fight for ten years, his final ring appearance.

Marvin's next trip to Philadelphia, on 14 September 1976, has been described as the crossroads of his career. He had lost controversially to Watts and Monroe in what is known as the City of Brotherly Love. What would happen against Eugene 'Cyclone' Hart, a local favourite described by *Ring* magazine recently as among the 100 greatest punchers of all time? The feeling was that if he lost to Hart, Hagler would become merely 'an opponent', a test for up-and-coming boxers. This time Marvin took no chances by stopping the Philadelphian in the eighth round. Hagler walked through his opponent's punches as though he was heading through a rainstorm before Hart's corner threw in the towel.

The win over Hart earned Hagler a rematch with Monroe in Boston on 15 February 1977, and with a more conclusive result. In the final three minutes of their 12-rounder, he caught Monroe with a tremendous right uppercut followed by a straight left jab that knocked Willie down. He attempted to rise but fell over just before the count reached ten. Six months later, they met for a third time, this time in Philadelphia, where Hagler crushed 'The Worm' in 1:46 of the second round.

Around this time, promoter Don King set up what he called the United States Boxing Championships. King had come on the scene several years earlier when he staged the famous

Rumble in the Jungle, the Muhammad Ali-George Foreman world heavyweight championship fight in Central Africa, in 1974. Now, three years later, he had the support of the ABC television network, as well as *Ring* magazine, and organised the new tournament which would, in his own words, 'be comprised of the best fighters in the USA'.

Many top boxers were ignored in the selection process, including Hagler, and it would come to light that virtually half the fighters had to sign up exclusively to King and his associates. *Sports Illustrated* endorsed the championships, with the magazine's usually respected boxing writer Mark Kram unabashedly defending both the King team and the tournament. A character known as Flash Gordon, who ran a sheet called *Boxing Beat,* which he sold outside Madison Square Garden for 35 cents a copy, was also brought on board. ABC gave King $2m and handed over another $200,000 in matchmaking fees for two of King's pals. The Petronellis refused to allow Hagler to have any part of it, preferring to go their own way.

'King and his people wanted to take over Marvin's career,' Goody later explained to sportswriter Jack Newfield. 'They insisted my brother and I surrender all rights to Marvin if they let him into the tournament. King would become his new manager if he won. We don't do business that way.' Goody revealed that even after being rebuffed, King attempted a back-door manoeuvre and approached Hagler's mother about persuading her son to gain a spot in the tournament in exchange for dumping the Petronellis. Mrs Hagler refused, saying she did not interfere with Marvin's career.

The US Championships would soon be hit by allegations of rigged ratings, undeserved boxers being 'placed' in their lists, controversial back-handers, rows over contenders being short-changed and ludicrous decisions. On one occasion, after a contentious verdict had gone against Scott LeDoux, the Minnesota heavyweight, LeDoux interrupted Howard Cosell's television interview with the winner, Johnny Boudreaux, by aiming a karate kick at Boudreaux. He missed and instead kicked Cosell's toupee off. Howard quickly tried to replace it and conducted the rest of the interview with his hairpiece on backwards. It could only happen in the crazy world of boxing.

As soon as the FBI started making allegations into the whole set-up, things began falling apart and eventually broke up. When George Kimble, columnist and boxing writer for the *Boston Herald*, was in Dublin for a big fight night in 2008, he remembered, 'I can tell you that *Ring* magazine's reputation was so devastated by the disgrace that it took decades to recover. Several journalists were also tainted by the scandal, among them Mark Kram, who was quietly dismissed by *Sports Illustrated*. Flash Gordon, who ran a boxing sheet, seemed to drop off the face of the earth and hasn't been seen around the boxing world for years.'

Meanwhile, Hagler continued his quest for a world middleweight title fight. Several contenders declined offers to meet him and even some who were down the pecking lists were cautious about tangling with him. Britain's Kevin Finnegan was not one of them. Something of a wild man inside and outside the ring, Kevin is probably best known to many as the younger brother of Chris Finnegan, the 1968 Olympic gold medallist. But he was a capable boxer in his own right. 'Kevin Finnegan belongs to the last days of the dark ages in British boxing when titles changed hands behind closed doors at men-only private sporting clubs in the West End of London,' wrote Steve Bunce in the *Independent*. 'He fought at a time when being the best in Britain and Europe was no guarantee that a world title fight would follow.'

Born in Ive Heath, Buckinghamshire, Finnegan had a successful amateur career. When his brother lost a verdict during the 1967 British ABA Championships at Wembley, Kevin clambered into the ring to protest. The incident was seen live on TV and Kevin was handed an 18-month ban by the ABA 'for bringing the game into disrepute'.

'I never really forgave the authorities for their action,' Kevin recalled. 'I was a marked man after that. I never got any international chances, and some of the verdicts I lost were farcical. I don't like the set-up in amateur boxing anyway. It seems to be run by the Old Boys' Brigade and they're not in touch with realities at all.'

Turning professional at the age of 22 in November 1970, Finnegan had spells as British and European middleweight champion. When he crossed the Atlantic to take on Hagler at the Boston Garden on 4 March 1978, he was no longer a champion but still a strong contender and would subsequently win both his titles back. The city was covered in deep snow with an Arctic wind blowing, and only a sparse crowd of 5,300 fans braved the elements. Promoter Rip Valenti shrugged his shoulders, 'We expected a bigger crowd as the weather wasn't too bad this morning, but it's suddenly changed and here we are, too late for a postponement.'

No betting figures were released but if they had been, Hagler would have been an odds-on favourite. Finnegan was greeted with mild applause while there were roars and cheers for the American. Scowling at the Britisher across the ring as the two boxers awaited the fight announcements, Hagler looked what he was, a man bent on destruction. Finnegan had told the press a week earlier at Freddie Hill's gym in south London, 'I can repeat what Randy Turpin said before he beat the great Sugar Ray Robinson – he's only got two hands.' It's just that Finnegan may have needed a sledgehammer to beat Hagler.

From the first bell, Hagler was on the attack, jabbing and hooking and always getting the inside position. Finnegan used the ring well in the opening round, jabbing the advancing Hagler, but Marvin simply brushed the punches away and kept advancing. Finnegan had cuts under and over his left eye by the second round and he was having difficulty seeing Hagler, let alone scoring. Good corner work allowed the British battler to make a lively start in the third round, when he got his left jab working and became more aggressive, but this was going to be a hard night at the office, and Finnegan knew it.

In the fifth, the crowd rose to Finnegan as he attacked Marvin but towards the end of the round, with his face a mask of blood, he was taking some heavy punishment, though he was still fighting bravely. Two strong right-hand blows actually shook Hagler in the sixth but in the seventh a powerful right from the Brockton fighter opened a bad gash on Finnegan's left cheek and it became apparent that he would not be able to complete the ten rounds. Still, he was always in there fighting and won the eighth on sheer aggression, although there were suggestions that Hagler was taking a breather, knowing the fight was already his. Just before the bell, Finnegan emerged from a clash of heads that resulted in a deep two-inch gash under his left eye, adding to cuts over both eyes and his forehead.

Finnegan's cornermen Freddie Hill and Mickey Duff knew it was futile their man carrying on and pulled him out before the bell was due to ring for round nine. Kevin would need 20 stitches back in his dressing room. 'His cheek was laid open almost to the bone, and he couldn't have carried on,' said Duff, 'but the fans loved him and they want him back as soon as the cuts heal. His purse was £5,000 and he can look for much more in a return.' Under a three-deck heading in *Boxing News*, the report said that 'Finnegan fought superbly against the fearsome Brockton contender'.

Ten weeks after the bout, they fought the return, again at the Boston Garden, although it seemed patently clear that, barring accidents, Hagler would win again. The only consolation for Finnegan was that he was getting 'a purse well in excess of £5,000', according to promoter Rip Valenti. Finnegan said on arrival in Boston. 'I gave Marvin a tremendous battle last time, only for the cuts to hamper me. I aim to do better this time.'

From the opening bell Hagler was on the attack, driving the Englishman back against the ropes with two-handed barrages. 'Finnegan gave Hagler a tremendous battle last time around but in this return fight, he failed to reproduce that form,' reported *Boxing News*. 'He was never in any danger of being floored or halted other than on cuts, but he was fighting uphill all the way after a clash of heads in the opening round reopened old scar tissue on his left cheekbone.'

Finnegan was still able to score effectively with a fine left jab, which he would often turn into a hook, but the American was relentless in his attacks. Finnegan nevertheless kept his composure and was in there fighting from bell to bell. As the rounds went by, however, it seemed only a matter of time before it was all over. Hagler seemed to ease up in the third and fourth rounds, knowing that he had the fight won, but he opened up in the fifth, jabbing with that powerful right hand and hooking and uppercutting with lefts. In spite of it all, Finnegan's sturdy chin stood up well and he was determined to maintain his proud record of never having been on the canvas, either as an amateur or a professional.

The decisive flurry came in the sixth, when Hagler reopened old cuts above and below Finnegan's left eye. The Bucks battler fought back bravely but at the end of the round, cornerman Mickey Duff threw in the towel. 'The important cut was the one-inch break at the corner of the scar on Kevin's cheekbone,' Duff said in the dressing room. 'It was certain to spread further and I didn't want to see him go through that again. Kevin agreed wholeheartedly with the retirement.'

Around this time, an African-American middleweight from Augusta, Georgia named Bennie Briscoe was calling out Hagler's name for all to hear. Some named him 'the Black Robot' but most stuck with 'Bad Bennie'. Bald-headed like Hagler, with his prowling, crouching style, Briscoe was a fearsome slugger who possessed a solid punch in both gloves and was virtually impossible to hurt. He was a professional in his teens and would be battling away when was almost 40. In the 1970s, he had inherited Rubin 'Hurricane' Carter's designation as 'the best middleweight never to win the world title', having come out on the losing end in three challenges for the championship. Briscoe was named 34th in the *Ring Yearbook 2003* list of all-time greatest punchers. Benny never gave anybody an easy night but it was not in Hagler's nature to duck anybody.

The match was made over ten rounds for 24 August 1978 at the Spectrum Arena in Philadelphia and attracted an attendance of 14,950, the largest crowd for a non-championship fight in Pennsylvanian history. Based in Philadelphia, Briscoe got a hero's reception while Hagler, the out-of-towner, was loudly booed. During the instructions from referee Tommy Reid in ring centre, Briscoe, who usually fixed opponents with a menacing stare, turned his back on Hagler and refused even the most basic acknowledgement of his rival.

It started off badly for Hagler. After a sudden clash of heads in the first round, he emerged with blood streaming from a nasty cut above his right eyebrow. There was huge concern in the corner in case the fight would be stopped but by the time the doctor climbed into the ring, the cut had been treated. He was satisfied and allowed the fight to continue.

'It was a bad one,' recalled Goody Petronelli. 'It might have been the worst cut I've ever worked on. Briscoe used that big, bald head of his and split Marvin's skin right open. Before the round was even over, I told Pat to keep the referee and doctor away from the corner because I was afraid they'd stop the fight. The cut was right above the eyebrow and at the end of the round I was up there in the corner even before Marvin got back. I slapped compression right on it and loaded it up with medication and held it there. When the doctor got up there and made me pull the compression away, the blood had stopped. They let the fight continue but I told Marvin to just stay outside and box.'

Once Petronelli staunched the flow of blood, Hagler was careful to keep out of harm's way for the rest of the fight, moving around, jabbing hard with his right and opening up Briscoe's defence. This was one fight in which he could take no unnecessary chances. He was keeping Briscoe guessing, moving one way then the other while keeping that stabbing jab in his opponent's face. 'Bad' Bennie was constantly coming forward, attempting to get under Hagler's long reach, and while he often succeeded with strong uppercuts to head and body, Marvin was still ahead on points.

In the last two rounds, Hagler took risks by slugging with Briscoe but he was still careful enough against one of the world's hardest-hitting 160-pounders. One good punch would reopen the cut over his right eye, so he was keeping those close forays to a minimum. In the final round, Briscoe was looking weak and a left hook knocked him back into a corner. The final 90 seconds saw both fighters go head to head but Hagler came out the strongest. Then came the final bell and referee Reid had no hesitation in walking over to Marvin and raising his right hand in victory. Hagler was the first to admit that it had been a hard-earned victory, but a victory, and an important one, nevertheless.

Briscoe's veteran trainer George Benton, a former world middleweight title contender and later dubbed 'the Professor' because of his coaching skills, said, "We have no arguments. Bennie fought with courage but tired towards the end. Hagler's jab was in his face all evening and Bennie could do nothing about it.' Hagler gave equal praise to Briscoe. 'This man will go down as a legend,' he said, offering to take on Briscoe's mantle as 'the baddest bald-headed fighter in the world'.

Pat Petronelli told the press gathering in the dressing room that the fight confirmed his belief that Hagler was now unofficially the best middleweight in the world. 'Our plan is now nearing completion and it needs just one more fight to cement it,' he said. One of the scribes present was George Kimble. In his report the next day in the *Boston Herald*, Kimble wondered whether Hagler's cautious and careful performance was due to the cut early on, or whether he showed too much respect for the always-dangerous Briscoe. 'All things considered, Hagler emerged from this fight with Bennie's "title" and from now on, people will be calling *him* the uncrowned champion.'

J Russell Peltz, director of boxing at the Spectrum in Philadelphia, thought it was a bit of both. 'You've got to remember that Bennie was 35 years old,' Peltz recalled, 'and in those days that was really old. Briscoe had no legs left, so his only chance would have been if Marvin had stood right in front of him and tried to go toe to toe. Marvin did that in the closing minutes of the last round but never early on. It would have been foolish to fight him [Briscoe] any other way throughout. Many people regarded Marvin as the uncrowned champion at the time but it was a double-edged sword as the managers of the other top-rated fighters seemed determined to avoid or sidetrack him.'

The pressure was now on the reigning undisputed world middleweight champion Vito Antuofermo to sign contracts for a title defence against his number-one contender Hagler. Antuofermo was born in Bari, Italy and his family moved to the US when he was 17. He learned how to fight in the tough streets of New York and before he was 20 had made up his mind to be a professional boxer. When he got into trouble with the police for various misdemeanours and was brought before a local court, the judge declined to put him in jail, instead telling the cop who arrested him to take him down to a gym on Snyder Avenue. 'If he wants to fight, let him learn how to box and have them teach him some discipline,' advised the judge. It was sound counselling because in 1970, a year after he had arrived in the US, Antuofermo won the New York Golden Gloves welterweight title.

Turning professional in November 1971, he ran up an impressive record with only three defeats and qualified for a world middleweight title fight inside eight years. On an open-air card outside the Royal Palace in Monte Carlo on 30 June 1979, Antuofermo outpointed Hugh Corro of Argentina over 15 rounds. The fight was jointly promoted by America's Bob Arum, who ran the Top Rank organisation, and Italy's Rodolfo

Sabbatini. In the main undercard fight, Hagler defeated another Argentine contender, Norberto Cabrera, in eight rounds. Arum had announced that he had agreed with the respective managers that the winners would meet for the title in Las Vegas later in the year. Vegas was by now establishing itself as the centre of world boxing, with major fights taking place in the grounds of hotels and casinos.

Arum was true to his word. On 30 November at Caesars Palace, Hagler, in his 50th professional bout and ninth year of activity, got his long-awaited and deserved chance at the middleweight championship. But much to his chagrin, the fight would not be top of the bill. It would be relegated to the undercard of Sugar Ray Leonard's challenge to Wilfred Benitez for the world welterweight championship, as recognised by the World Boxing Council. Leonard stopped Benitez in the 15th round, when the Puerto Rican's legs gave out. He took the mandatory eight count before referee Carlos Padilla intervened with six seconds remaining.

The two fights were, in fact, part of a TV triple-header, with former WBC champion Marvin Johnson going for Victor Galindez's World Boxing Association light-heavyweight title at the Superdome, New Orleans. Johnson won when he floored Galindez in the 11th round. As referee Jesus Celis started to count, the towel came fluttering in, with Celis waving his hands wide to indicate the fight was all over, 20 seconds into the round. All three fights were shown on giant screens, with the two Las Vegas bouts televised in New Orleans and the New Orleans match shown in Las Vegas by the same method.

Hagler was dismissive of the champion's punching powers and handed out souvenir fly-swatters at the pre-fight conference. Antuofermo dismissed the act as 'cheap publicity'. From the first bell, the fight turned out to be the most exciting of the three. Marvin, a 4/1 favourite, constantly switched from southpaw to orthodox but Antuofermo would say later that Hagler was more effective as a southpaw.

Vito showed impressive strength, ruggedness and courage as he went forward relentlessly. He realised he could not hope to match Hagler's greater speed or boxing ability and opted to force the fight inside. But Marvin could brawl as well as box and took an early lead. By the fifth round, Antuofermo began to get through with rights to the jaw but Hagler looked dominant in the sixth and seventh as he moved smoothly, ramming lefts and rights into the champion's face from both the orthodox and southpaw stance.

Vito punched away with both hands in the eighth, forcing Hagler back against the ropes. Marvin was not looking so effective now as Antuofermo battled his way back into the fight and was looking the stronger of the two in the ninth, jabbing with his left and following through with thumping rights. The fight swung one way then the other in the 10th and 11th rounds, but it was noticeable that Hagler was now landing the most effective punches, inside and outside.

Michael Katz of the *New York Times* felt Hagler had a good lead after 12 rounds. 'Hagler boxed conservatively down the stretch,' he remembered. 'I think it was more than protecting a lead. Remember, at this point, Hagler had never gone 15 rounds and he'd only gone 12 once. He seemed to be husbanding his energy to conserve himself and the more cautious he became, the more Antuofermo came in.'

In the 14th round Antuofermo, cut over both eyes, could sense his title was in danger and charged headlong into Hagler, resulting in a spirited exchange. In the 15th, the two men battled furiously but Hagler caught Vito with several sharp uppercuts that nearly lifted him off the floor. The final bell saw them punching away. It had been a real thriller but the judges' verdicts were still to come. Duane Ford had it 145-141 in Hagler's favour, reflecting the opinions of most ringside observers, but his scorecard was offset by that of Dalby Shirley, who made it 144-142 for Antuofermo. The third judge had it even at 143-143, thus rendering a drawn verdict that allowed Vito to retain his title.

There were howls of disapproval all over the arena and most ringside writers disagreed with the decision. Relatively few, including Dick Young of the *New York Daily News*, said a draw was fair. *Boxing News* said, 'Antuofermo looked fortunate to come out with his title. Hagler was the sharper hitter and there were times when he seemed to be cutting Vito to pieces at long range as he made full use of his six inches reach advantage.' Bob Arum said, 'I promoted both Antuofermo and Hagler but I thought Marvin won at least eight rounds and Vito no more than four.'

Looking back in later years, Michael Katz of the *New York Times* said, 'It was a terrible decision. If they'd had punch statistics back then, they probably would have had Hagler outlanding Antuofermo three to one – and remember, Vito couldn't punch.'

Pat Putnam of *Sports Illustrated* made Hagler the winner. 'Antuofermo's style is neo-caveman,' he wrote. 'Pressure is his game. He simply lowers his head and charges, and once inside, rains blows with unrelenting fury. It is a style that has taken him to the world title. Hagler is a switcher who prefers to fight from a distance, sharp and clean. He wears people down, taking them out with clusters of crushing, crisp combinations. Marvin's strategy was to circle the wagons, to stay out of the corners and off the ropes and, whenever Antuofermo got inside, to tie him up until the referee gave him a pass out of the danger zone. In the end, the decision was astonishing.'

As he left the ring, Hagler was intercepted by Joe Louis. 'You won that fight,' said the former world heavyweight champion. 'Don't give up. You'll get another chance.' In the packed dressing room, Marvin told the gathering of reporters, 'I know I won that fight. Vito knew I won, too. I could see it in his eyes. In my heart, I'm the champ. I did everything right. This result will just put bitterness in me and make be a better fighter. I'll become world champion eventually because that's my dream and that's my destination.'

Antuofermo, who had 26 stitches on his cuts, defended the controversial decision, 'I thought I won but I'm satisfied with the draw because it allowed me to keep my title. I knew I was behind coming out for the eighth round but I felt I was starting to control the fight by the tenth. Yes, I'd be prepared to give Marvin a return fight in all fairness, but that's up to my team and my promoters. I will leave everything to them.'

Hardly had the decision been announced when Bob Arum, standing at ringside, shouted that there would be an immediate rematch, much to the dismay of the World Boxing Council and the World Boxing Association. Alan Minter, the English southpaw, had been promised the next title fight no matter who won in Las Vegas. 'The WBC will not be led by promoters,' said José Sulaimán, the WBC president. 'We will have our convention in a week and we will talk about it. There is no doubt Hagler deserves another chance. But after Minter.'

As expected, it was Minter who got the title fight – leaving Hagler waiting on the sidelines. A southpaw like Hagler, Minter was a crisp hitter and clever boxer who knew his way around the ring. Born in Crawley, West Sussex, he had a distinguished amateur career, winning 90 of his 112 bouts. In the Munich Olympics of 1972, he won a bronze medal at light-middleweight, losing narrowly in the semi-finals to West Germany's Dieter Kottysch, who would go on to win the gold medal. 'Everybody agreed that I was robbed by disgraceful political judging,' Minter would lament. Turning professional in October 1972 with a knockout in six rounds over Maurice Thomas, Minter ran up an impressive 36-6 record, including 22 wins inside the distance, winning British and European titles in the process.

It was on 16 March 1980 that he climbed into the ring at Caesars Palace, Las Vegas to face Antuofermo with Vito's world middleweight championship on the line. It turned out to be a tough, gruelling contest rather than a spectacular one, but it was the Englishman who generally produced the cleaner punches. The Brooklyn-domiciled Italian, a 3/1 favourite, swung and swiped determinedly but his walk-in style seemed to suit Minter, certainly early on.

Antuofermo came on strong in the middle rounds with his aggression, often catching Minter coming in and landing with sharp left hooks to the body. Minter was ahead by the ninth round but he clearly lost the 10th and 11th, when Vito came on strong. The Crawley man did some of his best work in the 12th and 13th rounds as Antuofermo seemed to tire. In the 14th, Minter was dropped for the first time in his career. It was the only knockdown of the fight, although it seemed more of a slip.

In a stirring final round with the crowd on their feet, including the 1,000 British supporters, both contestants went toe to toe up to the bell. With the three judges' votes split, Minter won the decision and became the first British boxer since Ted 'Kid' Lewis in 1917 to travel to America as a challenger and return as champion of the world. Minter punched the air in jubilation then wept with joy during the post-fight interviews. 'I can't put into words how I feel,' he said. 'It was a hard fight but then all 15-rounders are hard. The one thing I always dreaded was a split decision and how I prayed when I heard the announcement.' Antuofermo complained that referee Carlos Padilla did not let him work. 'Every time I got close, he'd break us up,' the ex-champion said. 'I needed to have a referee who understands my style of fighting and this one didn't. They should suspend the two judges who gave Minter the fight. Robbery.'

After several attempts at becoming a top middleweight again, Antuofermo retired from boxing in 1985. Soon afterwards, he began to pursue an acting career. In 1990, he landed small roles in *Goodfellas* as a boxer and *The Godfather Part III* as a gangster. There was a story doing the rounds that during the shooting of a scene with Andy Garcia in *The Godfather Part III*, director Francis Ford Coppola said to Antuofermo to think back to Las Vegas in 1979, when he fought Hagler. 'I did, and punched Andy right on his nose,' he laughed. Antuofermo also had a part in the hit television show *The Sopranos* and has done stage plays.

Today, he owns a successful landscaping company in Long Island, New York.

* * *

Meanwhile, Hagler was watching the Minter-Antuofermo-Sulaimán-Arum scenario from afar. He knew it was only a matter of time, a short time, before he would put his signature on a contract to meet Minter. Boston, Las Vegas, London, Timbuktu – it didn't matter.

After protracted negotiations, the fight was set for Saturday, 27 September 1980 at Wembley Arena, with Arum joining up with British promoter Mickey Duff and Wembley impresario Jarvis Astaire. Surprisingly, Minter was installed an 11/10 favourite, with practically all the British press confidently tipping him to win, much to the puzzlement of the American scribes.

Boxing News correspondent Bob Mee, under a two-page heading 'Minter Will Take Him', said, 'In a desperately hard fight, I would pick Minter on points, or possibly, depending on the ability of Hagler to pace himself, by a stoppage in the last three rounds.' It is easy to be wise after the event, but that forecast, and the views of the home writers generally, seemed somewhat optimistic to say the least considering Hagler's frustration at being sidelined for so long and his mean, moody and menacing kill-or-be-killed streak. Was it being forgotten that Hagler had twice ruthlessly destroyed Minter's countryman Kevin Finnegan only two years earlier, and seemed unbeatable in America?

Two days before the fight, Goody Petronelli drove Hagler over to Wembley to familiarise himself with the venue. 'As we stood there looking at the empty seats,' he said, 'I reminded Marvin that they'd all be full on Saturday night – almost all of them with hostile British fans cheering for Minter.' Goody could hardly have imagined how much he had understated the situation.

George Kimble of the *Boston Herald* remembered, 'Possibly because they had been disappointed so often for so long, British boxing fans didn't need much of an excuse to become over enthusiastic, and Minter himself abetted the jingoistic frenzy in the run-up to the fight when he promised that "no black man is going to take my title." By injecting a whiff of racism into the issue, the champion ensured that Hagler's reception would be nasty.'

The unpleasant atmosphere was defined in the preliminaries when former champion Vito Antuofermo was jeered and booed as he entered the ring to take a bow. There was a substantial presence of the anti-immigrant National Front and gangs were engaging in football chants, with many bearing Union Jacks and dressed in beefeater costumes, the kind seen at the Tower of London. Nor did it help that traders were selling beer by the case. Leigh Montville of the *Boston Globe* recalled, 'I remember standing there in the lobby of the arena watching all these skinheads buying cases of beer, hoisting them on to their shoulders and trudging up the stairs to the balconies. I couldn't have anticipated what was going to happen but I remember thinking that no good was going to come of this.'

The bearers of the lone Hagler banner must have felt apprehensive as the atmosphere built to fever pitch. When Marvin climbed into the ring, he too was booed, being greeted with choruses of 'go home, you bum.' Bob Arum was shocked. 'I never saw anything like it,' the visiting American promoter said. 'It was disgraceful. Up in the stands, it was like a huge drunken orgy.'

Minter was cheered to the skies when he ducked between the ropes and his introduction was inaudible even to the ringside press as the roars drowned out the MC's words. The American anthem was likewise lost amid the boos and whistles. Hagler, who had been obliged to weigh in naked to scale exactly on the division limit of 160lbs, jigged constantly throughout. Minter led the singing of the British anthem, which was bellowed out with such intensity by the capacity crowd that, in the words of one writer, 'it was more of a hymn of hate than an expression of pure patriotism'.

The first bell went and inside 30 seconds a sharp right jab opened a cut beneath Minter's left cheek. The Crawley boxer counter-attacked with a couple of lefts as the crowd chanted 'Minter, Minter'. He even nailed Hagler with a strong left, but the American came back and opened a second cut on Minter's face, this time over his left eye. Minter fought bravely in the second round but it was an uphill battle. The Briton seemed to be fighting desperately now against the smoother skills of Hagler and at the bell, two of the judges had Marvin ahead by a point while the third had Minter in front by the same score.

By the third, it looked like the end was near. Hagler was pressing the attack, rocking Minter with right hooks and occasional left jabs, and the champion's face was a mask of blood. Hagler was now a fighting fury. 'It was as if all the frustrations of his career were being unleashed,' said Leigh Montville of the *Boston Herald*. Many of the hooligans were either so drunk or seated so far from the ring that they couldn't accurately gauge the extent of the damage to Minter's face, and they erupted angrily when referee Carlos Berrocal of Argentina stopped the one-sided fight and led the Englishman to his corner. The time of the finish was 1:45 of the third round.

Hagler sank to his knees, world champion at long last. Initially, there was a great roar before the powder keg exploded. A bottle sailed into the ring, bursting and sending a spray of beer that flashed under the ring lights. It did not take long for the mob to get the same idea. Bottles, full and empty, showered down and splintered on the canvas. Here is how Harry Mullan described it in *Boxing News*, 'The result precipitated a horror scene in which a cascade of beer bottles, cans and coins showered the ring and a racist mob howled obscenities at the black fighter and the referee. For the first time in a British ring, and probably for the first time anywhere, a new world champion had to be rushed from the ring as soon as the fight ended, without even waiting for the official announcement of his victory. It was a shameful, degrading spectacle. A black night for British boxing, one the sport would like to forget.'

Henry Cooper, the former British and European heavyweight champion, who was among the ringsiders, endorsed Mullan's view. 'It was a night of shame for British boxing,' he said in an interview in 1990. 'What should have been one of the most glorious moments in Hagler's life was turned into a nightmare by football-type hooligans among Minter's supporters. Hagler needed a police escort to get to the safety of his dressing room. I had never experienced anything like it in all my years of boxing, and it left me feeling sick to the stomach and fearing for the future of my sport. It made me wonder whether British fair play was a thing of the past.'

Hagler would make 12 successful defences of his world title in total. His 11th defence, against Thomas Hearns, in Las Vegas on 15 April 1985, is considered by many to be among the most memorable boxing matches in history. Hearns, then the world junior middleweight champion, had gone up a weight for the bout. The fight lasted just three rounds but in that time it delivered relentless action, drama and violent exchanges. In the third round, with his face a mask of blood from two bad cuts, Hagler dropped Hearns with a barrage of lefts and rights. Hearns clambered to his feet before the full count was reached, but he was in no condition to defend himself and referee Richard Steele intervened. 'I've been a referee for 15 years,' said Steele later, 'and have never seen such intensity in the ring.'

Hagler's final challenger was John 'The Beast' Mugabi. Born in Campala, Uganda on 4 March 1960, Mugabi had won a silver medal at the Moscow Olympics of 1980 as a welterweight. By the end of the year, he had turned professional under the aegis of Mickey Duff, the British matchmaker and promoter. Boxing mainly in West Germany, Mugabi shifted his operations to the US in late 1982 and settled in Tampa, Florida. When he was matched with Hagler in 1985, he had compiled an impressive 25-0 record, with not one opponent lasting the scheduled distance. The 15-rounder was originally set for November 1985 but rescheduled for 10 March 1986 at the open-air Caesars Palace, Las Vegas after Hagler injured his back in training.

On fight night, it had been raining earlier but while it was bitterly cold, the crowd of some 15,000 anticipated hot action – and got it early. Mills Lane, who refereed the fight, remembered it like this, 'I recall looking over at Hagler in his corner and saw steam rising from his bald head. With the imminent threat of more rain, vendors were selling garbage bags for $10 at ringside. Hagler was one of the most complete packages I've ever seen. He was a natural left-hander with a good right hook but he could switch to a right-handed style with no problem. Mugabi was also a tough customer, and he could knock you dead with one shot.

'He wasn't big as middleweights go but he gave Hagler all he could handle. Mugabi kept the fight close in the early rounds but then Hagler started nailing him with a left-handed lead and kept on the pressure. Mugabi almost went down in both the ninth and tenth rounds but somehow held on. Then in the 11th, Hagler clobbered him with eight or nine straight punches and Mugabi went down and I counted him out.'

Happy as he was in victory, the monster in Hagler would surface. 'I want to beat Carlos Monzon's record of 14 title defences, then I'll retire,' he told the media. 'Then, too, I might get some credit. If I'd lost to Mugabi, it would have been "Goodbye, Marvin." Everybody has been trying to get rid of mean Marvin for years so as a new champion could come on the scene. Everybody wants a new face. Nobody will give me credit until I'm done with the game, but I'm not finished yet.'

* * *

When Muhammad Ali's career began to wane in the late 1970s, boxing desperately needed a new superstar. Sugar Ray Leonard, a compact version of Ali, filled that role. Fast and powerful, Leonard fought with a flash and arrogance that both angered and entertained the fans. Borrowing his nickname from the great Sugar Ray Robinson, it did not take the new Sugar Ray long to prove he belonged with the greats. Named Fighter of the 1980s, he entered the decade a champion and left it a champion.

Born in Wilmington, North Carolina on 17 May 1956, Leonard first captured the public's attention with impressive performances as a light-welterweight in the 1976 Montreal Olympics, returning to the US with a gold medal. His professional debut on 5 February 1977 was televised by the CBS network and drew a record crowd of 10,170 to the Baltimore Civic Center. Leonard won a six-round decision over Luis 'The Bull' Vega and picked up a $40,000 cheque, at the time a record fee for a professional debut, while Vega got just $650.

Sugar Ray would win two world titles, welterweight and junior middleweight, before announcing his retirement in June 1982 following surgery for a detached retina in his left eye. He would return briefly two years later but not satisfied with his performance against the unheralded Kevin Howard, he retired again. Howard had knocked him down in the fourth round before Leonard recovered to stop his man in the ninth. After nearly three years of inactivity, Leonard felt the urge to make yet another comeback – this time against Marvin Hagler for the world middleweight title. Billed as The Super Fight, it was set for 6 April 1987 at Caesars Palace. The World Boxing Association refused to recognise the fight as being for the title because it was unhappy over what it called 'Leonard's suspect left eye' and declared the title vacant.

The World Boxing Council and the International Boxing Federation disagreed and felt Leonard had satisfied its medical people that he was physically fit to go ahead and sanctioned the fight as an official title defence. One way or another, the fight was definitely on but to satisfy everybody it was billed as being for the vacant title, even though Hagler was still seen officially as the world champion whatever the WBA said. 'They're still trying to pull me down out there,' mused Hagler.

The fight drew a capacity crowd of 15,336 and an estimated television audience of 300 million. It was the richest contest in boxing history up to then and Leonard would be attempting to become the tenth boxer to win world titles at three different weights.

By the time the two boxers entered the ring, Hagler was a 5/2 favourite. Of the 67 reporters at ringside, 60 went for Hagler. In the two opening rounds, Marvin abandoned his southpaw style and boxed out of an orthodox stance, seemingly an attempt to take Leonard by surprise. But Sugar Ray was prepared for anything Hagler came up with and won both sessions. In the third round, Hagler switched back to his more normal southpaw stance and had better success, getting through with solid jabs and driving Leonard back with two-handed hooks to head and body. Leonard's superior speed and boxing skill, however, kept him in the fight. But by the fifth, Leonard, who was moving a lot, began to tire and Hagler started to get closer.

Leonard was now clinching more frequently and Hagler continued to score effectively in round six. Leonard, having slowed down, was obliged to fight more and run less. In rounds seven and eight, Hagler's southpaw jab was landing solidly and Leonard's counter flurries were less frequent. Round nine was the most exciting round of the fight. Hagler hurt Leonard with a left cross and pinned him in a corner.

Sugar Ray was in trouble then furiously tried to fight his way out of the corner. The action see-sawed back and forth for the rest of the round, with each man having his moments. Leonard boxed well in the 11th. Every time Hagler scored, Leonard came back with something flashier, if not as effective. In the final round, Hagler continued to chase Leonard, backing him into a corner. Leonard responded with a flurry and danced away with Hagler in pursuit. The fight ended with Hagler and Leonard exchanging blows along the ropes.

The verdict was split, with two of the three judges voting for Leonard, giving him a majority decision. Even the ringside writers were divided over who was the better man, and even today, some three decades on, the controversy has scarcely abated. Hagler would say in his dressing room, 'How can they say I lost when the other guy won't fight? I beat him fair and square and he knows it. He told me so himself. "You beat me," he said. Isn't that enough proof? In my heart, I'm still the champ. The gods up there were always against me, and this proves it once again.'

Leonard called the fight a 'special conflict'. He said, 'To me, Marvelous Marvin Hagler is still the middleweight champion of the world. It wasn't his belt I wanted. I just wanted to beat *him*.' Fight statistics showed that Leonard threw 629 punches and landed 306, while Hagler threw 792 and landed 291.

Hagler requested a rematch but Leonard chose to retire for the third time. Marvin never fought again, finishing with an impressive 62-3-2 record. In 1990, with both well past their best, Leonard, now world super middleweight champion, finally offered Hagler a rematch that reportedly would have earned Marvin $15m, but he declined. By then, Hagler had settled down to a new life as an actor in Italy and was now uninterested in boxing. 'A while ago, yeah, I wanted him so bad, but I'm over that now,' he said. 'While we are on the subject, if you really want to know, Leonard never beat me that night. You never take the title away from a champion on a split decision.'

Chapter 11

Champ with a passion for pigeons

HISTORY may not be kind to Mike Tyson. He alienated the boxing fraternity with his escapades both outside and inside the ring. By the mid-1980s, the sport had forgotten the bad boys of the past and remembered the good guys such as Joe Frazier, Muhammad Ali and Larry Holmes, who restored dignity to the game. Now Tyson ruled boxing's most prestigious weight class as heavyweight champion of the world, a man with not only a troubled past and present but most certainly a turbulent future. He would spend three years in prison on a rape charge and once threw a television set through a window. He was also jailed for a road rage incident.

Tyson had a catastrophic marriage to the actress Robin Givens that ended in predictable and painful divorce. He sacked his long-time trainer Kevin Rooney, who had played such a significant part in his development. He split with his manager and friend Bill Cayton, who along with business partner Jim Jacobs owned a famous fight film collection that helped to heighten Tyson's interest in boxing. Between the ropes, Tyson brought disgrace on himself and the sport when his licence was revoked after he was was disqualified for biting Evander Holyfield's ears in their infamous championship fight in Las Vegas in 1997. Boxing writer and historian Bob Mee believes that Tyson wasted his potential and the opportunity to become the greatest heavyweight of them all. 'He always had the air of a man whose built-in self-destruct mechanism was ticking away,' says Mee.

If ever anyone deserved the title 'The Baddest Man on the Planet', it was surely Mike Tyson. Yet what must not be forgotten is that in his prime, Tyson, with his frightening knockout power and intimidating glare, ruled the division with an iron fist. Boxing people put him up there with legends like John L Sullivan, Jack Dempsey, Joe Louis and Rocky Marciano, all big hitters. Tyson unified all three world championship belts, those of the World Boxing Council , World Boxing Association and International Boxing Federation, at a time when they were fragmented and adding confusion to the sport.

In 1986, at the age of 20 years and four months, 'Iron Mike' became the youngest world heavyweight champion in history, a record he still holds. Tyson, a native New Yorker, was so intimidating and such a concussive puncher that many of his opponents were defeated before the first bell. Refusing to wear a robe or boxing socks, he was a portrait of menace as he climbed into the ring adorned in plain black trunks and black boots, and equipped with the most powerful fists in boxing. He was a godsend to boxing when the sport was looking for an exciting young heavyweight to replace the retired Muhammad Ali.

Born the youngest of three children on 30 June 1966, Michael Gerard Tyson barely knew his father Jimmy Fitzpatrick, who moved out of the family home in the rough Bedford-Stuyvesant district of Brooklyn, New York when Mike was ten. The children were raised by their mother, Lorna Tyson. She and Jimmy had never married and Lorna gave all the children her maiden name. When Mike was still very young, the family moved to an even tougher area, nearby Brownsville, another high-crime locality but where the rent was lower.

'You could feel the difference,' Tyson remembers. 'The people were louder, more aggressive. It was a very horrific, tough and gruesome kind of place. My mother wasn't used to hanging around those types of black people and she appeared to be intimidated. So were my brother and sister. Everything was hostile. There was never a subtle moment. Cops were always driving by with their sirens on. Ambulances were always coming to pick up somebody. Guns were always going off, people getting stabbed, windows being broken. One day, my brother and I were robbed right in front of our apartment building.'

Boxing people believe Tyson's ghetto childhood left an indelible mark on him, a lifelong sense of insecurity. Explosive violence was the most effective means of self-assertion. Paradoxically, the unruly lad with the ready fists had a softer side – his attachment to the pigeons he kept in a loft, perhaps an antidote to the pressures of the street. He stayed calm with these symbols of peace. It was when a bigger boy pulled the head of one of Mike's beloved birds that he first discovered his power. He set about the boy in a fury and beat him up.

By the time Tyson was 13, he had been roaming the streets and was picked up by the police 38 times, for crimes ranging from pickpocketing to armed robbery. He was in and out of a succession of juvenile detention centres and medium security facilities before ending up in the Tryon School for Boys, a correctional centre in Johnstown, New York, where he could be detained until he was 18. There, he came under the influence of Bobby Stewart, a counsellor and former professional welterweight boxer who was the school's athletic coach. Stewart could see Mike's potential. Tyson was an awesome physical specimen, and already a heavyweight, weighing a muscular 200lbs. Stewart encouraged the wild youngster to put on the gloves and promised he would teach him the rudiments of boxing in return for cooperation in class.

During his time at the Tryon School, his mother died. Tyson was 16. 'I regret to this day that I never saw my mother happy with me and proud of me for doing something,' he remembered. 'She only knew me as being a wild kid running the streets, coming home with new clothes that she knew I didn't pay for. I never got a chance to talk to her or know about her. She detested violence in all forms. She was a very gentle and timid person. I had only my sister to play with because my brother was five years older, so I guess I picked up a lot of gentle, sort of effeminate habits [from her]. In fact, when I was a kid, they used to call me a little fairy boy. My mother's death had no effect on me professionally but it was crushing emotionally and personally.'

Stewart continued to coach Tyson and had him enrolled in the USA Junior Olympics, America's most visible youth athletic development programme, in 1981 and 1982. In both competitions, Tyson won gold medals and holds the world record for the quickest knockout in Junior Olympics when he flattened Kelton Brown after eight seconds of their contest in 1982. Tyson had hoped to represent the USA in the heavyweight division in the summer Olympics of 1984 in Los Angeles, but dropped two controversial decisions to Henry Tillman, the second one in the Olympic trials. As a result, it was Tillman who made it on to the team and ended up winning the gold medal. Six years later, their paths would cross as professionals.

It was around this time that a friend of Stewart named Cus D'Amato came into Mike's life. D'Amato was a famous 72-year-old boxing manager and trainer who had a gym in the Catskills in Upper State New York. Stewart reasoned that if D'Amato took over the young Tyson, it would mean that Mike could be released from the Tryon School and enrolled in the Catskill High School under D'Amato's care. Although Stewart had not yet put the proposition to D'Amato, he felt Cus would agree.

The seventh of eight sons from the Bronx in New York, D'Amato went into the army in the mid-1930s and became a boxing coach, later a sergeant. By his own admission, he fell in love with the noble art as a child when he got into fights with neighbourhood kids. He decided to learn as much as he could about boxing so he could take care of himself. 'Boxing,' he would repeat again and again, 'is a contest of character and ingenuity.

The boxer with more will, determination, desire and intelligence is always the one who comes out the victor.' D'Amato worked out of the Gramercy Gym on 14th Street and honed young boxers in the finer points of the sport. It was said that the role he played in the gym was that of a master sergeant ordering his soldiers around. Cus commanded his boxers rather than advised them.

A number of good boxers worked out at the Gramercy Gym as it was one of the best known in New York. One who trained there from time to time was a raw newcomer named Rocky Graziano, who would become middleweight champion of the world inside a few years. But the two fighters always associated with D'Amato were Floyd Patterson and José Torres. He became their trainer/manager and guided both to world titles – Patterson to the heavyweight championship and Torres to the light-heavyweight title. Both had also excelled as amateurs in the Olympics, with Patterson winning gold as a middleweight in Helsinki in 1952 and Torres capturing silver at light-middleweight in Melbourne four years later. As it happened, both also later became chairman of the New York State Athletic Commission.

In the 1980s, D'Amato was running a small gym over a police station in the Catskills, not far from a 14-room house where he lived with his lifelong companion, Ukranian-born Camille Ewald, whose sister had married one of Cus's brothers. Cus was still very much interested in boxing and always had the dream of finding another young boxer he could develop into a champion. When Stewart called him and said he wanted D'Amato to look over a kid he felt had great potential, Cus agreed. The next day, Tyson walked into D'Amato's gym and, as Cus recalled later, 'I was looking at a future heavyweight champion of the world.'

D'Amato's association with Tyson brought the veteran boxing figure back into the spotlight. Newspapers and magazines began writing favourable pieces about them and forgot about D'Amato's unwarranted 'protection' of Floyd Patterson when Floyd was world champion in the 1960s. They had accused D'Amato of dodging or delaying title defences on behalf of his boxer. Now all was forgotten. Cus promised he would make Tyson his third world champion. D'Amato worked constantly in the gym with Mike and the pair shared a seemingly unbreakable bond.

After Tyson's mother died in 1982, D'Amato became Tyson's legal guardian. Mike was 16. Under D'Amato's care and guidance, Tyson experienced stability and a structured existence for the first time. Cus treated him like a son, always making sure he had warm clothes in winter time and food on the table. DAmato's pet hobby was reading biographies of all the world's great leaders, and he filled young Tyson with tales of what could be achieved with the right attitude and discipline.

To get Mike started, D'Amato got the finance together from two wealthy backers, Jim Jacobs, a former handball champion, and Bill Cayton, a one-time New York advertising executive. Both owned a huge library of fight films going back nearly 100 years that were featured in the long-running TV documentary series *The Great Fights of the Century*. Tyson watched open-mouthed as the images flickered on the screen – Jack Johnson's win over James J Jeffries, Jack Dempsey knocking out Georges Carpentier and Luis Firpo, Joe Louis's two dramatic fights with Max Schmeling and Sonny Liston's rise and fall against Floyd Patterson and Muhammad Ali.

The trio came up with the idea of Tyson entering the ring in black shorts and boots, without socks, just like Dempsey. The attire would be several cultures away from the tasselled, designer shorts and colourful robes used by modern champions but it would give their fighter a look of menace, one of kill-or-be-killed. Teddy Atlas, a respected coach from New York and son of a doctor, had also been employed to assist D'Amato in the training of their young heavyweight prospect.

Together, they taught Tyson all the classic bobbing and weaving movements that are so vital to allow a boxer to move in close to an opponent without getting hurt. They did not need to show Tyson how to punch. That came naturally. However,

Atlas and D'Amato fell out over a personal matter and Kevin Rooney, another New Yorker, was brought in as a replacement. A former professional boxer with a 21-4-1 record, Rooney picked up where Atlas had left off.

After the disappointment of failing to make the 1984 Olympics, Tyson yearned to turn to the paid ranks. He had no intention of waiting around for the 1988 Olympics, scheduled to take place in Seoul, South Korea, and in any case he wanted to make some money.

Tyson made his professional debut on 6 March 1985 in Albany, New York when he knocked out Hector Mercedes in 1:47 of round one. Before the year was out, he had run up an impressive 15-fight winning streak, including 11 knockouts in the first round. Boxing writers and fans alike were beginning to take notice of the explosive teenager who was being guided by Floyd Patterson's former mentor.

Sadly, D'Amato died of pneumonia eight months later and never got to witness Tyson's subsequent domination of the world heavyweight scene. Tyson said his last farewell to D'Amato on 4 November 1985. It is the belief of many experts that the turning point in Tyson's life was D'Amato's passing. Mike still had a strong management team in place as well as a respected trainer, but D'Amato had been very much a father figure to him, the father he never had growing up. Cus was not only his mentor but his best friend. Whenever he had a problem, D'Amato was always the first person he would turn to for sound advice. Now it looked as though Tyson had nobody to properly guide him or take care of him. It was a concern, especially as Mike was something of a loose cannon, ready to explode at any given time. The boxing world waited, hoping for the best but still concerned about the future.

Tyson, meanwhile, continued his rampage through the heavyweight ranks. A powerful knockout puncher with both hands, Tyson had an almost barbaric approach to boxing. He would later say in a quote that he subsequently tried to dismiss as a joke, 'I try to catch him [the opponent] right on the tip of the nose, because I try to push the bone into the brain.' The purists were shocked.

This was not the way boxers went about their business. Sure, Muhammad Ali boasted and bragged about what he was going to do with opponents but it was usually done, with the very odd exception, with tongue in cheek. Tyson's comment was something entirely different. Those close to him, including his trainer and management team, would say that Mike was not joking, or anything of the sort. He really meant it, and opponents had better watch out.

Tyson continued his winning run with 11 more victories up to September 1986, with only two opponents lasting the scheduled distance. His 27th win, over the former WBC cruiserweight champion Alfonzo Ratliff in his first appearance in Las Vegas, qualified Tyson for a world heavyweight title fight. The man in the opposite corner would be Trevor Berbick, the World Boxing Council champion. This would be Tyson's first real test, at least on paper. The match, promoted by Don King, was set for the Hilton Hotel, Las Vegas on 22 November, the 23rd anniversary of President Kennedy's assassination. While most of the country would be commemorating the day with solemnity and sadness, in this self-absorbed city of entertainment, gambling and razzmatazz, it was all Tyson and Berbick. The memories of Kennedy, Lee Harvey Oswald and Jack Ruby did nothing to diminish the hoopla.

Born in Jamaica, where he started boxing, Berbick represented his country in the 1976 Montreal Olympics. He had only had 11 bouts previously and his lack of experience was evident throughout the early stages as he was beaten by the eventual silver medallist Mircea Simon of Romania. But Berbick received a lot of praise as a promising young heavyweight and vowed to continue – but this time in the professional ranks. Berbick moved to Canada soon after, settling in Montreal and then Halifax.

Turning professional in 1976, Berbick won his first 11 professional fights, ten inside the distance, before suffering his first defeat against another rising contender, Bernardo Mercado from Colombia, whom he had beaten as an amateur. All the evidence was that Berbick had a strong chin but with the first punch of the fight, Mercado landed a right hook and knocked him cold in ten seconds. It would be the only time Berbick was counted out in his career.

Berbick went on to challenge Larry Holmes for the world heavyweight championship in April 1981. He lost but had the satisfaction of being the first man to take Holmes the full distance. Three months later, Berbick won the Commonwealth title by knocking out Conroy Nelson in two rounds. Later that year, he beat a pathetically inept Muhammad Ali over ten rounds in the Bahamas in what was Ali's last fight. In March 1986, Berbick caused an upset by winning the WBC title from Pinklon Thomas on a unanimous points decision and, by all accounts, looked a formidable opponent for the rising Tyson.

As champion, Berbick announced he would be wearing all black, Tyson's trademark attire, hoping to force the challenger into wearing another colour. In the end, Tyson wore his usual black anyway. Commission rules stipulate that both boxers cannot wear the same colours for the purpose of identification on TV so Tyson, as challenger, was risking a fine. It was Berbick who won the fashion stakes by wearing a spectacular, floor-dusting black hooded robe. He also made a statement about Tyson's no-socks look by wearing knee-length black socks himself, which he had bought just hours before the fight.

Berbick had Angelo Dundee, Ali's former trainer and mentor, in his corner, having failed to come to a financial agreement with his usual cornerman, the knowledgeable 75-year-old Eddie Futch, who had guided the likes of Joe Frazier, Ken Norton and Larry Holmes to the world heavyweight title. The problem was that Dundee, one of the best strategists in the business, had had fewer than four weeks to get his fight plan together.

Futch shrugged off the summary dismissal of his services and gave his expert analysis on how the fight could go. 'Trevor has the nerve, the equipment and the ability to win but it all depends on which Trevor Berbick gets into the ring,' he said. 'He is never the same fighter two contests in a row. The important thing is for him to stay off the ropes and out of corners. He must dictate the fight from the middle of the ring and keep backing up Tyson and not let him get to close quarters. Many of Tyson's opponents freeze up and wait to be slaughtered. If the right Berbick gets into the ring, he won't be intimidated and has the best chance.'

Dundee predicted at the weigh-in, 'Tyson is going to find Berbick much tougher opposition than the ones he's been knocking over. He'll be sliding this way and that, going from side to side and taking Tyson's momentum away. I think he'll stop Tyson late in the fight.'

At the bell, Tyson came out fast from his corner, taking the fight to the champion. Berbick stood his ground and attempted a left hook but Tyson got there first and drove his man back. Berbick tried a right uppercut but it was short as Tyson moved in with a cluster of punches. Berbick kept looking for an opening that never came. Tyson landed two heavy rights to the head and Berbick was forced to hold on. Mike was now the Great Dictator, the All Conqueror. He was fighting like a man possessed. A powerful left hook from long range sent the Jamaican staggering back across the ring as Tyson followed him. When they came together, Berbick held with both hands and as Tyson was attempting to shake him off, the bell clanged and referee Mills Lane separated them.

Tyson began round two with a tremendous overhand right to the chin that sent the champion reeling backwards as though a carpet had been pulled from beneath him.

Another big right turned him completely around like a spinning top before he was sent crashing to the floor. Dazed and hurt, Berbick was up with only three seconds of the mandatory eight count gone but was on shaky legs and hanging on desperately.

Tyson was now out for the kill. With about a minute left in the round, he dropped the champion for a second time with what seemed only a grazing left hook to the temple. Berbick tried to haul himself up by the ropes but fell backwards again before rising. He lurched forward but collapsed for a third time before zig-zagging to a corner as referee Lane ended the bizarre walkabout at 2:35 of the second round. 'Berbick's last dance as champion had the look of a death rattle,' said José Torres, the former world light-heavyweight champion now at ringside in his new role as a boxing writer and author. Mike Tyson had become new heavyweight champion of the world, the youngest ever, at 20 years and four months.

'I saw fear in Berbick's eyes when we first came into the ring,' said Tyson at the post-fight conference. 'I knew I'd get him, and quick. Winning this title is the moment I waited for all my life.' In October 2006, 20 years after the fight, Berbick was murdered outside a church in Norwich, Jamaica by his nephew over a land deal dispute.

Meanwhile, boxing writers were taking a closer look at Tyson, who was something of a phenomenon. Sure, he was the youngest heavyweight champion but he was also one of the smallest at 5ft 11ins. Only Rocky Marciano, at 5ft 10ins, and Tommy Burns, at 5ft 7ins, were shorter. His weight of 221lbs was within the modern range. His short legs were strong enough to move his immensely muscled body around the ring quickly. Tyson's most noticeable feature was his thick neck, which looked like it was bolted on to his body. While it was still untested, it looked well capable of absorbing most of the force of any blow to the head. Tyson's physique gave him terrific power in his punch and he had also great hand speed. Equally, he had the confidence that had been instilled in him by D'Amato.

Less than four months after taking the title from Berbick, Tyson returned to the Hilton Hotel, Las Vegas, to face rival champion James 'Bonecrusher' Smith, from Magnolia, North Carolina, on 7 March 1987. Smith was anything but a stereotypical heavyweight having earned a bachelor's degree in business administration before becoming a boxer. Turning professional in 1981 at the late age of 28 to help feed his young family, he ran up an impressive record and gained international recognition when he met Britain's unbeaten heavyweight hope Frank Bruno at Wembley in May 1984. Trailing on points going into the tenth and last round and heading for defeat, Smith opened up with a desperate barrage of punches that sent Bruno down and out for what would be the first and only knockout defeat of his career.

Against Tyson, Smith possessed enormous advantages in height, reach and weight but it was Tyson who entered the ring as an 8/1 favourite. Tyson was already the World Boxing Council champion and this fight was also for Smith's World Boxing Association title. To the surprise of most, the battle of the big punchers went the full 12 rounds. With Smith holding like a limpet at every opportunity, Tyson was constantly forced to pull himself free from his opponent's clutches.

At the final bell, the result was inevitable. Tyson had won by a landslide on the cards of all three judges. Criticised by the media at the post-fight conference for failing to knock out Smith, Tyson said, 'How can you fight somebody who is hanging on and holding for dear life? This is showbusiness and people want a performance, but Smith fought only to survive. He was there not to win but to be on his feet at the finish.'

Tyson's dream now was to unify the heavyweight championship. After stopping Pinklon Thomas in six rounds in May 1987, he met Tony Tucker, unbeaten in 34 fights and holder of the International Boxing Federation title. The match was set for the Hilton Hotel, Las Vegas for 1 August 1987. Promoter Don King trumpeted, 'Not since the days of Muhammad Ali has there been one king on the throne, one champion to respect and admire as the greatest heavyweight on God's earth. Now we are clearing up the mess of all these champions, just like I promised we would, and after this fight we will have just one man to whom we shall bow the knee. Glory hallelujah!'

King was conveniently forgetting one thing. Unbeaten Michael Spinks was considered by most as the best contender around, having beaten America's great white hope, Gerry Cooney, on a fifth-round stoppage. But Spinks had refused to do business with King, who wanted him to take part in his so-called elimination tournament to find an undisputed champion. Tyson had to go the full 12 rounds against Tucker but he won the unanimous decision. Tyson said after the fight, 'He gave me great pain in the first round when he trod on my toe. It broke my toenail and my right foot was throbbing throughout the fight. By the halfway stage, I knew I would get him. He gave me my toughest fight. He took some good shots and came back very well. One time he got cocky and gave me the Ali shuffle and that made me more determined to win the fight.'

There was now just one champion, Mike Tyson, but it was generally accepted that the true unification fight would have to be against Spinks to settle all differences. Butch Lewis, Spinks's promoter, said, 'If that's the best Tyson can do, then he can kiss his titles goodbye. He is made for Michael's left hand, and I can see him in all kinds of trouble with my man's lethal right uppercut.' The hype had started and the official unification bout would have to happen. It's just that Spinks was in no great hurry to accommodate Tyson, so Mike was happy to pick up easy money against other opponents.

Tyson stopped Tyrell Biggs, the 1984 Olympic super-heavyweight gold medallist, in seven rounds in October 1987 in Atlantic City, New Jersey. Three months later, again in Atlantic City, he came up against the former great world heavyweight champion Larry Holmes, who was then 38. Before the fight, Holmes accused Tyson of using what he called 'dirty, gutter tactics' at every opportunity. 'He hits after the bell, butts with his head, uses his elbows and hits opponents when they are down,' he proclaimed. 'If he tries any of those tricks with me, I can be just as dirty.' It was all over early. The fight was stopped in Tyson's favour with five seconds of the fourth round remaining, with Holmes down three times in the round.

Tyson had invited three beautiful women to ringside to see the fight – the US sitcom star Robin Givens, British model Naomi Campbell and the reigning Miss America, Suzette Charles. He invited them back to his hotel later for drinks. Two weeks later, having already collected his $10m cheque, he married Robin in a secret ceremony attended only by a few close friends. It was now that Tyson's personal life was about to fall apart like a house of cards. His co-manager Jim Jacobs was not at the fight as he was in New York's Mount Sinai Hospital, seriously ill with leukaemia, which he had been battling for eight years. He died two months later. Earlier, Tyson had signed a contract that in the event of Jacobs's death, the latter's associate, Bill Cayton, would become his sole manager, with Jacobs's widow continuing to share a one-third interest in Tyson's ring earnings.

Robin Givens resented this arrangement and, with the assistance of her businesswoman mother, began to take a strong interest in her husband's finances. Cayton was served legal papers alleging that Tyson was duped into the signing, not knowing Jacobs's condition. Conspicuous at Jacobs's funeral, the scheming Don King, who had a strong interest in most of the heavyweights of the day, now began a concerted campaign to take over Tyson's contract. Meanwhile, a mere five months after Tyson's wedding, Givens's sister revealed that Mike had abused his wife, who suffered a miscarriage.

In the middle of all this turmoil, Tyson managed to fit in a title defence against Tony Tubbs, a Californian by way of Ohio, in Tokyo on 21 March 1988. Tubbs was not expected to provide any serious opposition but Tyson wanted to keep busy while waiting for negotiations to be completed for the big showdown with Michael Spinks. True to form, there was only one man in it and it was not Tubbs. Allowing the challenger a honeymoon period in the first round, Tyson opened up in round two and Tubbs didn't know whether he was in Tokyo or Timbuktu. After a blitz of punches from both hands, a left hook wobbled Tubbs like a drunk before he hit the floor. Referee Arthur Mercante had seen enough and waved his hands wide after 2:54 of the round.

Meanwhile, arrangements were set in motion for the long-awaited match with Spinks. It was finally set for the Convention Center, Atlantic City on 27 June 1988. Yet questions were still being asked: Was Tyson in the right frame of mind to take on the formidable Spinks? Was the turmoil in his personal life getting to him? Should he not have waited until his head had cleared and then signed for the fight? Or was it all too late? Tyson told reporters that he would answer them in the most important place – the boxing ring.

Born in St Louis, Missouri, Spinks was a class act. In the 1976 Olympics, he became middleweight champion, one of five Americans to win gold at the Montreal Games, including his light-heavyweight brother Leon, who would go on to win the world heavyweight title in 1978 by defeating Muhammad Ali. Michael accomplished what no other light-heavyweight had ever been able to achieve and that was to move up a division and win a heavyweight title. Historians would note that around the turn of the 20th century, England's Bob Fitzsimmons also held both titles, as well as the middleweight championship, but the Cornwall boxer was heavyweight and middleweight champion *before* winning light-heavyweight honours.

Spinks is rated by both the International Boxing Research Organisation and BoxRec as being among the ten best light-heavyweight champions of all time. With an impressive record of 31 wins in 31 fights, he looked capable of testing Tyson, even beating him, particularly bearing in mind the trouble and chaos in Mike's personal life.

Tyson entered the ring in his usual all-black attire, without a robe or socks. He looked menacing as he prowled around, intent and pent-up during the preliminaries, acknowledging familiar faces at ringside, including Donald Trump, the future president of the United States. Spinks came into the ring dressed in a white dressing gown trimmed in black, looking confident, and knelt in his corner to pray. Finally, referee Frank Cappuccino called both boxers together for the pre-fight instructions, greeting them with words not usually heard from referees, 'Good evening, gentlemen.'

At the bell Tyson came out fast, like an unstoppable tank, and landed a high right to the head. Surprised at the quick start, although he should not have been, Spinks jabbed once, twice, three times but each punch was short of the target. He tried a looping right that he called his 'jinx punch' and which had accounted for many of his opponents. Tyson ignored it and let fly a straight right that landed high on Spinks's forehead. The former Olympic champion was stunned for a moment but the blow had not hit the right spot. Still, unable to escape the relentless pressure of a stronger, charging opponent, Spinks looked for refuge by staying close to the champion and attempted to hold.

Tyson shook him off and, backing Spinks to the ropes, he let loose a left uppercut that jolted the challenger's head back. This was followed by a thumping right to the body and Spinks sank to his knees. He got up at two but his face was clouded with doubt while Tyson's own face had 'bad intentions' written all over it. Spinks tossed a right, more in hope than anything else, but Tyson walked inside it and fired his own right to the point of Spinks's jaw. Spinks crashed back as though he had been shot and hit the canvas, his right elbow pressing hard over his right ribs.

He would have only heard in the misty distance Cappuccino starting to toll the ten-second count. At four, he rolled over on his side and tried to rise as Tyson made an unnerving sign to Spinks's voluble manager Butch Lewis down at ringside by running his glove across his throat. The executioner had done his job. Spinks was still trying to get up as the count reached ten. The time of the knockout was 91 seconds flat.

Not only had Tyson established himself officially as the world's best heavyweight but his unification win was the fourth fastest finish in the history of the division. Afterwards, he delivered another knockout blow – to the media. Admitting he was clearly unhappy with the treatment he had received in the previous months, he said, 'I wasn't too appreciative of what you did to me. You tried to embarrass me, you tried to embarrass my family, you tried to disgrace me. Some of you are my friends, some of you are *******. All my life has been chaos. Since I was 12, I was groomed for this. I knew what you would do to me. But my job has to be done regardless of what happens in the ring.' He ended by saying what few, if any, would have disputed, 'There's no fighter like me. I can beat any man in the world.'

Spinks, two weeks short of his 32nd birthday, was left to count his $7m purse while Tyson's take was around $22m. 'I came to fight like I said I would,' Spinks told the media gathering. 'I wasn't intimidated at all. If I was afraid, I wouldn't have turned up. I felt 100 per cent going into the ring. I just got caught. I've no excuses.' He refused to be drawn on Tyson's apparent level of dominance in the heavyweight division. 'There's always somebody on earth that can beat someone else. Nobody is invincible.'

How good was Tyson? It was being said that he had not been fully tested, though newspaper columnists and magazine writers heaped praise on him. The historian and boxing writer Bob Mee wrote after the Spinks fight, which he attended, 'Tyson's place as one of the great heavyweight champions in history is becoming increasingly certain with each defence, and his performance against Spinks might just go down as his most awesome of all.' *Ring* magazine joined in the praise, 'Tyson is a reminder of the great days of Dempsey, Louis and Marciano.' *Boxing News* said, 'It's hard to see anybody around the scene at the moment who could take him more than even a few rounds. Spinks was steamrolled by a man at the top of his form.'

There was trouble ahead, however, with issues in his private life going from bad to worse. Scheduled to meet Frank Bruno at Wembley, London on 24 June 1988, Tyson's personal problems caused a succession of postponements and changes of venue, which kept the Londoner, a model of persistence and hard work, hanging around for what would be eight months. In that time, Tyson suffered a litany of private and personal disasters.

They included (a) indulging in a street fight with former opponent Mitch Green and fracturing his hand; (b) driving his wife's BMW into a tree, which some believed was a suicide bid; (c) causing a scene in a Moscow television studio where his wife was filming and chasing her and her mother through a hotel lounge; (d) threatening to hang himself; (e) smashing a TV camera whose crew had been filming him in training; (f) sitting with his wife on a TV chat show as she confirmed many of the stories and said he was a manic-depressive; (g) smashing up his mansion and ordering his wife and mother-in-law out into the street; (h) signing an exclusive promotional contract in defiance of his manager Bill Cayton; (i) sacking his trainer Kevin Rooney, who had been with him all his professional career, because he supported Cayton; (j) accused by two women of sexual harassment; and (k) flying to the Dominican Republic in Don King's plane to finalise his divorce, his marriage having lasted one year and eight days.

Finally, on 25 February 1989, Tyson climbed into the ring to meet Bruno, not at Wembley as originally planned but at the Las Vegas Hilton. It was the sixth date set for the fight in eight months. No world champion in any division in boxing history had ever had such a stormy, muddled and confused build-up to a championship defence.

Born in Hammersmith, west London, Bruno was a good boxer with a solid punch in both gloves. His only problem, and it was a big one, was an apparently suspect chin. His first attempt at becoming Britain's first world heavyweight champion of the 20th century in July 1986 when, after being behind on points against Tim Witherspoon, he was stopped in the 11th round at Wembley Stadium. Nine years later, he would finally win the title by outscoring Oliver McCall, again at Wembley.

Over the years, Bruno never lost his popularity, remaining a much-loved character throughout his career. He enjoyed a passionate British following and not since the days of Henry Cooper a generation earlier had the nation taken a boxer to its heart in quite the same way. Now he was going in against the formidable Mike Tyson. Had Bruno a real chance? The experts said 'No,' even taking into consideration the Londoner's heavy punch and the fact that Tyson would most likely be rusty, having been out of the ring for eight months due to his unsettled personal circumstances. But it was wishful thinking.

During all the preliminaries Bruno looked impressively calm, keeping his eyes locked on Tyson as the champion prowled the ring perimeter. 'Iron Mike' made an explosive start as a booming right to the head caused Bruno to lose his footing. Tyson moved in quickly and sent the challenger jerking backwards, his composure gone, his legs out of control, and down on to one knee. Tyson landed a full-blooded right while Bruno was still on the canvas for the mandatory eight count but incurred no warning from referee Richard Steele. Yet on resuming, Bruno was soon cautioned for rabbit punching. Towards the end of the round, Bruno rocked Tyson with a terrific left hook followed by a jarring right uppercut. Ringside writers would agree later that had the Englishman followed through, he might well have put Tyson down and out, but Mike held on until his head cleared and landed a stray elbow into Bruno's face.

Bruno never got another chance. As the rounds passed, Tyson gradually shook off the effects of his enforced inactivity. He bombarded the Britisher with hooks and uppercuts, and landed a strong right after the bell to end the third round, which brought boos from the crowd. In the early rounds, Bruno had been able to push the smaller Tyson away in the clinches but by the fourth, the New Yorker's powerful body blows were draining his strength. In the fifth, Tyson cut loose with a series of hammer blows before two final right uppercuts reduced Bruno to helplessness and referee Steele moved in to rescue him just as manager Terry Lawless threw in the towel. The time of the stoppage was 2:55.

Tyson was quick to acknowledge Bruno's strong challenge and courage afterwards. 'He really came to fight,' he told the media gathering. 'He hurt me, I hurt him, but we are in the hurting business. The body punches started to break him up. I heard him grunt from a left hook and from then on I knew he'd go. But look, how dare these boxers challenge me with their somewhat primitive skills? They're as good as dead.'

While Bruno was praised in the media for standing up to Tyson for five rounds, and was never afraid to have a go, particularly in that dramatic opening round, Tyson generally came in for heavy criticism. Colin Hart of *The Sun* said, 'Bruno not only provided Tyson with by far his roughest and toughest championship defence, he also exposed him as being vulnerable and decidedly beatable.'

Ron Wills of the *Daily Mirror* wrote, 'Frank Bruno was right. Mighty Mike Tyson, his emotional life shredded by a messy divorce, bitter courtroom wars and a back-street punch-up, was vulnerable and ready to be taken. Sadly, Bruno was not up to doing the taking. He did not have the expertise, the aggression, the know-how or the fire in the belly that sets champions apart from ordinary men.'

Hurt by the assault on his ring ability, Tyson vowed to prove he was still the best heavyweight in the world and the undisputed champion. Don King matched him with 29-year-old Carl 'The Truth' Williams, a ranked contender from Belle Glade, Florida, who claimed he was the only man capable of ending Tyson's reign of terror. He recalled that six years earlier he had got the better of Mike in gym sessions. 'Oh boy, did I give him some lessons,' he said. 'I couldn't miss him with my left jab.' That was not the way Tyson remembered it but at least it gave Williams some confidence. Williams had won all but two of his 24 fights and fought Larry Holmes in a title fight in 1985, losing a disputed decision after 15 rounds. Now he was getting a second chance against Tyson and promised he would make up for the loss to Holmes. The fight was set for Atlantic City on 21 July 1989.

Once the bell sounded, Tyson got to work. Jabbing and hooking the challenger and driving him back, Mike would say later that Williams was ready to be taken at that stage. Midway through the round, Tyson slipped inside a left jab and loaded up with what one reporter described as 'one of the most devastating counter-punches of his career', a left hook knocking Williams backwards and sending him down. With one hand on the bottom rope, he managed to pull himself up at a count of eight but referee Randy Neumann looked into Williams's eyes and decided he was not in a position to continue. He waved the fight off after just 93 seconds.

Williams launched a mild protest to the referee and ringside judges, but to no avail. He believed the fight was stopped too early and he was not given more of an opportunity to demonstrate to Neumann that he was not disorientated after the knockdown. In a post-fight interview in the ring, Williams appeared to be uninjured, spoke clearly and expressed disappointment that he was not given the chance to 'show my stuff'. Later in the dressing room, he said, 'I was standing upright and in control of myself. I've been down before and got up to win. I deserved the chance to carry on. This was a world title fight and I had worked my butt off to get in the best possible shape.'

Tyson shrugged off Williams's complaints. 'That's the way it goes,' he said. 'OK, the referee was a bit quick in stopping it but it just proves once again that when I hit them, they have to go.' Williams called for a rematch but it never happened. King had other plans for Mike, a seemingly easy defence against an also-ran in the heavyweight stakes, one James 'Buster' Douglas, in Japan. The Japanese fans had already seen Tyson, albeit for a short time, in 1988 when he stopped Tony Tubbs in two rounds. King told the US media that his connections in Japan were anxious to see Tyson back in their country again, and for a longer period this time.

It's just that the flamboyant promoter was not telling the full truth. Yes, of course Japan would welcome a world heavyweight championship fight but this fight belonged in America. The problem was that King could not get financial backing for the fight in the US, not even from the high-rollers in Las Vegas and Atlantic City, because television executives, who would provide most of the finance, considered it an outrageous mismatch against a no-hoper and rejected it. King now had no alternative but to put it on outside America – and Tokyo took the bait.

The match was signed, sealed and ready to be delivered on 11 February 1990 at the domed Korakuen Stadium, Tokyo. As predicted, Douglas was a huge underdog in the weeks leading up to the fight, with Tyson installed as a prohibitive 42/1 on favourite. They were the longest odds in boxing history, dwarfing the lopsided 15/1 betting on Max Baer when he defended his world heavyweight title against James J Braddock in 1935. Braddock won that one. Could Douglas pull off another shock, an even bigger one, this time? The knowledgeable boxing followers shook their heads. No way.

Tyson was already lined up to defend his title against the unbeaten Evander Holyfield, the number one contender, in a $25m defence later in the year and nobody believed the Douglas match was anything other than an easy defence, 'a stroll in the park,' as one writer put it. Douglas had been knocking around the fight circuit for many years, mainly as a supporting player.

Nobody took him seriously, least of all Tyson's team and King. Sure, he was 6ft 4ins, five inches taller than the champion, but he was not a great puncher, only managing to polish off 18 of his opponents inside the distance.

In his only previous crack at the big time, in 1987, he went in against Tony Tucker, a subsequent Tyson victim, for the vacant International Boxing Federation version of the heavyweight title. Running out of stamina and ambition, he was punched to a standstill in the tenth round. In the run-up to the Tyson challenge, Douglas said his loss to Tucker was 'a mistake', without fully explaining what that meant, but that he would be a different fighter against Tyson. It's just that nobody quite believed him.

Tyson looked unbeatable, despite the occasional blip, notably against Bruno. He had won all his 37 fights, 33 inside the distance, and hoped to better former champion Rocky Marciano's tally of 49-0. On the other hand, Douglas claimed he was in the right place at the right time. He brushed aside suggestions that he was just a fall guy in the plans of team Tyson and King. When somebody showed him a copy of the *Los Angeles Times* with the blaring headline 'Tyson in the mood for Buster's last stand', he pushed the paper away and laughed, 'No, this will be Tyson's last stand.' When the Associated Press boxing writer Ed Schuyler arrived at Tokyo International Airport and was asked by the passport inspector how long he intended to work in Japan, he said, 'Oh, about one minute and 33 seconds.'

Douglas was born in Columbus, Ohio on 7 April 1960 and taught to box by his father Billy Douglas, who had been a highly rated middleweight and light-heavyweight in the 1950s but was never fortunate enough to get a title fight. Douglas Sr had the last fight of his career just two months before his son turned professional in May 1981. Buster had preferred basketball to boxing and was a formidable force on the court, but opted for the sweet science after winning a Junior Olympic title. When the Tyson fight was signed, his manager John Johnson, a former football coach at Ohio State University, forecast a surprise and explained how Douglas was going to win. But nobody took him seriously. At 29, Douglas was six years older than Tyson.

After referee Octavio Meyran brought the two boxers to the centre of the ring, a strange hush fell over the stadium. Douglas made a good start, jabbing the oncoming champion with long lefts and crossing the right. Using his 11lb weight advantage to the full, he hurt Tyson with stinging uppercuts in the second round, the perfect counter for Mike's walk-in style. Surprisingly, Tyson did little to avoid them. In the past, he had oozed menace and violence, moving forward, stalking his opponent, but on this night he looked strangely ordinary.

After six rounds, Douglas had a commanding points lead. Amazingly, 'Mr Nobody' was turning into 'Mr Somebody'. In a sensational eighth round, Tyson came back into the fight, dropping Douglas with a powerful right uppercut for a nine count. Tyson's promoter Don King would later claim that Douglas benefited from a long count, a protest that was eventually rejected. In the tenth, Douglas opened up and floored Tyson for the first time in his professional career. Mike scrambled to his knees at the count of five, clawed around pathetically on the canvas for his lost mouthpiece and put it in upside down. He wobbled to his feet at the count of nine but Meyran waved the fight off, hugging the beaten champion before leading him to his corner. The time: 1:23 of round ten.

Tyson declined to meet the media and left the stadium for the airport straight away to catch an early-afternoon flight home. Douglas, beaming with delight, said, 'The win was for my mother [who had died a short time earlier]. I wanted this for her. I was relaxed out there. I wasn't afraid of Tyson. In my career I was mediocre sometimes but I knew my day would come, and it has. It's a great, great feeling to be heavyweight champion of the world, it really is.'

Douglas lost the title in his first defence eight months later on a third-round knockout to Evander Holyfield, the same opponent who had been signed to meet Tyson before Buster shattered his plans. Meanwhile, Don King was progressing with arrangements for a Tyson-Holyfield match and talked of guaranteeing Mike between $22m and $25m. King forecast it would be the richest fight of all time – but it would not happen for another six years.

In July 1991, with talks for the Holyfield bout progressing, Tyson took himself off to Indianapolis, where he checked into a lavish hotel suite but spent most of his time on the town. In a nearby hotel, where the Miss Black America contest was taking place, he met the entrants. The youngest, 18-year-old Desiree Washington, Miss Black Rhode Island, was taken back to his room at 2am, where she alleged he raped her. Tyson was indicted and sentenced to six years' imprisonment at the Indiana Youth Center. After a shaky start, Prisoner 922335 became a model inmate and earned remission after less than three years.

After embarking on a ring comeback in the summer of 1995, Tyson won back his WBC title in March 1996 by stopping his old rival, an earnest Frank Bruno, in three rounds in Las Vegas. Tyson then regained his WBA belt six months later by crushing a scared-stiff Bruce Seldon after 109 seconds of round one, dropping him twice. By now, negotiations for Tyson's postponed world heavyweight championship fight against Evander Holyfield had restarted. A bronze medallist at light-heavyweight at the 1984 Olympics in Los Angeles, Holyfield was from Atlanta, Georgia and had been an outstanding world cruiserweight champion, dominating the division before moving up to the heavyweight class and winning the title.

The Tyson-Holyfield fight was set for 9 November 1996 at the MGM Grand, Las Vegas, with Tyson installed as a 6/1 on favourite. As happened in the fight with Douglas, Tyson was up against another opponent who was not intimidated by him. The fear factor had been an integral part of Mike's armoury throughout his career and now stripped of it, he suddenly seemed normal.

No sooner had referee Mitch Halpern called the two boxers together than Tyson sent Holyfield reeling backwards with a smashing right cross. Holyfield made a quick recovery and tied

Tyson up. Using his superior strength, Holyfield hammered 'Iron Mike' with powerful left and right hooks before the bell. Tyson was having trouble getting his combination punches off as Holyfield continually drove him back and broke up his attacks. This was Holyfield's strategy. While Tyson threw one punch at a time, Holyfield would shove him back, upsetting his balance and then scoring with clusters of punches.

As the rounds passed, Tyson was unable to adjust and found himself being thoroughly outboxed and outfought. In the sixth, a butt opened a cut over Tyson's left eye but Halpern ruled it accidental. In the same round, the fight turned decisively in Holyfield's favour when he floored Tyson with a left uppercut. By the eighth, Tyson was still missing with wild punches and absorbing counter punches. At the end of the tenth, Holyfield sent his opponent staggering across the ring. Holyfield chased him into the ropes and landed a series of devastating blows. At the the sound of the bell, Tyson was out on his feet and defenceless, but his corner still allowed him out for the 11th. It was futile as Holyfield gave Tyson a severe drubbing, prompting Halpern to intervene with just 37 seconds gone in the round.

While the Douglas defeat could be considered a fluke, on this occasion Tyson had been soundly beaten by a superior boxer. Not satisfied that Holyfield was his master, Tyson demanded a return fight. It was set for 28 June 1997, again at the MGM Grand. 'I'll be more prepared next time,' he promised. 'Tyson has had it,' said Holyfield. 'What I did before, I can do again.' On fight night, it was a lacklustre Tyson who walked down the aisle and climbed between the ropes. Bob Mee, who reported the fight for *Boxing News*, would remember, 'As Tyson walked restlessly around the ring before the start, it was not the fearsome prowl of old. He looked a dull-skinned, ageing athlete.'

In the opening round, Holyfield came straight out and jabbed Tyson off balance. Mike moved back before tossing a left hook but Holyfield ducked inside it. Referee Mills Lane warned both fighters for rough stuff in the clinches. As in the first fight,

Tyson did not seem able to get his clusters of punches together and was continually out of range. It was no better in the second, though he slightly improved towards the end of the round when a left hook shook Holyfield. In the third came the sensations. Coming out of a clinch, Tyson tugged Holyfield in and bit down hard on the champion's right ear as Holyfield bounded up and down in agony, frustration and outrage. Seconds later, Tyson chomped on Holyfield's left ear, causing his opponent to jump around like a scalded cat. Amazingly, Lane allowed the round to finish before announcing that he was disqualifying the challenger.

For this outrage, Tyson was fined $3m and banned from boxing for 12 months. More trouble loomed when, four months later, he crashed his motorcycle, leaving him with a punctured lung and broken ribs. Resuming his career in Las Vegas in January 1999, he knocked out South Africa's Francois Botha, billed as the 'White Buffalo', in five rounds. Soon after, Tyson found himself jailed for assault in a road-rage incident and later tested positive for marijuana. Matched with Lennox Lewis on 8 June 2002 in Memphis, Tennessee, he started a brawl at a media conference and bit the Londoner in the leg. Lewis stopped him in eight rounds. Now nearing 40, Tyson continued to tread a forlorn comeback trail before calling it quits after losing two successive fights, a knockout in four rounds by London's Danny Williams in July 2004 and a retirement after six rounds against the Irishman Kevin McBride almost a year later.

Looking back on his turbulent, rollercoaster life inside and outside the ring, Tyson reflected, 'I don't do regrets but I certainly would have done things differently if I had my life to live over again. But it's all come out right in the end, I guess. That's the important thing.'

Chapter 12

Two Ton, the octopus, the kangaroo and the bear

THEY called him 'The Beer Barrel Palooka,' 'Two Ton Tony', 'Mr Two By Four 'The New Jersey Fat Boy' and 'The New Jersey Night Stick'. What's more, all the labels fit Tony Galento like a comfortable slipper. As well as taking on the best boxers and sluggers of the 1930s and 1940s, the brawling New Jersey heavyweight boxed an octopus and a kangaroo, each wearing boxing gloves, and even matched up with a 250lb bear, all in the name of publicity.

Galento's statement before fighting Joe Louis for the world heavyweight title in the summer of 1939 has long gone into the dictionary of boxing's most famous quotes. Pointing to a picture of Louis hanging behind the counter of the Galento bar in his hometown of Orange, New Jersey, known as The Nut Club, he proclaimed for all to hear, 'I'll moider da bum.' He nearly did, too, for a few moments.

To say that Galento had only a nodding acquaintance with the rules of boxing is putting it mildly. It is quite possible that he had never even heard of the Marquis of Queensberry Rules drawn up in 1886, and may well have answered a query with, 'Marquis what? Marquis who? I'll moider da bum.' Tony fought by Galento Rules. Butting, mauling, hitting with the inside of the glove, gouging, using his elbow and brawling were an essential part of his repertoire, like it or loathe it. 'Fat, short and with all the finesses of a charging rhino,' was how boxing writer Bob Mee described him.

Peter Wilson of the *Daily Mirror* said Galento was a genuine throwback to the old knock-down-drag-'em-out style of bruiser. This was a reference to the old-time battlers of the 18th and 19th centuries who fought with their bare fists. Fights would last as long as the fighters could stand, often 70 or more rounds, when terrible injuries were the rule and death often occurred.

It would not be true to say that Galento had no skill. He fought out of a very low crouch and would feint his way into a position to launch his feared left hook, his favourite punch that many experts consider to be one of the hardest of all time. Tony could also use a decent left jab when he wanted to. But his going-forward style of brawling was his forte. He was certainly one of the roughest, toughest heavyweights the division had ever seen, and would have given any heavyweight in any period in history a run for their money. He was simply a 'no-holds-barred' battler who feared nobody.

'I never allowed such niceties as ring rules or sportsmanship or any of that guff to interfere with my work in the ring, and that work was to knock out the other guy in the fastest possible time,' he once explained. 'Promoters and managers put them up and I put them down, usually for keeps. That's how it was with me, like it or leave it.'

Tony earned his most famous nickname 'Two Ton' early in his career. He used to deliver ice around the streets of Orange. One night, when he was due to box at a local arena, his manager Harry 'Pop' McKinney was at ringside anxiously looking at his watch, with no sign of Tony. When he went outside to the car park, he met his fighter casually making his way in with just ten minutes to fight time. 'Where the hell have you been?' barked McKinney. 'You're just about to go on, do you know that?' 'Hold on a minute, Pop,' replied Galento. 'I had two tons of ice to deliver on my way here, up and down flights of stairs. What did you expect?' So Galento became 'Two Ton Tony' there and then, and that was the way he was introduced in the ring.

Standing no more than 5ft 9ins in his boxing socks and generally weighing between 235lbs and 240lbs, give or take a few ounces, Tony hated training. No long miles of roadwork for him. No chopping trees. No long sessions in the gym. No extended sparring sessions or regular workouts with hired help. He reckoned bag-punching and working on the speed ball to test reflexes was for sissies. Tony was said to do his 'training' after dark, with nobody around to see him. Asked by a reporter why he did not train like every other boxer during daylight, he replied, 'Cos I fight at night.'

Galento achieved his level of fitness by eating whatever he wanted, much to the horror of his handlers. A typical meal for Tony would consist of six chickens and a generous helping of spaghetti, all washed down with half a gallon of red wine or beer, often both, at one sitting. He modelled his drinking on John L Sullivan, the former world heavyweight champion known as the 'Boston Strong Boy'. 'Old John L drank heavily and it never bothered him,' Galento said. 'He could drink as well as he could box.'

Whenever Tony did go to his training camp, and usually reluctantly, he would foil his trainer's attempt to modify his diet and many times eat his sparring partners' meals in addition to his. 'He just ate all day,' recalled Harry Mendel, a former sportswriter and promoter who managed the New Jersey brawler for a time. 'You know how most fighters worry about having the right diet and a special chef at camp. That was not for Tony. He would just eat, eat, eat, even for big important fights coming up.'

Galento feared nobody and fought many of the leading heavyweights of his day. True, he was unorthodox to the extreme and would do just about anything to attract publicity. He was only happy once he got his name and picture in the newspapers.

The second of four children, Galento was a holy terror at school and how the teachers kept him in check is something that will never be known. He played truant regularly and was beaten up by his father for missing lessons. 'You'll never get anywhere in life without an education, and here you are throwing it all away,' said Tony Sr.

Boxing would be Galento's outlet. He was bitten by the boxing bug at the age of 12 when the Jack Dempsey-Georges Carpentier world heavyweight championship fight was put on in a newly built wooden stadium known as Boyle's Thirty Acres in Jersey City in July 1921. Tony could not afford to buy a ticket. In any event his father, to his dying day, never approved of boxing and never even saw his son in the ring. But Galento read all about the fight in the local newspaper, the *Star Ledger*, the next day. Promoted by Tex Rickard, it drew over 85,000 fans and became boxing's first million-dollar gate, with receipts actually totalling $1,789,238.

Boxing was thriving in the New Jersey and New York areas then, with fight clubs widespread. Along with a neighbourhood pal and in spite of his father's objections, Tony built a makeshift gymnasium in the backyard of the family's modest home in Orange, with a punchbag suspended from the ceiling and filled with sand. Soon, he would join a proper gymnasium in the town and learn the rudiments of the sport – not that he would ever fully put them into practice later on. Now 12 years of age, he enjoyed the camaraderie of the ring. His amateur career, which was on and off and spread over seven years, would consist of 31 bouts, including 28 wins, mainly around his local area. Turning professional at the age of 18 in March 1928 at the Laurel Garden in Newark, New Jersey, he faced the promising Babe Farmer, who had high ambitions of his own.

When Galento climbed into the ring, there were hoots of laughter. With a 38ins waist, Tony had weighed in at 238lbs. For two rounds, Farmer outboxed, outfoxed and outmanoeuvred the lumbering New Jersey battler with every scientific punch in the book: left jabs, uppercuts and hooks. Galento could simply do nothing right against this speedy prospect and swung all over the place, his arms swishing through the empty air as fans laughed, much to Tony's embarrassment and frustration.

The laughter ended a minute into the third round. Galento missed with a long left hook but the following right swing caught Farmer on the side of the jaw and sent him down as though a trapdoor had opened under him. As the referee counted to ten, Galento went over, picked up the stricken battler and brought him to his corner. But no sooner had Galento propped him up, Babe regained his senses and thinking the fight was still on, suddenly crashed a hard right on to Tony's exposed chin. Enraged, Galento swiftly landed a short right cross to the jaw and Farmer slid to the canvas – out to the world. 'Jeez, they should pay me twice for taking on a guy like that,' said Galento as he left the ring.

'Two Ton' was on his way. Filled with ambition, he vowed to win the world heavyweight championship no less, and as quickly as possible. The title was vacant at the time, Gene Tunney having retired as undefeated champion a year earlier. It would take Tony 11 years to get a crack at the title but along the way he certainly livened up the heavyweight division and sent many fighters home, and often to hospital, with cuts and bruises, sore heads and jaws, not to mention shattered dreams.

Galento fought all over the US. He won some, he lost some, but he was a big attraction with fans and promoters because he was exciting, and the pay was good. He did not mind the boos that greeted his illegal tactics. 'It's all part of the game,' he would say. 'Fans and sportswriters would often accuse me of fouls and call me a dirty fighter, but they got it all wrong. I'm not a dirty fighter. I take showers every night, just like other fighters.'

In his book *Champ In The Corner*, author John Jarrett recalls the story of Galento's trainer Jimmy Frain and his experience one night when Tony went in against another rough brawler like himself. 'The fella fouled him, butted him, elbowed him, did everything, and the referee did not say anything to the hometown fighter,' said Frain. 'So Tony got mad. He ran this guy against the ropes, grabbed him and threw him down, then pretended to trip and fell on him. Tony weighed 240lbs. He was the first to get up. He puts his hand on this guy's head, carelessly pushes himself upright, meanwhile grinding the guy's dome into the canvas. Believe me, after that it was the cleanest fight you ever saw. The other guy was as tame as a kitten.'

On 1 May 1931 in Detroit, Galento took on three opponents one after the other and knocked two of them out – Frankie Kitts in one round, Joe Brian also in one round – and beat Paul Thurman over three. When he sought out the promoter at the end of the show, he demanded three purses. 'Look bud,' said the promoter. 'I hired you for tonight to fight, and fight you did. One purse, and one purse only.'

Galento was now already on to his second manager, Pete Dodd, after he found his first one, Max Waxman, was devoting more time and energy to the promising Italian-American Vince Dundee, who would go on to win the world middleweight title. Dodd matched Tony with the 6ft 4ins Arthur De Kuh, a noted puncher, on 11 April 1932 at Dreamland Park, Newark. Half an hour before the weigh-in, Galento was missing. Dodd sent out a search party to check Tony's usual haunts, with no success. A local reporter put an item in the afternoon newspaper and the owner of the Newark Cinema recognised Galento as the fellow snoring through two movies. He called Dodd and the manager came to pick up his errant boxer.

After several expletives were exchanged between fighter and manager, they made their way quickly to the venue. Galento told Dodd what had happened. Earlier that day, at a local bar, he had eaten 50 hot dogs for a bet. For good measure he ate two more and then crawled into the cinema, where he digested the food pleasantly before falling asleep, snoozing longer than expected and snoring heavily. Rushed to the dressing room at the arena, he found he could no longer fit into his trunks, so one of his handlers slit his waistband and managed to get them up.

De Kuh, annoyed at the long delay and anxious to get going, went out fast at the opening bell and punched Galento around the ring. This went on for three rounds. Before the start of the fourth round, Tony told Dodd he was feeling less stuffed by now. 'Then get out there and knock the stuffing out of this guy,' advised Dodd. Galento charged from his corner like a rhino. Catching De Kuh flush in the face with a hard left hook, he followed through with a swishing right that sent his opponent down to be counted out. De Kuh was never the same boxer afterwards. His career over, he later got involved in all-in wrestling, a kind of last resort, before fading into obscurity.

'A potential heavyweight contender was discovered at Dreamland Park last night,' wrote Tony Marenghi in the *Newark Star-Eagle*. 'His name is Tony Galento. He ought to go places in boxing if he attends to his duties in the ring, trains hard and takes advice from his handlers.'

Galento's motto was never to duck anybody. His record is scattered with wins and losses but he was an exciting battler. On 7 June 1932, he faced Ernie Schaaf at the Dreamland Park Arena in Newark, New Jersey. Born in Elizabeth, New Jersey, Schaaf moved to Boston after a spell in the navy and built up an impressive record with wins over name contenders. He had all the appearances of a future champion.

The Galento-Schaaf bout had already been postponed three times because of heavy rain and was being referred to as a jinxed fight. It went the scheduled ten rounds, with the decision going to Schaaf on his better boxing. He finished stronger, too, and had Galento floundering at times. But there was much infighting and brawling, with both men guilty of infringements. Galento was the main culprit. He repeatedly struck Schaaf on the back of the neck with right-hand chops known as rabbit punches. Schaaf complained of headaches for over an hour as Galento sauntered back to his bar.

Despite his victory, Schaaf was exhausted and dazed when he got to his dressing room and lay on the table for over two hours. He was never the same again and his career spiralled downwards, culminating in a bad defeat in ten rounds by big-punching Max Baer and a loss in 13 to the Italian giant Primo Carnera. Against Carnera, Schaaf was caught with a light left hook that sent him to the canvas to be counted out. Carried from the ring on a stretcher, he underwent an emergency operation for bleeding on the brain and died the following morning. It was said that Baer's powerful punching earlier was the root cause, but sportswriters would claim that the blows he received from Galento had done the damage.

Tony, meanwhile, continued to eat – and drink. 'Beer never hurt anyone,' he once said. 'Of course, I have my limitations.' But nobody believed him. He just loved the booze. Perhaps, too, he came along at the right time in history. With the rise in alcohol consumption around the world in the first half of the 20th century, drink bans were introduced in Canada, the Russian Empire, Iceland, Norway, Hungary, Finland and North America. Rum-running became widespread and organised crime took control of the distribution of alcohol. Distilleries and breweries in Canada, Mexico and the Caribbean flourished as their products were either consumed by visiting Americans or illegally exported to the US.

Chicago became notorious as a haven for prohibition dodgers during the time known as the Roaring 20s. Prohibition generally came to an end in the late 1920s or early 1930s in most of North America and Europe, although a few locations continued prohibition for many more years.

The repeal of the law was welcome news for drinkers like Tony Galento as it ushered in a national love of tomfoolery with the booze. On the advice of his latest manager, Joe 'Yussell the Muscle' Jacobs, Galento put a deposit on a bar on Day Street in Orange and opened for business. 'If anyone had been born to be a barkeeper, it was "Two Ton" Tony Galento,' recalled the boxer's biographer Joseph Monninger. 'Jacobs, who believed boxers needed a business besides fighting, told Tony the publicity he received in boxing would attract patrons. One of his former managers, Pete Dodd, had started a sporting tavern and dollar signs danced before his eyes.'

In his inimitable style, Tony found a 250lb bear in a local circus and bought it so he could put on sparring exhibitions. On a little stage with a seven-inch cigar stuck in one corner of his mouth, and a white bar-apron tied around his expansive girth, Galento soon had the customers rolling up. While the New Jersey Boxing Commission greeted the prospect of a boxer running a bar with a nervous glance, not to mention sparring with a mighty bear, newspaper reporters found the combination irresistible.

Meanwhile, 'Two Ton' carried on his ring career, seeking out and getting the big names but also taking on the small ones. By the beginning of 1936, his eighth year as a professional, he was in the Top 10 ratings issued monthly by *Ring* magazine, the accepted rankings in boxing. If boxers got into one of those lists, from flyweight to heavyweight, they were, to use a modern term, the real deal. The heavyweight champion was, by coincidence, another New Jerseyman. James J Braddock had been champion for six months, having taken the title from Max Baer in a stunning upset. Braddock's leading contender was the promising Joe Louis, who would figure in Galento's plans inside three short years.

On the night of 28 April 1937, Galento ducked between the ropes at the New York Hippodrome to take on one of the top contenders, Arturo Godoy, the son of an Argentinian fisherman, who was moving up the ratings. Godoy, a cagey fighter with a good dig in both gloves, would be best known for his two world heavyweight championship fights with Joe Louis in 1940. The first went the full 15 rounds, with Louis winning a disputed split decision, but in the return Godoy was stopped in the eighth.

Against the rough-and-tumble Galento, Godoy outsmarted the New Jersey battler over ten rounds but not before he had been butted and elbowed several times. In the sixth round, Galento hit the South American on the break and Godoy responded with a head butt. Referee Arthur Donovan took Godoy aside and warned him to behave himself, to which Godoy replied in broken English, 'Yes, but tell that to Galento, too. He's been fouling me all night.' John Kieran of the *New York Times* reported: 'The two fighters were funny. They made if a free-for-all, catch-as-catch-can match and used everything except spurs on one another.'

Not convinced that the Chilean battler was his master, Tony openly challenged his man to a return. He got one two months later at Chicago's Comiskey Park and once again Godoy won the decision, this time over six rounds in another no-holds-barred, free-for-all battle. This time, both fighters were repeatedly warned and how they were not thrown out and the fight declared a no-contest will forever remain a mystery. No encounter with Galento was ever going to be an easy ride, win, lose or draw.

Tony was now competing in the big league and there was serious talk of a match with Louis for the world title. Following the second Godoy victory, Galento ran up 11 straight wins, all either by countouts or stoppages. *Ring* magazine featured him on its cover in its August 1938 issue, calling him 'New Jersey's Heavyweight Hope'.

Galento's manager at the time was Joe 'Yussell the Muscle' Jacobs. The son of a tailor, Jacobs was born on New York's Lower East Side to Hungarian immigrants. He was the quintessential boxing manager of the 1920s and 1930s, a cigar-chomping, fedora-wearing, streetwise, brash, combative, argumentative and fast-talking individual. Jacobs had earlier managed three world champions, featherweight André Routis of France, light-heavyweight Mike McTigue of Ireland and his most famous charge, heavyweight Max Schmeling of Germany. 'Jacobs knew nothing about boxing, but he knew how to negotiate and get his man the best deal possible,' recalled Schmeling.

In his fight for the vacant world heavyweight championship on 12 June 1930 at the Yankee Stadium, Schmeling was knocked down in the fourth round by a low blow from Jack Sharkey. Jacobs jumped into the ring screaming, 'foul, foul' at the top of his voice until the bewildered referee Jim Crowley disqualified Sharkey. It was the first time the heavyweight championship was decided on a foul. When the two boxers met in a rematch for the title on 21 June 1932 at the Long Island Bowl, Sharkey won a controversial 15-round decision, leading Jacobs to utter to a national radio audience what became a classic sports quote and an entry in *Bartlett's Familiar Quotations*, 'We wuz robbed!'

Another *Bartlett's* quote from Jacobs that became part of the language occurred when he attended the 1935 World Baseball Series in Detroit on a very cold and windy day. 'I shoulda stood in bed,' he remarked in the stands.

Among Galento's victims after the second Godoy fight were big names such as Leroy Haynes, Charley Massera, Harry Thomas, Natie Brown, Jorge Brescia and Abe Feldman. Galento challenged Louis for the world heavyweight title at the Yankee Stadium in New York on 28 June 1939. The fight would be promoted by Mike Jacobs and marked Louis's seventh defence of the title he had won from James J Braddock in June 1937. On paper, it looked a horrible mismatch – the little fat guy against the great 'Brown Bomber', who looked unbeatable. Louis had lost only once in 42 fights, and that defeat, by Max Schmeling in 1936, had been avenged two year later. Galento had 76 wins, 23 losses and five draws.

The experts agreed that Galento was a brawler with a fair left jab, but he had a powerful punch in both hands, particularly that ponderous left hook. If he could land even one shot on the champion's jaw, anything could happen. Moreover, Galento had yet to be put on the canvas, even for a short time. It was, and still is, a maxim in boxing that the puncher always has a chance. All that mattered now was getting Galento into the fittest physical condition of his career, a task that was not going to be easy.

'Trying to get Tony fit was a farce,' remembered Ray Arcel, who trained Galento at one time. 'The roly-poly pug with the bulging paunch and the sledgehammer punch was tough enough. I'm not denying that. He was as strong as an ox, and his powers of endurance, his ability to soak up punishment and absorb pain bordered on the freakish. Moreover, he could fight dangerously in an ugly, brawling roughhouse fashion, and he did not lack guts. But outside the ring he was nothing but a comic, noisy man whose circus-tent antics and crazy eccentricities certainly brought no credit to the game.

'He dragged his training down to a comic-strip level. What indeed could anyone make of a fighter who conditioned himself on gallons of beer and nine-inch cigars, who did his roadwork on a motorcycle because he said running made him tired and who was want to waddle into the ring with rolls of surplus fat like motor tyres billowing around his mid-section? It all sounds very amusing, and certainly the hairy-chested, barrel-shaped slugger kept hitting the headlines with his capers. Right in the middle of training, he might disappear for a couple of days. On the other hand, he was just as likely to roll into the gymnasium full of beer at midnight and begin belting punch bags clean from their moorings.

'How I got involved with Galento in the first place was in 1933, when Tony was managed by Jack Dempsey, the former heavyweight champion of the world. Jack called me one day and asked me if I were interested in training Galento. I told Dempsey he was wasting his time in having anything to do with Tony and that it would be a waste of time and money as he hated training. Dempsey said he felt Galento had the makings of a world-beater and that I would be the very man to accomplish that. So, since Jack and I were old friends, I agreed to give it a try.'

One day Dempsey strolled into Stillman's Gym while Galento was working out with Arcel. Jack walked upstairs to the balcony to have a look at his fighter and at this time, as Arcel remembered, 'Galento was fatter than ever, hopelessly out of condition and obviously doing nothing about it.' He didn't see Dempsey and continued waddling around the ring, clowning and wisecracking as he fooled around with sparring partners. After watching for a couple of rounds, Dempsey went down to ringside, wearing a beautifully cut light grey suit, tan shoes and a white silk shirt. When Galento caught sight of him, he shouted out a big 'hello' and gave Jack a big hug. 'You look like a million bucks this afternoon,' Tony said. 'Never mind how I look, you bum,' replied Dempsey. 'Let's see you do some work.'

While Galento continued to loaf, Dempsey asked Arcel to get him some boxing gloves. Stripping to his white silk underpants, Dempsey said to Galento, 'I'll show you how we used to do it.' Arcel recalled, 'What Dempsey did in those three minutes was nobody's business. He ripped punches into Galento's torso from all angles, split his lip with a terrific left and sent the blood squirting from his nose with a right. Even when Galento threw his arms up to stop, Dempsey chased after him, throwing punches until I called time.

'Still breathing easily, Dempsey ducked under the ropes and began to dress while Galento stood shaking his head in a semi-daze trying to wipe the blood from his face with the back of his boxing gloves. When dressed, Dempsey gave him one contemptuous look. "That's how we used to fight, Galento," he said. "Now I'm through with you. You can find yourself another manager." Then he turned to me and said, "You were right, Ray. It's a waste of time trying to make a champ out of this chump."'

Would Dempsey be proven wrong? Would New Jersey have another world heavyweight champion? Or would Louis show Galento who was the real boss of the world's heavyweights and keep his prized crown? The fight drew a crowd of 34,852 and Louis started as a 10/1 favourite to win. But Galento and his manager scoffed at the odds. 'They're crazy,' barked Jacobs, taking the fat cigar from beneath his clenched teeth. 'My man punches too hard for Louis, and the fans are going to find that out very soon. Wait and see.'

Louis, essentially a quiet man outside the ring, rarely predicted how his fights would go, leaving all that to his handlers. If any statements did come out, one could assume that they were made by his publicity people. Not so Galento. At a press conference a week before the fight, he made his famous statement, 'I'll moider da bum.' Asked if he were fit for what was the biggest and most important fight of his career, he said, 'Sure I am. I haven't even taken alcohol for two days.'

Galento also emphasised he did not want a repeat of Dempsey's fight with Luis Firpo. This was a reference to the 1923 battle when Dempsey was knocked through the ropes and landed on the typewriter of Jack Lawrence of the *New York Herald Tribune* before being pushed back into the ring. Galento said he had asked the New York State Athletic Commission to instruct the first two rows of newspapermen to let Louis remain where he landed in the event that he sailed out of the ring. 'If da bum flies out, let him make his own way back, if he can that is,' proclaimed Tony boldly. Many put all this down to good publicity but some felt that Galento really believed it.

It was also disclosed that often late at night, Galento had dialled Louis's number in Pompton Lakes, New Jersey, where the champion trained. In whispered tones, he told Louis what he intended to do to him in the ring. He called Louis every name in the book, questioned his manhood, talked about his race and made sexual references about Joe's wife Marva. Years later, Galento apologised publicly for the phone calls and the two became friends, with Louis often visiting Tony's bar.

But at the time, the phone calls were mocking and strictly in bad taste, publicity or not. It was clear that Galento wanted to get under the champion's skin, anger him, pry open Louis's deadpan expression. Unfortunately for Galento, it had the opposite effect and made Louis all the more determined to show up his opponent and make him pay for all the insults. This was going to be a grudge fight, just like Louis's second bout with Max Schmeling, who had knocked out Louis in 12 rounds in 1936 and was a close associate of Adolf Hitler and the so-called master race.

At the weigh-in on the day of the fight, Galento scaled 233lbs and Louis 200lbs. Tony would use his weight advantage to the full. His trainer for the fight was a legendary figure in boxing, Whitey Bimstein. A native New Yorker from his beloved East Side, Bimstein would preside over the careers of hundreds of champions and near-champions in the city's Stillman's Gym and was still to be seen in the corner on big fight nights in boxing's most famous venues up to the late 1960s. He promised to get Galento into the best possible shape, maybe not 100 per cent because of Tony's somewhat erratic lifestyle, but certainly 75 per cent.

At the bell, Galento came out crouching and rushed in with a hard left swing to the body, which surprised Louis and sent him back on his heels. An estimated 40 million listeners moved closer to their radio sets. Gathering his composure, Louis tied up the challenger. As they came out of the clinch, the 'Bomber' jabbed two lefts to Galento's scowling face. A second later, Tony suddenly crashed over a thunderous left hook to the champion's jaw. Joe's legs buckled, his eyes became glassy and he reeled back into a neutral corner.

Louis was hurt, seriously hurt, and he instinctively covered up. The wild-punching barman was unable to reach him with another punch. Looking deadly serious, Joe boxed his way out of danger as Galento continued to chase him, firing away with both gloves and desperately seeking another opening. But the champion was proving a difficult target as he jolted his man with a left and a right. At the bell, Galento was credited with having the better of the round.

Louis went to work in the second round, as if to make Galento pay for his behaviour in that first session. He nicked Tony's left eye with a snappy left jab and a follow-through right to the jaw almost lifted the 33lb heavier challenger off his feet. Louis then connected with a fast combination, a left to the body and a right to the jaw that sent Galento wobbling into his own corner. Louis followed his foe relentlessly, smashing away with both hands as Tony fought back and the crowd were now really on their feet. As Galento rushed in, Louis clipped him with a short right uppercut and followed with another fast, hard combination, culminating in a powerful left hook that lifted the New Jersey battler off his feet and deposited him on his broad beam. Galento refused to take a count and was back fighting shortly before the bell rang.

Coming out for the third round, Louis was now in charge but Galento was always dangerous, although he was bleeding from his right eye, nose and mouth and his left eye was looking the worse for wear. Suddenly, as they were parting from a clinch, Tony whipped across a smashing left hook that caught the unprepared champion on the chin. As Louis dropped to the canvas, 'the stadium became a veritable madhouse', according to *Ring* magazine editor Nat Fleischer, who described it at ringside. Louis bounced up immediately and instead of retreating and keeping out of danger, he went straight on to the attack and found a willing mixer in Galento. Weary and battered as he was, Tony was running out of steam and Louis had little difficulty in fending off his attacks.

Louis went out for the fourth round to finish the job and hammered the roly-poly contender at will. Galento reeled back like a drunk under the champion's determined attack. In his own corner, he fell back against the ropes and propped himself there while Louis hammered away. His legs sagged and he sank to his knees as referee Arthur Donovan moved in, pushed the champion back and called it all off. The time of the round was 2:29.

Back in the dressing room, Galento complained that 'da bum referee stopped the fight too soon', but not one of the sportswriters agreed. However, his cornerman Bimstein said, 'I still think Tony could have licked him if he had been 100 per cent fit and obeyed orders. He wouldn't listen to my advice to stay cool after putting Louis down, and so paid the price.' When Galento was asked by one writer if he planned to re-establish himself by taking on other contenders, he said in his mangled New Jersey accent, 'Look, dere all bums, every one of them. I'd have moidered dem all.' When another seeker of knowledge suddenly changed the subject and asked Tony what he thought of Shakespeare, he replied, 'Shakespeare? Shakespeare? Listen, if he was one of dem foreign heavyweights, I would have moidered him, too.'

Jack Mahon covered the famous fight for the *New York Daily News*. Looking back nearly a quarter of a century later, he recalled in *Boxing and Wrestling* magazine, 'All of us writers, to a man, knew that Galento was hopelessly overweight and disdained all standard and training methods. He had been beaten 22 times, mainly by stumblebums of every kind in all parts of the country. But he feared nothing or nobody and would have gotten into the ring with King Kong. He was a throwback to the dark ages of the sport. Also, he had the best manager of the previous 25 years, Joe "Yussel the Muscle" Jacobs. He talked the promoter Mike Jacobs into putting Galento in with Louis. We all knew that Galento did not belong in there with the champ yet the memory of other second-raters who had staggered Joe on occasions was fresh in our memories.

'But in that amazing third round, the bizarre barroom challenger electrified everybody in the ball park by knocking Louis off his feet for the first time in his defence of the championship. The crowd, the newspapermen, could not believe their eyes. Here was the man who was being called the greatest heavyweight in history lying there, hurt and frightened. When he got up, he went on his bicycle for the rest of the round but Galento had proved his pre-fight boast. He said he would have the champion on the floor. In the fourth round, systematically and relentlessly, Louis went to work on his man, hammering him mercilessly until referee Arthur Donovan stepped in and halted the fight. There wasn't a heavyweight fight in years that produced such unexpected drama. Galento, though beaten, went out a hero.'

If Galento's clash with Louis was the most exciting fight of the year, then Tony's next fight three months later was the dirtiest. This was his clash with Lou Nova at the Municipal Stadium in Philadelphia on 15 September 1939. The encounter would surpass even the modern foul-filled battle between Riddick Bowe and Andrew Golota, which set off a full-scale riot at Madison Square Garden in 1996. *Boxing News* referred to the Galento-Nova fight as 'one of the goriest in history'.

Of Irish and German heritage, Nova was one of the leading heavyweights in the 1930s and 1940s. Born in Los Angeles in March 1913, he later moved to Philadelphia, where he would be based during his ring career. He had a very successful amateur career, winning the National Amateur Athletic League title in 1935 and, the same year in Paris, the International Amateur Championships, which was effectively the world championships. Nova turned professional in January 1936 and went unbeaten in 20 fights before dropping a decision to the former world light-heavyweight champion 'Slapsie' Maxie Rosenbloom. Lou ran up another six wins, including a points win over the Welshman Tommy Farr and an 11th-round stoppage of ex-world heavyweight champion Max Baer, before signing to meet Galento.

For the first two rounds, Nova jabbed Galento so often that Tony must have thought his opponent had two left hands. In the third, Galento shouted to Nova, 'Come in close and fight, ya bum.' Lou accepted the challenge, only to find himself flat on his back from a wicked left hook. When Nova rose, Galento rushed in to finish the job but Nova boxed him off until the bell.

From the fourth round onwards, Nova was subjected to one of the worse beatings any boxer ever received. His face was a mass of cuts and bruises. Galento head-butted, stuck the thumbs of both his gloves in the Californian's eyes, used his elbows repeatedly, grabbed and pushed Nova into the ropes, spat at his rival and made a complete mockery of what purists like to call 'the noble art'. Why referee George Blake, an experienced official, did not disqualify Galento remains a mystery to this day. By the 11th, Nova was a thoroughly beaten man and the fight should have been mercifully and compassionately stopped.

The 12th and 13th rounds both went to Galento as he continually charged while he punched and fouled. Nova's remaining strength was fast ebbing away. It was a miracle the fight had lasted so long. A mighty right swing in the 14th round put Nova down. He staggered up at nine before another blow, this time, a massive left hook, floored him again just as referee Blake finally called, 'That's enough!' The bloody battle, or rather the war, ended at 2:44 of the round.

Galento decided to take a break for a few months to look after his bar and make public appearances. Feeling the urge to fight again, he took on Max Baer at the Roosevelt Stadium, Jersey City on 2 July 1940. Baer, from Omaha, Nebraska, but fighting out of California, had something of a dual personality. He was a flashy performer who clowned his way through life, but he also happened to be one of boxing history's biggest hitters, possessing a deadly right hand. On the night he fought Galento, the former world heavyweight champion was past his best but still a dangerous foe.

On the afternoon of the fight, Galento decided to stop off at his bar with his brother and had a large bowl of spaghetti and meat balls, washed down with more than generous helpings of beer. At the end of the meal, the siblings got into a heated argument, resulting in his brother throwing a beer glass in Tony's face, which severely cut his lip. Galento was forced to get the cut stitched up, with just a couple of hours to go until fight time. When the bout started, Baer reopened the cut in the first round, forcing the New Jersey battler to swallow blood for the remainder of the fight. The one-sided battle was stopped in the eighth round.

Max's brother Buddy completed the family double nine months later by stopping Galento in the seventh round in

Washington DC. Out of the ring for over a year, Tony pulled on the gloves again in June 1943 and ran off three wins over nonentities before calling it a day by the end of the following year. He was back in the news in 1944 as a professional wrestler and took on the Irish heavyweight Jack Doyle, who had also turned to his new sport. They clashed at Harringay Arena in London. Frank Butler, sports editor of the *News of the World*, recalled, 'Galento showed up at our offices and displayed his strength by picking up my secretary and holding her with one hand and in the other did the same with a fairly well-built member of the sports staff.'

Galento beat Doyle in the second round when he fell on the Irishman. Two of Doyle's ribs were broken and he had to be taken to St Mary's Hospital in Paddington, where he was bandaged up. Doyle would recall later, 'When Galento held me down, it was like being under a steamroller.' Inside three months they met again, at Tolka Park football ground in Dublin. This time Doyle was the winner before a turnaway crowd of 25,500.

Michael Taub aptly described the occasion in his book *Fighting for Love*, 'Jack hoisted Galento's "Two Ton" frame on his shoulders and spun him like a roulette wheel, gaining such momentum that both men went crashing out of the ring. Galento's head hit the concrete and he was out cold. Fortunately for Doyle, his fall was broken by a chair. He was able to clamber back in the ring before the count was completed and be declared the winner.'

By the 1950s, Galento realised he was getting too old for such strenuous activities as wrestling and turned to Hollywood, where he got roles in movies such as *On the Waterfront*, *Guys and Dolls*, *The Best Things in Life are Free* and *Wind Across the Everglades*.

In January 1976, Galento appeared alongside his old rival Joe Louis in a sports nostalgia programme on US television. When Louis was asked by veteran fight commentator Don Dunphy if he had any ill feelings towards any of his opponents, he denied stories that he 'hated' Max Schmeling, who once knocked him out. 'We were good friends,' he stressed. Pointing then to Galento, he said, 'But that little fellow. He really got me mad all right. I was so angry with him after he said such nasty things about me before the fight that I decided to punish him. But after he knocked me down in the third round, I changed my mind and knocked him out as quickly as I could.'

Boxing's most colourful and eccentric contender died in his hometown of Orange, New Jersey on 22 July 1979 at the age of 69. The cause of death was complications brought about by diabetes. Tony Galento left behind a respectable record of 80-26-5. Fifty-seven of his wins were by the short route, a clear indication of his tremendous punching power.

Selected bibliography

Assael, Shaun., *The Murder of Sonny Liston*, Macmillan, 2016

Benson, Peter., *Battling Siki*, University of Arkansas Press, 2006

Collins, Nigel., *Boxing Babylon*, Robson Books, 1991

Duran, Roberto., *I Am Duran*, Macmillan, 2016

Eubank, Chris., *Eubank,* Collins Willow, 2003

Fleischer, Nat., *The Ring Record Book*, The Ring Book Shop, 1957

Gallimore, Andrew., *Bloody Canvas*, Mercier, 2007

Giudice, Christian., *Hands of Stone*, Milo Books, 2006

Graziano., Rocky., Barber, Rowland, *Somebody Up There Likes Me*, Simon and Schuster, 1955

Heller, Peter., *In This Corner,* Dell Publishing, 1973

Jarrett, John., *Toy Bulldog*, McFarland Press, 2013

Monninger, Joseph., *Two Ton*, Steerforth Press, 2006

Mullan, Harry., Mee, Bob., *The Ultimate Encyclopaedia of Boxing*, Carlton Books, 2010

Paxton, Bill., *The Fearless Harry Greb*, McFarland, 1966

Roberts, James B, Skutt, Alexander G., *The Boxing Register*, McBooks Press, 2006

Shetty, Sanjeev., *No Middle Ground*, Aurum Press, 2014

Zale, Thad., Moyle, Clay., *Tony Zale: The Man of Steel*, Win by KO Publications, 2014

Index

INDEX